I AM OF IRELAND

Also by Elizabeth Shannon

Up in the Park:
The Diary of the Wife of the American Ambassador to Ireland,
1977–1981

I AM OF IRELAND

Women of the North Speak Out

Revised and Expanded Edition

Elizabeth Shannon

UNIVERSITY OF MASSACHUSETTS PRESS
AMHERST

Printed in the United States of America
LC 97-20261
ISBN 1-55849-102-3 (pbk.)

Library of Congress Cataloging-in-Publication Data
Shannon, Elizabeth, 1937-
I am of Ireland: women of the North speak out / Elizabeth Shannon. — Rev. and expanded ed.
p. cm.
Includes bibliographical references.
ISBN 1-55849-102-3 (pbk.: alk. paper)
1. Women—Northern Ireland—Interviews. 2. Women in politics—Northern Ireland. 3. Northern Ireland—Politics and government—1969-1994. I. Title.
HQ1599.N67S47 1997
305.4'09416—dc21 97-20261
CIP

British Library Cataloguing in Publication data are available

This book is published with the support and cooperation of the University of Massachusetts, Boston.

For Liam, Christopher, and David Patrick
with love

Contents

Maps appear on pages x through xiii

Acknowledgments

EACH TIME I VISITED Northern Ireland, I knew I had a home with John Fairleigh, whose hospitality and endless help changed the face of Belfast for me. Mrs. Toy, his housekeeper, supplemented John's hospitality and I am grateful to both of them.

Lady Faulkner, Pauline Ginnity, Jennifer and David Gilliland, and Maurna Crozier also opened their homes to me, and their kindness soon made Northern Ireland seem a familiar and welcome place.

When I conceived of writing this book, the first person I talked to about it was Leila Doolin, an Irish journalist who has spent much time in Belfast. She generously gave me the names of her friends to interview and suggested places that I see; her help was the starting point of my trips to Northern Ireland.

Midway through writing the book, I discovered the efficacy of having a place away from home in which to work. For the use of his library and his word processor, and for the company of Xina, his dog, I am grateful to William Doering.

My agent, Helen Rees, always makes me think my book projects are "wonderful," and I think she is, too. Her enthusiasm and support sustained me all the way through. Jennifer Josephy, my editor at Little, Brown and Company, made this an infinitely better book by her meticulous, thoughtful editing, her suggestion for the title, and, damn it, even all that important material she ruthlessly cut.

My husband and sons suffered from many missed meals throughout my trips to Northern Ireland (although their cooking improved), and I am grateful for their patience, and especially for Bill's careful reading of the manuscript and his always-right editorial suggestions.

But especially — and foremost — my gratitude goes to all the women in this book and many others not mentioned by name, for their honest, helpful, and enlightening talk. It is through them that I have seen Northern Ireland.

Author's Note

IT IS HELPFUL to be familiar with certain key dates in the current sequence of events in Northern Ireland, as well as the names of people, places, and organizations in the country. Rather than break into the text of the book each time an organization is mentioned, or to stop and give the significance of a certain date, I have organized a glossary and a chronology at the back of the book. The reader may refer to either while reading the book, if an event or organization is unfamiliar.

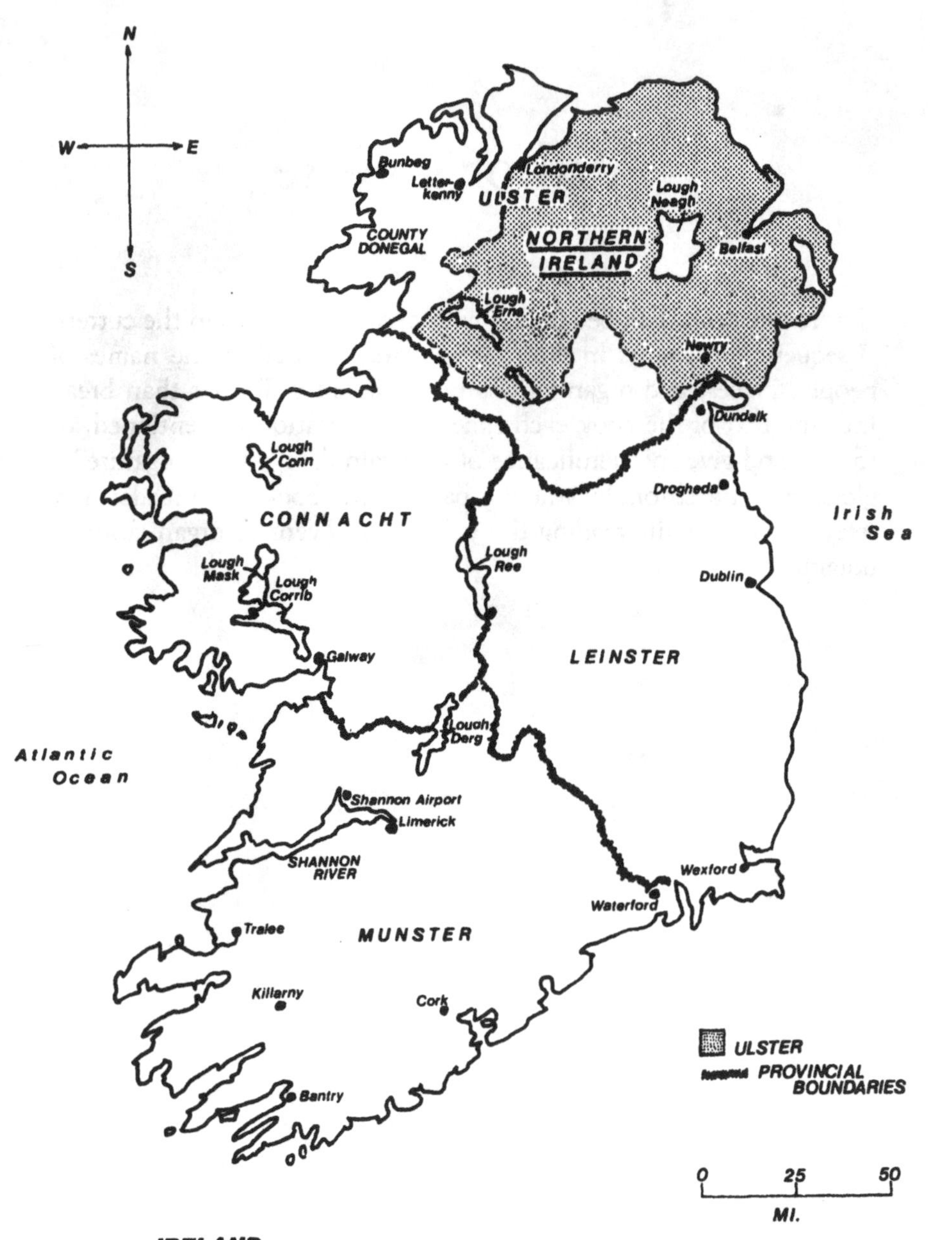
N
W
E
S
Bunbeg
Letterkenny
Londonderry
ULSTER
Lough Neagh
COUNTY DONEGAL
NORTHERN IRELAND
Belfast
Lough Erne
Newry
Dundalk
Lough Conn
Drogheda
CONNACHT
Irish Sea
Lough Mask
Lough Ree
Lough Corrib
Dublin
Galway
LEINSTER
Lough Derg
Atlantic Ocean
Shannon Airport
Limerick
SHANNON RIVER
Wexford
Waterford
Tralee
MUNSTER
Killarny
Cork
ULSTER
PROVINCIAL BOUNDARIES
Bantry
0
25
50
MI.

IRELAND

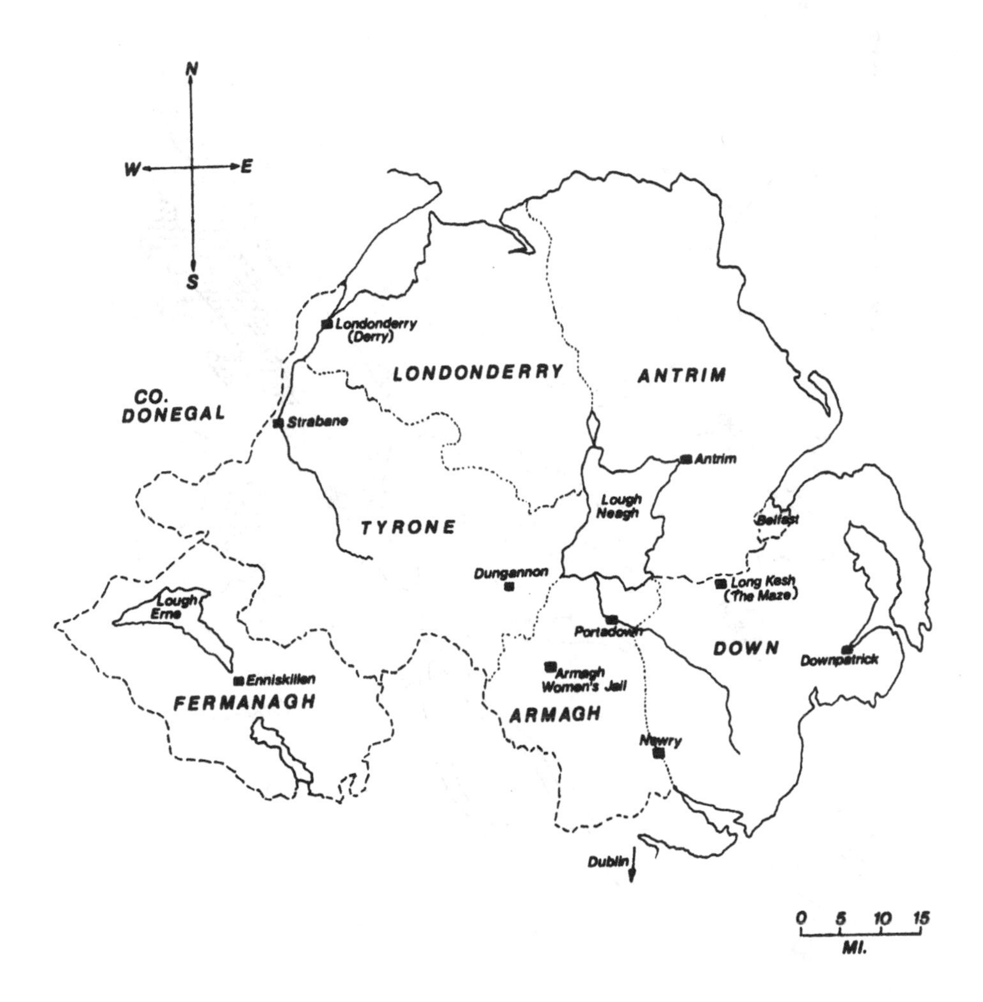

NORTHERN
IRELAND

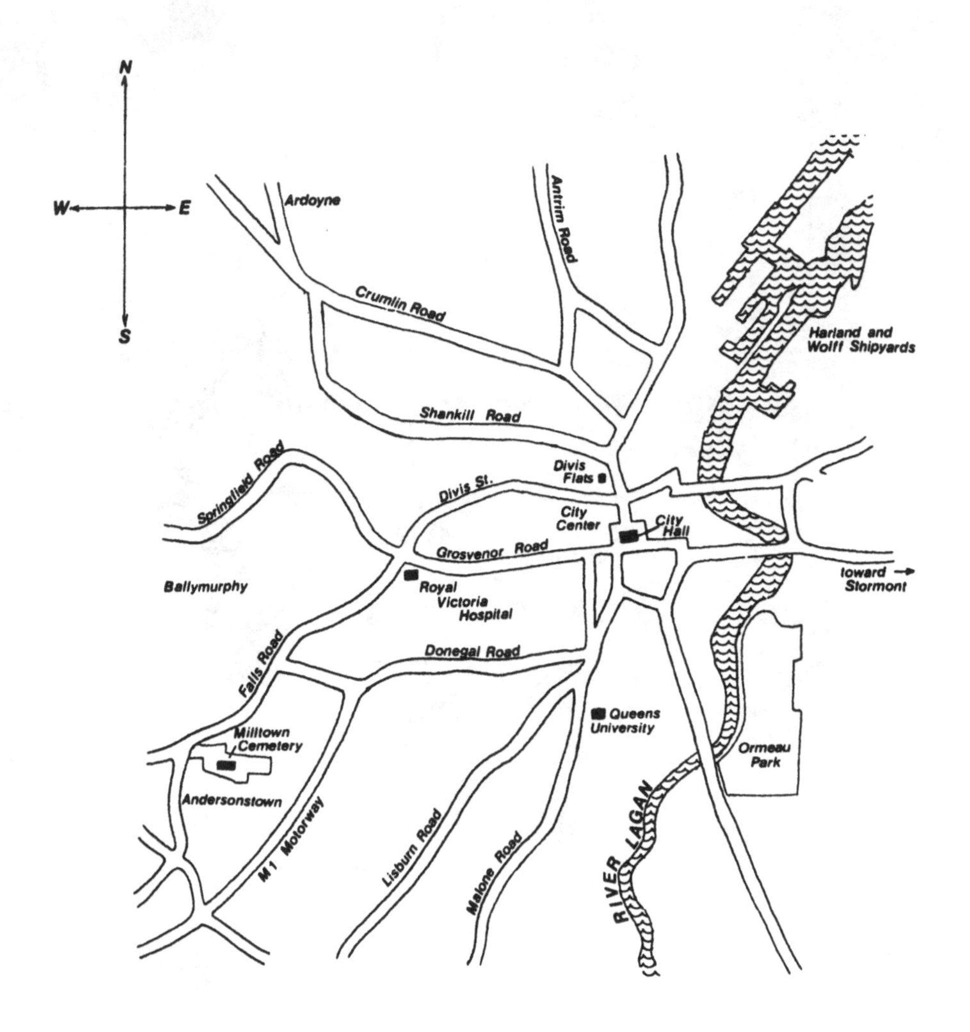
N
W
E
S
Ardoyne
Antrim Road
Crumlin Road
Harland and Wolff Shipyards
Shankill Road
Springfield Road
Divis Flats
Divis St.
City Center
City Hall
Grosvenor Road
toward Stormont
Ballymurphy
Royal Victoria Hospital
Donegal Road
Falls Road
Queens University
Milltown Cemetery
Ormeau Park
Andersonstown
M1 Motorway
Lisburn Road
Malone Road
RIVER LAGAN

BELFAST

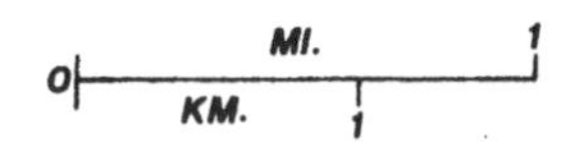
MI.
1
0
KM.
1

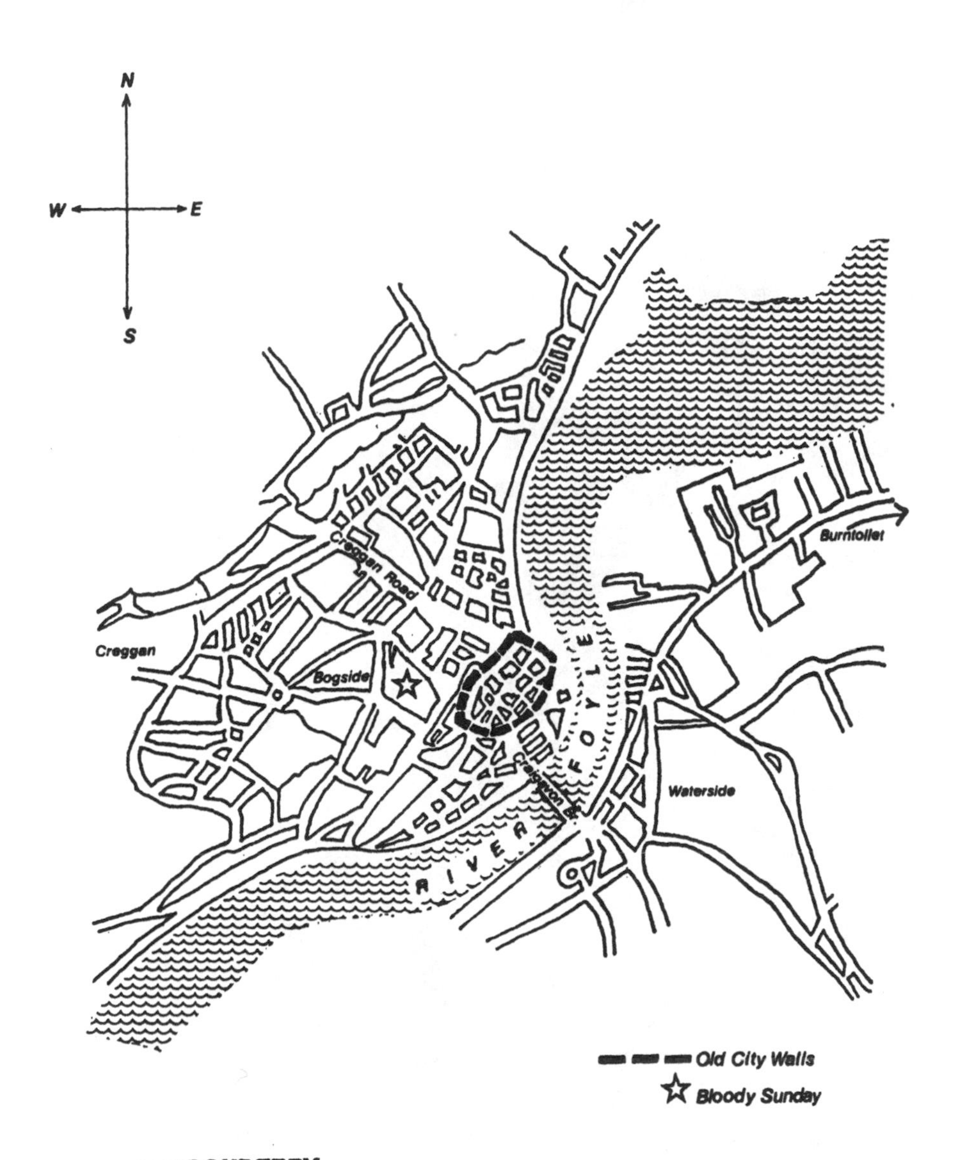

LONDONDERRY
(DERRY)

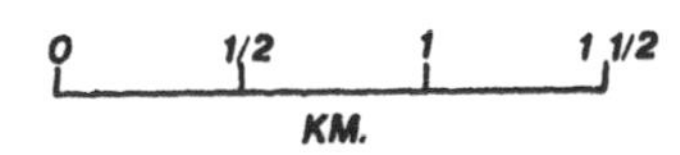

Introduction to the Revised and Expanded Edition

IT IS A PRIVILEGE to be able to bring out a new edition of *I Am of Ireland.* Many events have changed the course of history in Northern Ireland since this book was first published in 1989, and neither the political texture of the country nor the role that women are playing there is the same as it was when I began doing research for the first edition of this book.

As I sit and write today in the autumn of 1996, having just returned from Northern Ireland, it appears that the political situation there is at another crisis period and that the future of the all-party talks seems threatened even before substantive progress can be made. The ceasefire was a period of hope and celebration for the short time it lasted. Perhaps within the next few months a firmer resolution to maintain the spirit and the promises of the Downing Street Declaration and the Framework Document will have been achieved, and then the process might get back on track. This is what the vast majority of the people of Northern Ireland want and what they deserve.

Many friends made during my first visits to Northern Ireland, and new ones made since, are still there, sharing their hospitality, their experiences, and their humor with this American woman who appears on their doorsteps every June. John Fairleigh's home in Belfast is still my home away from home, and he opens his door with generosity not only to me but to my friends. I am grateful to have the chance to thank him.

There have been tragic losses in Northern Ireland in the years since this book was published, and losses closer to me.

My husband, Bill Shannon, died of cancer just before the book was published. I will always be grateful that he was able to read the manuscript.

My traveling companion on many trips to the North, Marie Hawke, of Washington, D.C., succumbed four years ago to the same enemy that killed Bill. Marie was a gentle, perceptive, selfless friend, a blithe spirit who would drop everything and pack her bag the minute the mention of a trip to Ireland was made. She read the maps while I drove. She was supportive and enthusiastic about the research we did in Northern Ireland, and her extensive knowledge of Irish literature and history was an indispensable resource. She flagged only once: We were seated, shivering and somewhat timorous in a dank room, waiting to meet a woman who would have appalling stories to tell us, when Marie muttered, sotto voce, that perhaps my next writing project could be entitled "Women of the Sunny Mediterranean."

Joyce McCartan, whom I wrote about in the 1989 epilogue of this book after attending her son Gary's wake, died early this year. She was an indomitable spirit, one who chose a commitment to healing and reconciliation over bitterness when Gary was murdered and who used her energy for helping those in her community. She reached out to everyone; Protestant or Catholic, it made no difference to Joyce. I last saw her in the Women's Information Center offices in Belfast in June 1995, puffing on her ever-present cigarette. She was frail looking but as invincible as ever. We were talking about political prisoners: their rights, their potential release as a result of the cease-fire, and their rehabilitation. Joyce spoke up for victims' needs. "A lot of people here have sons and husbands who were murdered. I think their murderers should serve their time in prison. That's the only thing that helps ease the pain," she said. Joyce tried and was able to succeed in helping many people in Northern Ireland ease their pain.

During President and Mrs. Clinton's trip to Northern Ireland in November 1995, Joyce took great pride in showing Hillary Clinton around The Lamp Lighter, her fish-and-chip shop on the Ormeau Road. Before her death, Joyce received honors from Queen Elizabeth II and an honorary degree from Queens University, Belfast. She was highly amused by the latter honor, having quit school at the age of fourteen to help support her family.

Mairead Farrell, a young Belfast republican who had just finished serving a ten-year prison sentence when I met her in Belfast, was shot dead in Gibraltar some months later by the Special Air Services of the British Army. Mairead could have been, had she lived and chosen a constitutional path to express her political gifts, a leader among the disaffected minority in Northern Ireland.

Ronald Brown, the United States Secretary of Commerce, and his deputy, Charles Meissner, had been deeply involved with economic initiatives in Northern Ireland. Their enthusiasm had won the hearts of men and women in the North. They were killed in April 1996, in a plane crash in Croatia. Both men helped lay the groundwork for the White House Conference for Trade and Investment in Ireland. In December 1994, Secretary Brown had become the first cabinet-level American official to visit Northern Ireland.

WHERE ARE THEY NOW?

Lady Faulkner of Downpatrick is semi-retired in the countryside of County Down, running a rare-book business. She took time out of retirement to serve as one of the members of the prestigious Opsahl Commission. Her wise and balanced views are still welcomed in the tumult of emotional, sometimes angry, response to the problems facing the people of the North.

The Charabanc Theatre Company officially closed its doors in 1995, but all but one of its talented members are pursuing their theatrical careers elsewhere. It was a shock to learn that one of their members, Rosena Brown, the young mother of nine children whose natural acting ability would have taken her far in the theater, was imprisoned a few years ago when a large bomb was found in the trunk of her car during a routine search. Her former Charabanc colleagues were equally stunned by the discovery. I don't think any of them realized the depth of her political affiliation.

Marie Jones, the talented writer and actor and a founder of Charabanc, has scored one success after another with her plays. *A Night in November*, her one-man play, was produced in London and New York. *Women on the Verge of H.R.T.* will open at the Opera House in Belfast during the 1996–97 season. It has already been seen at the Gaiety Theatre in Dublin, the Pavilion in Glasgow and will go to London's West End. It has received rave reviews in all its venues. Her latest play, *Stones in His Pockets*, opened in the 1996 Theatre Festival in Dublin.

When Marie left Charabanc, she joined another Belfast theater company, Double Joint, as associate director.

Eleanor Methven and Carol Moore, two of the original Charabanc members, are now part of the Rough Magic theater company and continue their careers.

Mary McMahon has left the Workers' Party and is now devoting her time, energy, and compassionate help to the Travelling Community in Northern Ireland.

Eileen Evason is a prominent professor at the University of Ulster. Her rapid-fire delivery, her articulate intensity, and her irony have not dimmed. An afternoon's conversation with her is a mini-course in social economics. We sat in her garden in the sunshine of the extraordinary weather of the summer of 1996 and caught up with the past ten years and the social changes that have taken place in England and in Northern Ireland. I felt that we were just picking up where we had left off that summer twilight sitting in the back garden of the Charabanc Theatre home in Belfast. Her analysis of the economic forces that are changing Northern Ireland sounded eerily similar to the situation in the United States.

"Ten years ago when we were having arguments as feminists, we would talk about the way the health service doesn't serve women, but that has almost become a simple issue because now the argument is: Are we going to have a health service at all? We've had such deep changes that in the past the idea was women should have more rights, and women should have child care, and all the rest of it. But now what we're talking about are the very deep changes that have occurred in the kind of employment that is available to people.

"You're probably aware that our government has a particular strategy which is deregulation of the labor market. What that means is basically that nobody should have a secure job. What we are seeing is a massive growth in insecurity. So now we have large numbers of people who are unemployed and more who are badly employed, and a shrinking proportion of our labor force that has secure, permanent employment. That is having effects all over the place.

"For example, there is a serious problem here for single parents because part-time work is no use to them. They need a full-time job, that is how they get off benefits, that is how they increase their living standards. But that is not what is available. The bulk of new jobs are part-time jobs and that is destabilizing the family and how people can plan their lives. It is having an extraordinary devastating effect . . . so I've become interested in all these changes."

As part of her current academic research, Eileen is involved in a large and long-term project on the single-parent family.

The Gillespie sisters are happily married and, I hope, have put the deplorable events that landed them in prison behind them. The injustice of their imprisonment must always be a bitter legacy for them, but if, like so many other legacies left to the people of Northern Ireland, it can be used in a positive manner to combat injustice everywhere, it is not in vain.

Their friend from prison, Anne McGuire, is free now and trying to reestablish her life in London. Anne, her husband, brother, and two sons were arrested on suspicion of making bombs. Their arrest was based on a "confession" made by her nephew Gerard Conlon and his friend, Paul Hill, in the case of the Guildford pub bombing, which was publicized in the movie *In the Name of the Father.* Anne spent eleven years in custody, much of it in prison in Durham with Eileen and Ann Gillespie. The three women sustained each other through some difficult days in prison. Her imprisonment was described by Sir John May, in his report on the case to the British Attorney General, as "the worst miscarriage of justice that I have ever seen."

Berna McIvor is still enthusiastically involved in Social Democratic and Labour Party (SDLP) politics. When we visited during the summer of 1996 in Derry, she was rueful about the lack of women entering the political stream in Northern Ireland.

"It's been frustrating listening to women talking about politics. They want to share in the action and yet they will not join political parties. Too many middle-class women stay out of politics and play bridge and golf instead."

I said that a lot of the women I had spoken to thought they would lose the respect of their communities if they joined a political party.

"That's a shame! It really is. It has annoyed me intensely over the years to see that it's not respectful. And as the years go on, we get fewer in numbers. And I say that both for unionists and nationalists, it's exactly the same thing. They must have political views; there are social issues, economic issues. They care about people, and that's what politics is all about. You can only get change inside a political party. Most of the women I know would feel exactly the same as I do on social and economic issues.

"I've been working on education for the past seven years. We are a group of people who are unionists and nationalists, clergy, both Catholic and Presbyterian and others as well, trade-union representatives, and we are all working and cooperating together. The education boards are a model for the rest of the North. We can and do work together. We are simply for the young people of the North in our own area. There's no big problem. We have the same goals and we work in unity towards them.

"I'm a member of the Western Educational Board for the past seven years and chair for four. I was the first woman to chair an education board in the North of Ireland. It was while I was on the board that I met Lady Jean Mayhew. She's marvelous. It's wonderful what she has done here.

"And of course I'm still John's [Hume] campaign manager. I'm very optimistic about the future. Even in the worst days here, there were so many good people around, working hard. There's just an innate sense of decency about so many people. John has worked very, very hard; he's a hero. It took a lot of courage to do what he has done, and there was criticism about what he was doing. It hasn't been easy. He knew what he was doing, and he's been working towards that for some time, but it wasn't easy. You've come at the right time! You can see the peace, you can feel the peace!"

When I asked Berna what she thought about the American involvement in the peace process, her answer was resoundingly affirmative: "I think the Americans are absolutely crucial to the whole thing. The support of President Clinton has been wonderful. I have met Nancy Soderberg, too; she's been over here. She's made a marvelous contribution."

Dodie McGuinness has continued her involvement in Sinn Fein politics and is a respected activist and member of her community. She did not run for reelection for City Council in 1993, deciding instead to become more involved in internal party politics. She is now serving as the Six-County Director of Elections for Sinn Fein. We spoke recently in Boston where she attended, along with many other politicians from Northern Ireland, a seminar at Harvard's Kennedy School of Politics.

"One thing is different than it was when we talked back in the 1980s," she said. "The role of women in the party has progressed. Women are not being held back if there is a role they wish to play in the party."

She, like everyone else I spoke to in Northern Ireland, feels that Sinn Fein must be at the all-party talks if they are to make any progress toward a peaceful settlement.

Bríd Rodgers is also still in the forefront of SDLP politics in Northern Ireland. The Orange parade that caused the eruption of violence near Portadown in July 1996 is near her home, and she was, as she had been ten years ago, involved in conciliatory actions to contain the emotional reactions of the provocative march.

Annita and Austin Currie did finally leave Dungannon and move to the South of Ireland. Austin has continued his political life and was the Fine Gael candidate for the Irish presidency. He was defeated by Mary Robinson.

Many of the other women I wrote about are still soldiering on, trying to make a better world for themselves and their families. Their selflessness and their willingness to subordinate their private needs and desires into the greater good of their communities are indicative of the generous character that personifies women in Northern Ireland. I admired them from afar when I began to write this book. All these years later, that admiration has remained and grown.

THE POLITICS OF THE 1990S

To understand what has taken place in Northern Ireland since the late 1980s, one must review the shifting political landscape, which changes quickly and recklessly but nevertheless has moved the possibility of peace in that province to the position of a conceivable option.

The peace process in Northern Ireland has received invaluable impetus from the Clinton Administration. From the beginning of his campaign for the presidency, President Clinton had signaled that he was responsive to exerting U.S. pressure on the British government to move ahead with peace talks and that his administration would support such talks. He followed up on his commitment when elected President.

Nancy Soderberg, Clinton's Deputy National Security Advisor in the White House, previously had been an aide in Senator Edward Kennedy's office and had followed the Northern Ireland political scene. Her expertise and her scrutiny of the Anglo-Irish negotiations during the first year of the Clinton presidency were crucial.

In January 1994, President Clinton made a bold move and offered a forty-eight-hour visa to Gerry Adams, the President of Sinn Fein, so that he could visit the United States. Both the British government and the U.S. Department of State were incensed at the decision. Clinton stuck by it, and Adams came to the United States on a brief visit in February 1994. On February 1, he addressed a packed invitation-only Conference on Northern Ireland sponsored by the National Committee on American Foreign Policy; he was preceded by John T. Alderdice, leader of the Alliance Party and John Hume, leader of the Social Democratic and Labour Party. Adams ended his speech by saying: "It is our firm intention to remove and to see the removal of the gun from Irish politics."

His trip to the United States resulted in a media frenzy; he was hailed in some quarters as a conquering hero and received a standing ovation when he spoke at the Kennedy School of Politics at Harvard. Although the adulation he received in the United States is a far cry from the skepticism with which he is viewed by many at home, the visibility he received in America gave him the credibility he needed to persuade the IRA to announce their cease-fire.

December 15, 1993 After months of talks and negotiations, private and public, Prime Minister John Major of Great Britain and the then-Taoiseach of Ireland, Albert Reynolds, issued the Downing Street Declaration, a joint declaration that acknowledged that the most urgent need of their people was to "remove the causes of conflict, to overcome the legacy of history and to heal the divisions which have resulted."

The Prime Minister stated on behalf of the British people that they have "no selfish strategic or economic interest in Northern Ireland."

On behalf of the Irish government, the Taoiseach stated that he "considers that the lessons of Irish history, and especially of Northern Ireland, show that stability and well-being will not be found under any political system which is refused allegiance or rejected on grounds of identity by a significant minority of those governed by it. For this reason, it would be wrong to attempt to impose a united Ireland, in the absence of the freely given consent of a majority of the people of Northern Ireland. He accepts, on behalf of the Irish Government, that the democratic right of self-determination by the people of Ireland as a whole must be achieved and exercised with and subject to the agreement and consent of a majority of the people of Northern Ireland." The declaration challenges those who use or support violence to stop.

This historic document was achieved by establishing mutual trust and from the understanding that grew out of a genuine friendship between John Major and Albert Reynolds. It is an extraordinary achievement and builds upon the goals of the Anglo-Irish Agreement of 1885 and the long years of sporadic "talks" between the two governments.

August 31, 1994 The IRA announced their "complete cessation of military operations." It appeared that Gerry Adams and the nonviolent faction of Sinn Fein had succeeded in persuading the IRA that their political options were better than their military options. This announcement was met with universal joy in Northern Ireland.

October 13, 1994 The Loyalists announced their cease-fire.

February 22, 1995 A document called "Frameworks for the Future" was launched in Northern Ireland by Prime Minister Major and the new Taoiseach, John Bruton. Called "A New Framework for Agreement," it sets out the British and Irish governments' proposals for relationships within Ireland and between the two governments.

Shortly thereafter, a document called "A Framework for Accountable Government in Northern Ireland" was promulgated separately by Prime Minister Major, which gives the British government's own proposals for possible new democratic institutions in Northern Ireland.

May 1995 President Clinton continued his commitment by appointing former Senate Majority George Mitchell to be his special adviser on economic initiatives in Northern Ireland. Assisted by an able and highly efficient staff headed by the indefatigable Martha Pope, Senator Mitchell organized a White House Conference, for Trade and Investment in Ireland, hosted by Clinton.

November 1995 President and Mrs. Clinton made their historic visit to Northern Ireland and the Republic of Ireland. While the President addressed the business community, officials, politicians, and the plain citizens of Northern Ireland, Mrs. Clinton visited with women who have been involved in community work for years, many of whom who have appeared in this book.

Moving on to Dublin, she addressed an impressive gathering of four hundred women leaders from the North and South of Ireland at the National Gallery of Art in Dublin. In her remarks to the assembled crowd (speaking to "tumultuous applause, roars and the occasional tear"), she talked about the women she had met in Belfast: "The women I spoke with yesterday are not high-level diplomats or professional negotiators. They have not yet been elected to office. But they are women, Catholic and Protestant alike, whose lives and families have been affected by the violence. They took it upon themselves to go door-to-door in their neighborhoods to say: Stop the bloodshed. Their grief became their and our call to action."

She quoted Katharine Tynan, the Irish poet:

> I am the pillars of the house;
> The keystone of the arch am I.
> Take me away, and roof and wall
> Would fall to ruin utterly.

During the ovation after Hillary Clinton's speech, Hilda Tweedie, a woman's rights campaigner of many years, said: "She said all the things we tried to say for years. That was Hillary Clinton speaking. Not Bill Clinton's wife."

Gemma Hussey, the former Minister for Education in Ireland, and a longtime political activist and writer, said: "Hillary's speech at the Gallery was a tour de force. She spoke clearly and diplomatically . . . she struck the right note exactly, without a hint of patronizing or preaching."

The Clintons' visit to Ireland was a high point on the road to peace in Northern Ireland. The people of the North of all political backgrounds were jubilant. The spirit of the Christmas season and the still-existent cease-fire combined to make it a joyous moment. They felt that, at last, there was an American President who took their cause seriously, whose involvement, support, and political pressure would help them "win the gold"—the peace that has been so elusive for so long.

January 1996 Senator George Mitchell was sent to Ireland by President Clinton to head up an international body to provide an independent assessment of the decommissioning of arms issue, which had led to an impasse, one side arguing that decommissioning should take place before the talks began, and the other that it could only take place after a settlement at the talks had been reached.

Senator Mitchell, aided by General John de Chastelain of Canada and Harri Holkeri of Norway, submitted their report on January 22. They had held meetings in December 1995 and January 1996 in Belfast, Dublin, and London, with oral and written presentations from government officials, political leaders, church officials, and representatives of organizations and institutions. At that time, the cease-fire had been in place for a year and a half.

In the excellent report the Mitchell Commission submitted, a recurring theme was that because of a lack of trust, "steeped in history" among all parties even well-intentioned acts are often viewed with suspicion and hostility. While condemning punishment killings and beatings, they urged all paramilitary organizations to agree to a total disarmament, verifiable to an independent commission, and to renounce the use of force to influence the outcome of the all-party negotiations, and that decommissioning should suggest neither victory nor defeat. The commission suggested that decommissioning should take place during the process of the all-party negotiations

February 18, 1996 The IRA cease-fire ended with the bombing of the Docklands in Manchester, England.

May 30, 1996 Elections were held for the establishment of the Northern Ireland Forum.

June 10, 1996 The all-party talks began, without the presence of Sinn Fein.

July 12, 1996 Violence spread again in Northern Ireland as an aftermath of the annual Orange parades; particularly provocative was the march from the Drumcree parish church near Portadown down the Garvahy Road, through a mainly Catholic, nationalist neighborhood. Royal Ulster Constabulary Chief Constable, Sir Hugh Annesley, reversed his decision to ban the parade as the marchers grew in numbers and threatened violence if the parade was not allowed to follow its planned route. This decision was looked upon by the nationalist citizens of the communities involved as a clear acceptance of "might over right" and a denial of their own rights to be protected by the police.

It was to the great relief of the citizens of Northern Ireland, Catholic and Protestant, that subsequent parades during the "Marching Season" passed off with relatively little violence. There was a sense that leaders of the different communities involved tried to employ both common sense and conciliation to defuse potential confrontation and violence.

Boston, Massachusetts
August 1996

I AM
OF
IRELAND

"I am of Ireland,
And the Holy Land of Ireland
And time runs on," cried she.
"Come out of charity,
Come dance with me in Ireland."

William Butler Yeats

Prologue

My ties with the North of Ireland are both inherited and cultivated. In 1832, my great-great-grandparents left a small, rocky patch of land at Warrenpoint, near Newry, in County Down, which is now one of the six counties of Northern Ireland. They sailed to Baltimore, Maryland, on an immigrant ship. He, Owen McNelly, eventually made a success of raising sheep in Virginia. She, Catherine Killian, had a one-year-old baby boy to care for on the journey to America and was expecting her second child. The one-year-old became my great-grandfather, and he continued the family's farming tradition in south Texas. It was probably a good thing that they emigrated when they did, despite the broken hearts they left behind: they were Catholics, and in County Down in 1832 that was not the fast track.

As a child I had become infatuated with stories of Catherine Killian and her journey from Ireland to America. There were only snippets of family history about her, but I happily embellished them and created my own fantasy about this young Irish woman, poor, pregnant, gallant, babe in arms, making that arduous Atlantic crossing to face unknown hardships. As her story wove its way into my creative imagination, she became the measure of my own pluck, courage, and stamina. How could I not work hard in school when she had taught herself to read and write? If I was green with morning sickness, who was I to groan when she had been pregnant on an immigrant ship without stabilizers? If my husband came home and announced out of the blue, when we had a small child and a baby, "We're moving to London for the year, pack up," how could I demur when *she* had left her family forever to begin a new life in a new land? (No letters of introduction in *her* trunk.) When life was hard, sad, or boring, how could I wallow in self-pity when my mind's voice would bring me up short, saying: "What would Catherine have done?" I don't know the secret route by which another person enters one's imagination and works those tricks, but I do know that she became my oracle, critic, censor, and straw boss.

I had thought one day to write a novel about her, to make her into the kind of heroine my imagination longed for her to be. Then I could bask in her image. But before that novel got written, I moved to Ireland, began visiting the North, met women there, and marveled at the brave good humor they maintain in circumstances designed to break one's heart. I decided I didn't need to create a romantic fictional woman to tell the story of Northern Ireland. The women living there now, in Belfast and Derry, in the country and in small towns and villages, in their stoic acceptance of the horrors going on around them, are heroines enough.

I also wanted to write about the women of Northern Ireland because the country seems to me to be like a secret society for men. They belong to all-male clubs, invent childlike mysterious handshakes, march to loud drumbeats, make deals, stir up hatreds, and try — some of them — to find the solutions to the problems that they and men of previous generations have created. They have excluded women from the struggles that produced the North's awful sectarian and political dilemma and from their unsuccessful efforts to resolve it. Women's voices, which might have had a moderating effect, have gradually faded and died away in Northern Ireland.

I wanted to listen to the women in the North in a way that only an outsider can. The barriers created by their religious and cultural differences are so high now that they don't cross them to talk to each other. Although an outsider can never fully understand the nuances of the lives of others, she can report what they say. Why the women there will open their hearts and homes to a stranger, but not to each other, is one of the many enigmas of this tormented land. An irony of my research in Northern Ireland is that I found — without a single exception — all the women I have met there to be hospitable, open, willing to talk to me, and helpful to an extraordinary degree. (Once when I asked Lucy Faulkner, the widow of the last Prime Minister of Northern Ireland, if she was offended by so many people coming to her country and questioning the attitudes there, she laughed and said: "Heavens, no. We all enjoy the national psychoanalysis.")

I had my first opportunity to visit Northern Ireland when my husband was appointed Ambassador to the Republic of Ireland in 1977.

Although we lived in Dublin, we were both intensely interested in the political situation in the North. Since that first trip (visiting Newry, my ancestral grounds, and walking over the rocky land of nearby Warrenpoint), I have been back many times. When I began, I knew three people in Northern Ireland. My circle widened as everyone I spoke to suggested another name. The "research" was done in kitchens, sitting rooms, in the front seat of a car, or on a park bench. I didn't intend to write another analysis of the political situation in the North, nor is this book meant to be an apology for one side or the other.

I have veered from despair to optimism, believing on one trip that everything seemed so much better than the last time, then returning to find nothing changed. With an American's belief in the "quick fix," I looked for logical solutions in a situation where logic has ceased to exist. And I became engrossed in the corrosive effects that violence, hatred, fear, and bigotry have on people over a period of years, particularly women. I grew up in an American town untouched by violence and with bigotry hidden behind good manners. I have one vague memory of walking home from school one day and being called a "Cat-Licker" for Catholic, a term I thought as funny as the name-callers must have thought it derisive. In Northern Ireland I was confronted with a cult of nationalism (on both sides) that glorified bigotry and made economic and cultural differences impassable. I saw women as the innocent victims of this cult, not as the perpetrators.

When I first moved to Ireland, one of the many misconceptions I had was that the "Irish problem" would preoccupy the Irish people of Dublin. The Women's Peace Movement had caught the imagination of Americans, and women in the United States were involved in it. I was, therefore, stunned in my first month in Dublin to hear a group of women journalists, whom I had invited to lunch, talk about Irish issues and to find that their interest in Northern Ireland was nil. They scoffed at the Women's Peace Movement and said, in effect, that there were enough other problems facing Ireland. As far as they were concerned, the people in the North could solve their own problems, most of which they had brought on themselves. There were even dark hints that if the six counties were to fall away from the mainland of Ireland and disappear into the sea, mourning would not be universal.

That attitude toward Northern Ireland continued to be the major theme I heard through my years of living in Ireland. There is likely to be far more heated and lively discussion about the pros and cons of the IRA in a bar in South Boston than in any pub on the quays in Dublin. But my own interest did not diminish. In seven trips to Northern Ireland, five of them between March 1986 and May 1987, I visited the homes, farms, offices, shops, and schools of many women, of all political shades and social and economic status. These are the stories I heard from them, the women whose soft voices have too long been muted by the drums of violence.

Three Towns

I am free of all prejudices. I hate everyone equally.

— *W.C. FIELDS*

PORTADOWN: MARCH 1986

WE RENTED A CAR in Dublin and drove to Northern Ireland via Newry. No one bothered to stop us or even look our way as we drove across the border, although cars from the opposite direction, coming into the Republic from the North, were being stopped and searched. It was a week before Easter, traditionally a tense time in Northern Ireland, when celebrations and marches on both sides can end in "sectarian violence" with the beat of a drum or the hurling of a rock. I was on my way to Portadown and Belfast, traveling with an American friend. It was my first trip to the North since 1981, and the first for this book.

Newry looked prosperous and bustling, much more so than the dreary, barricaded little town I had visited five years ago when I was angrily stopped by a British soldier for trying to take a picture of my father standing beside a road sign. Then the town had been filled with soldiers and tanks, and the main streets were cordoned off with rolls of barbed wire and cement-filled barrels. There was none of that in sight today.

As we drove down the main street, which runs parallel to the river, a hailstorm suddenly belted down so hard we had to pull over and wait five minutes for it to subside. Shoppers and children dashed into shops for cover. It drummed on the roof of the car, drowning out conversation, and hailstones the size of pecans bounced off the water of the narrow river, turning its surface into tiny volcanoes of white foam. It was over as suddenly as it had begun, and brilliant sunshine glistened on the wet pavement. People poured out of shop doors, cars shifted into gear, and movement on the streets began again. Northern Ireland's whimsical weather can alter the tempo of life as suddenly and as unexpectedly as a lethal paramilitary action. People here are so used to both interruptions that they return to normality instantly.

Just outside Newry we were stopped by a roadblock. Young British soldiers asked for identification and seemed inclined to chat. They were very amused at the "purpose of my visit" and made obvious remarks about helping me with my "research." ("I could tell you plenty about the women here," they assured me, not even well into manhood themselves.) They wanted to know what Boston was like. They were lonely and homesick in Northern Ireland, they said, and counting the days until they could return home to England.

Maria, my traveling friend, had lit a cigarette and rolled down the window to blow her smoke out; she suddenly let out a little yelp and nudged me. There, inches from her side of the car on the narrow country road, were ten or twelve soldiers in camouflage, faces blackened, belly-down on the grassy verge of the road, with rifles pointed directly at us. They were so still and so quiet, and their green and brown fatigue suits merged so smoothly with the grassy ditch, that I hadn't seen them as I stopped the car to hand over my identification to the soldier on the road. Their presence seemed like such a discordant contrast to the quiet, serene countryside that it was more like stumbling by mistake upon a movie set than witnessing a deadly serious military operation.

We arrived in Portadown in midafternoon. Famous for being perhaps the most bigoted town in all of Northern Ireland (in a highly competitive field), Portadown has carefully nourished its prejudices through the decades. Edward Carson, the Unionist delight of the 1912 era, once said proudly, "The Home Rule Bill might pass Parliament, but it will *never* pass Portadown."

I planned to interview two women in Portadown. Both are sisters of friends; one is Catholic, one Protestant. My first stop was the small, whitewashed stucco house on a quiet, tree-lined residential street where Christine, the Protestant, lived. She is a young American woman who had met and married a Northern Irishman while both were students at Trinity College in Dublin. Her American background made her an ideal interviewee for my transition to Northern Irish attitudes. An "outsider" by Portadown standards, Christine has made an extraordinary transformation from a Massachusetts, Irish-Catholic girl into a quintessential North of Ireland Presbyterian wife, mother, professional librarian. Her North of Ireland accent is indistinguishable to my ears from anyone else's in Portadown. Even her living room, with its little red-brick fireplace, floral rug, and knickknacks on the mantel, show no signs of American decorative taste.

"I always felt like those people you used to read about who have had sex changes," Christine laughed, pouring tea for us and her friend Kay. "You know, they'd say, 'I felt that I was the wrong person in the wrong body,' or something like that. Well, I felt like that in America. When I first came to Ireland, to Dublin, in fact, to go to university, I suddenly felt like I had come home. And then I met my husband and came to live in Portadown and was even more at home. The southern Irish were always too lazy for my taste. Even though I'm still an American citizen, I have adopted a tribe here, and I feel comfortable in it; of course I have none of the tribal instincts, none of the historical subconscious that everyone here has.

"I've invited friends in to talk to you, a wee Protestant this afternoon, a wee Catholic tonight." She grinned. "So you see, we *can* have Protestant and Catholic friends. The street we live on is mixed." It is an attractive, well-tended block, like any English middle-class neighborhood.

"The Troubles are a class thing, Christine," Kay, the "wee Protestant," interrupted. "I drove to Armagh the other day with a Catholic friend, and if *my* neighbors knew I'd done that, they'd reckon the car should be fumigated. I'm not exaggerating." Kay lives in a Protestant housing development; unlike Christine's mixed street, bigotry and suspicion are a way of life in the strictly segregated housing developments of Portadown.

"It *is* a class thing," Christine agreed, "but that being the case, you would think that education would change you, but it doesn't. In Ireland, you can't buy an education, you can only earn it. Poor people have a chance of getting a university place, and it seems that while they are at university they mix easily, but that doesn't carry over to their lives afterwards. Being educated doesn't necessarily change them."

"I was the only Protestant growing up in a rural area near here,"

Kay explained. "As a child, I was never conscious of any differences. They went to their school, we went to ours. When they passed a chapel, they made the sign of the cross, and I always wondered why. Only once was I bullied in my whole childhood: a group of children shouted: 'You're a dirty Prod!'

"'No!' I shouted back. 'I'm not a Prod, I'm a Presbyterian!'

"But things are so much worse now. I left Ireland in nineteen sixty-two and came back in nineteen sixty-seven, and things had changed so much. For one thing, the Reverend Ian had come on the scene."

Christine made a wry face as Paisley's name was brought up. "As a Christian, I guess I have to love him as a human being, but there's not much love for that man among my friends," she said. "My own Presbyterian Church is against violent action; it stands for talk and consultation. We don't even consider the Free Presbyterians [Paisley's church] Presbyterians at all. I work with a DUP man [the Democratic Unionist Party, Paisley's political party], and I have to listen to him preach at me all the time. Believe me, a discreet or reticent DUP man doesn't exist! All we hear about is how the Anglo-Irish Agreement must go. They're against it on principle without stopping to think. You can't reason with him. The DUP is *always* right. If you disagree ever so slightly, even with their methods, you are a traitor. I try to ignore him, but he pushes me so hard that I really have to control myself, especially because I'm his boss!"

A few weeks before our visit to Portadown, there had been a one-day general strike in Northern Ireland, called by the DUP to protest the signing of the Anglo-Irish Agreement. The stories in American papers had talked about intimidation by Protestant extremists, and I asked the women about that.

"The level of intimidation was dynamite!" Christine burst out. "I was intimidated by someone I know. He came into my office and said: 'You must stay home; it's your duty, and if you come to work, there's people in this town who will know it, and you won't have much of a house left. And your husband will have no business. *And* I know you have a wee child.' I was in tears and called my husband to tell him about it, but he said: 'Ach, he's a big pudding! Ignore him.' But I'm bloody-minded, too. I might have stayed away on Monday [the day of the strike] just to get a day off work, but once he came in and started all that talk, I was determined to go to work. And I did. Actually, most of the staff tried to get in, too, but they couldn't get through the roadblocks. Of course 'they' [the DUP] claim full support. It's not support, but who's going to stop them? Nobody. Intimidation works. It has before, and it will again. They don't go in for killings, but they would be very happy to come and break your windows."

"Women here are so different than women in the South," Christine said. "It's a matriarchal society down there. Southern women wait on men in a way we *never* would. They treat the men like children and that gives them a certain power. But more women in the North work outside their homes; that's always been our tradition."

Working-class society is unique in Northern Ireland. Employment opportunities in the nineteenth and early twentieth centuries, such as in the shirt factories of Derry and the linen mills of Belfast, relied heavily on female workers. So women there have a long tradition of working outside their homes, of being wage earners (sometimes the *only* wage earner) in a post-Victorian society that kept middle-class women tied to their homes. The self-reliance that developed from providing for their families turned these women into a strong, dominating force in Ulster. They gained their power not by dominance in the home but by bringing home the bread.

The paradox of women taking both the social and financial responsibilities of home away from the men turned those men into childlike figures. Idle, resentful, their sense of inferiority bred by generations of frustration, they were easily turned toward political violence. The gun and the bomb, or close proximity to them, gave them a sense of machismo that their everyday life had denied them.

"Given that tradition of self-sufficiency and confidence among the women," I asked, "why aren't any women taking a leadership role in politics, in working toward a solution for Northern Ireland's problems? The Women's Peace Movement is dead; one never hears anything about Bernadette Devlin McAliskey these days. You can count female politicians on one hand. Are there any women in Portadown trying to establish formal talks with each other, getting together and exchanging political ideas with other women?"

"No," Kay answered. "There's no feeling here about getting together with women to talk . . . certainly not about politics."

"You see," Christine added, "the longer you live here, you see that there is no solution. There are very good, law-abiding citizens here who want to remain British, and that's important to them. They fear the Anglo-Irish Agreement. Nothing in the world will change them.

They can never accept the concept of a united Ireland. Never. As long as they are in the majority, that's out."

"We won't ever be a united Ireland," Kay agreed. "Paisley's lot will make certain of it. And as long as the six counties exist, you'll have a disaffected nationalist population. So you can't win."

The two women were talking fast, interrupting each other, each wanting to make emphatic the point that there was no solution.

"I have a neighbor," Christine said. "She's more orange than orange. She says: 'There's going to be a war with dead bodies all over the place!' I think she relishes the idea!"

I knew that I would hear the "no solution" answer over and over again; I'd been hearing it since I first visited Northern Ireland. The first time I was shocked . . . and indignant. But obviously, when thoughtful people say it, they believe it. So what does it mean? That they will go on forever as they are now?

One can make an analogy in this country with our crime problem. To non-Americans, it seems dreadful, an untenable situation. No one in the United States "approves" of our high crime rate. No one thinks that old people should be afraid to go out of their houses at night, or answer their doorbells, for fear of rape, mugging, burglary, or murder. But I and my women friends don't meet with each other to try to find solutions to the crime problem.

It was getting dark and raining again when Kay stood up to leave us. She had to go home to prepare dinner for her husband. Christine urged us to stay and have dinner with her. "My husband is working late and won't be home for dinner. I made vegetable lasagna. Do stay." It didn't take more to persuade us. She and her husband were making improvements on their home and we complimented her on her pretty, cheerful kitchen.

"My friends thought I was daft, but the first thing I did was to put in a dishwasher. I guess I'm still that American." Her talk, as we sat at the small round table in the kitchen, was intelligent and thoughtful, and totally lacking the ponderous intensity that some American women affect when talking "seriously." Her insights were spiced with humor and a wry, Northern wit, and despite the grim and dismal story of political life in Northern Ireland, she showed no signs of stress because of the political hotbed in which she lives.

Before we left the table, another friend came in, a quiet Catholic woman, who, like Kay and Christine, deplores the sectarian violence around her but also, like them, sees no end and no solution.

"I don't know," she sighed. "It seems to me that the only answer is in prayer. Nothing anyone else has tried has done any good. The good people in Northern Ireland are being held ransom."

We left Christine at eleven and spent the night in a small local hotel. Stopping off in the bar to have a nightcap, we watched a group of teenagers arrive for a late-night drink. They were well-dressed, laughing, good to look at, like middle-class teenagers everywhere. Were they Catholics? Protestants? Mixed? I hadn't been there long enough to tell by their looks.

Unlike Christine, Pat Hughes was born and brought up in the North. She met us for coffee the next morning at the hotel. Despite having seven children under fourteen, she managed to arrive promptly at nine looking like a model on assignment, in a white leather suit, pink shirt, and pink socks. Her lovely, pale skin could only have been Irish. Pat is not interested in politics; she is busy with her children, her two homes, and her husband's business. She feels no anger, bitterness, or antagonism toward any religion. Catholic herself, she has Protestant and Catholic friends, derides the extremists on both sides with equal scorn, and stays as far away from the Troubles as she can. Her husband, a prosperous Portadown businessman, is so unaware of politics, Pat said, "that when a man came to our house soliciting funds for the 'Alliance' [a political party], Connor thought he said 'The Lions' and gave him a donation.

"Protestants shop in my husband's stores all the time," Pat said. "If anything, it's Catholics who are jealous of his success." Envy of success is a common trait here, one that runs deep in the Irish psyche; when you are down and out, you can't have a better friend than the Irish. Hit a run of luck, and watch out. Quoting the old refrain that the Northern Irish Protestants are more loyal to the half-crown than to the Crown, she feels they have more respect for a successful Catholic businessman than the Catholics do themselves. "The Protestants know the worth of money," she said with a smile, lighting another cigarette. "They may not approve of smoking or drinking, but that's because it costs money!"

"What about sex?" I asked.

"Sex is okay, if it's free," she laughed.

After we finished breakfast and checked out of the hotel, Pat offered to take us on a driving tour of Portadown. "I'd like to see the Tunnel," I told her. The Tunnel is a working-class Catholic section of Portadown, so called because a railway tunnel used to run through it. An Orange Order parade had been planned to march through the Tunnel in a week, on Easter Monday — a provocative act that was sure to cause trouble. Orange Order leaders had been asked to reroute the parade, a simple means to a peaceful compromise, but so far they had refused.

Founded in 1795, the Orange Order is the largest Protestant organization in Northern Ireland, with 100,000 members. It takes its name from William of Orange, and its largest march, the July 12 parade, celebrates King William's victory over King James II at the Battle of the Boyne. Its spokesmen are openly hostile to the Roman Catholic religion. Two of its main purposes are to maintain the status quo of the Unionist tradition in Northern Ireland and to protect Protestants against civil disorder. Thousands of Protestant men march in Orange parades. They wear orange sashes, which they revere, passing them down from father to son, and they beat big drums. Membership in one of the lodges of the Orange Order is a necessary requirement for Protestant politicians in Northern Ireland.

When we drove through that day, the Tunnel was peaceful and quiet, with the down-at-the-heels, silent dreariness of so many poor Northern Irish neighborhoods. Rows of small gray stucco houses, their windows lace-curtained, lined the streets. Some graffiti and a boarded-up shop were the only visible signs of the Tunnel's past troubles.

Four Months Later

I returned to Portadown four months after my first visit. This time the town was festooned with Unionist flags and symbols in preparation for the big July 12 parade. Overhead, the streets were draped with swags of red, white, and blue bunting. British flags hung from every Unionist house. Curbstones were painted red, white, and blue. Balloons of the same colors bounced around in the breeze. A huge poster in the center of the town square said "Portadown Still Says No!!" (In February the poster had just said "Portadown Says No," signaling opposition to the Anglo-Irish Agreement.) There was an air of festivity in the town; heavy traffic crowded the streets and pedestrian shoppers filled the sidewalks. It seemed like the prelude to the Fourth of July in the United States, except for the un-July-like chill rain coming down hard, the hum overhead of army helicopters, and the young soldiers on the streets in their black and green uniforms, carrying rifles, peering into the windows of parked cars.

I met Pat Hughes again, and she took me for a drive through the Protestant sections of Portadown to see all the banners and flags. Built in every vacant lot were huge bonfires that would be lit over the next few nights as part of the celebration. It is the custom for people to save all their old junk for the year and throw it on the bonfires to burn. Some of the piles are three stories high.

We passed through another neighborhood with more flags, more banners, and another bonfire laid in the center of a little rubble-strewn park. I asked Pat to stop while I got out to take a picture of it. A very tough-looking gang of teenage boys started walking in tandem toward me. I made a tentative decision to hold my own and not appear to be frightened off. As they got nearer and I could see their tattoos, their earrings, their punk hairstyles, and the very ugly expressions of their faces, I realized my decision had been a bad one. I took one quick, unfocused picture and beat it.

I had planned to spend the night in Portadown, but Pat and her husband both thought that my rented car with a southern Ireland license plate put me in unnecessary danger. It would be better, they suggested, if I stayed in a small hotel in a nearby town, where tensions wouldn't be running as high as they were in Portadown for that July 12 celebration. I took their advice.

The next day I drove back into town to watch the parade. I parked well away from the planned route and simply followed the noise and the crowds until I stood where the marchers were to pass. I was surprised to see that so many of the onlookers were drunk: I had the idea that loyalist Protestants in the North of Ireland were teetotalers.

I could hear the parade drums. Is there another sound like lambeg drums? Loud, insistent, aggressive, sepulchral, their dull, slow beat reverberates through the air. The sound of the drums grew closer, a solemn, ponderous warning of the march to follow. A dangerous sound. "Once you have heard the beat of a lambeg drum, you never get the sound out of your head," a Northern Irish friend said to me.

The marchers came on and on and on, their feet thudding on the pavement in tandem with the beat of the drums. Dozens, then hundreds of them, all dressed in black suits with black bowler hats that sat squarely on their heads, and orange sashes or aprons or little streamers pinned to their lapels. Many carried banners avowing their loyalty to God and country. Some wore uniforms that didn't fit. They looked strangely akin, like half brothers. Pale faces, overweight, serious. The only females in the parade were the drum majorettes, also in ill-fitting uniforms. All the marchers came from different lodges around the country and were identified by their lodge.

Boom. Boom. Boom. The drummers flicked their drumsticks in a high circle over their heads, then brought them back against the drumhead with arrogant force. Pipers followed, their high, tinny notes livening up the tempo. They sang songs, they marched on. The crowd loved them; they were much happier and more enthusiastic than the marchers. They waved and yelled and clapped, getting drunker. Small children darted in and out of the street as the marchers passed by. Usually I am a lover of parades, always tempted to join in, but there was something ominous and funereal about this one.

I read in the papers the next day that there had been fights, rioting, and general disturbance at various points the parade had passed. In my spot, the only disturbance was some pushing and shoving among the wee drunks, lots of obscene language and innuendo, and much good-natured bantering. The parade itself was a big bore.

BELFAST: MARCH 1986

After the tortuous bends of the narrow, dangerously picturesque roads of the Republic of Ireland, where drivers are kept alert dodging potholes, stray cattle, and aimless sheep, the highway system in Northern Ireland is a dream. The well-maintained four-lane motorway that leads into Belfast picks up traffic as it nears the city, giving a stranger the feeling that she is approaching a large metropolitan center. It's a surprise, then, to find oneself entering not a bustling city, but a big, lumbering town. It doesn't have the stunning Georgian architecture of Dublin, but its warm red-brick Victorian buildings are handsome, and there is a well-cared-for, prim, satisfied air about the neat, middle-class neighborhood I entered from the motorway.

My route followed the Malone Road, with its ornate brick houses and large, well-tended gardens, into University Road, past Queens University, and, after an awkward U-turn, up the Stranmillis Road. Shoppers and pedestrians were hurrying along Stranmillis, which is lined with small boutiques, meat and vegetable shops, bakeries, newsagents, and a large, well-stocked wine store — all the necessities of a prosperous, middle-class neighborhood. Late lunch-goers drifted out of restaurants with flushed animation on their faces. I was staying with a friend whose house is just behind Stranmillis, facing the Botanic Garden. Its manicured lawns were filled with the annual March offering of yellow daffodils, a certain announcement of spring despite the wintry chill in the air. This is not the Belfast of the evening news; no army patrols, smashed storefronts, or crowds of surly-faced teenagers huddled on street corners here. This is a serene neighborhood. Students from Queens University saunter out of the back gate of the Botanic Garden, dressed in jeans and sneakers; only their paler faces and longer hair make them look any different from American students. Rows of cars are parked bumper to bumper half on the street, half on the sidewalk to make more room in the narrow road.

I unloaded my luggage from the trunk of my rented car, proud of myself for having arrived without mishap and very grateful to have a friend with whom to stay. I had no doubt that as I grew to know it, Belfast would become a familiar place, and familiarity would make it seem ordinary. To a stranger, knowing only television coverage of the city's troubled neighborhoods, its very name conjures up an image of menace lurking behind every closed door. I dragged my suitcase up the long, narrow flight of stairs in my friend's house. A small conservatory built on the side of his second-floor living room is filled with plants and trailing vines, and I paused there to admire the view. It looks out over the street and beyond to the green parkland and neat gravel walks of the Botanic Garden below. All is peaceful and quiet. This is the other Belfast.

In Twinbrook, a working-class housing development in Belfast, thin, rough-coated dogs bark and snarl at strangers and roam the dismal, littered open fields in packs of three and four, looking ill-fed and mean. Rows and rows of gray stucco two-story houses, attached in groups of five, dot the littered fields. No trees or shrubs soften the landscape, no daffodils bloom here. Twinbrook was built to be a model development, integrated, comfortable, and spacious, a good place to bring up children. Fifteen years ago, any working-class family in West Belfast would have jumped at the chance to live in Twinbrook. Today it looks like a sad and dreary place. The Protestants have fled, intimidated and fearful. Behind closed doors and lace-covered windows, the stress of political violence and economic depression takes its toll on the residents. Bobby Sands, the first of the hunger strikers to die, was from Twinbrook. His body lay in the family house while thousands of mourners lined up to pay their last respects.

The big, bankrupt DeLorean car factory stands desolate and empty in the back of Twinbrook, a symbol of the area's desperate unemployment. Over 50 percent of the men here are out of work, with all the ensuing social problems. Men spend their empty days drinking, watching television, loitering, playing the odd game of snooker . . . a pointless social round certain to destroy initiative, sap self-confidence, and strain family life. Wife-beating is common. Half of the married couples are separated. Some of the men are in prison, others have disappeared, some have gone to seek work elsewhere. Here, as everywhere in Ireland, the mothers hold the fort. They take care of the children, manage the house, visit the school, and pray daily that their teenagers won't get into trouble. They make prison visits if their husbands or sons are inside. In Twinbrook, when a kid is in trouble, he faces a double threat: not only does he have the police to contend with, he is also a target for the IRA. They act as an alternative police force, a diligent and vicious vigilante corps who regard any action that might bring the RUC (Royal Ulster Constabulary) to Twinbrook as "anti-social behavior," punishable swiftly and thoroughly by "one of their own." Punishments used to consist of "kneecapping" — shooting the victim through the knee — which caused agonizing pain, a prolonged recuperation period, and usually permanent damage to the knee. More recently, they have discovered that a shot through the ankle bone is more effective. It creates longer-lasting and more severe disability.

The most seductive and dangerous pastimes for the bored, restless, and aimless teenagers is joyriding. Stealing a car from somewhere in the city, they drive it at high speed through town, crashing barricades, egging on the police to give chase, and end up wrecked or cornered.

If they escape the police, they abandon the car back in Twinbrook. When caught by the police, they are hauled up to juvenile court and sentenced to a detention home. The severity of the sentence depends on their past criminal record. When caught by the IRA, there is no court and no trial, just a quick pull of the trigger, a smashed ankle bone . . . and a limp for life. The "organization," as the IRA is called, is relentless in its pursuit of these delinquent teenagers. They are eager to maintain their reputation as authoritarian defenders of the neighborhood, which was the rationale for their reemergence in the early 1970s. They are also quick to spot an easy profit: when the injured offender is reimbursed by the government for having been shot, the IRA collects 25 percent of the reimbursement for its own coffers, a bizarre racket among many others they run. Their extortion network is all-pervasive: shops, pubs, taxi drivers, delinquent teenagers — no one is exempt.

Some of the Twinbrook mothers who had suffered through their sons' involvement in joyriding got together in 1984 to give each other community support. I met them the day after my arrival in Belfast, in the home of one of the women. Nine of us crowded into her cozy living room, warmed by a coal fire. A picture of the Sacred Heart of Jesus hung on one wall; two pictures of small children in their First Communion finery, knickknacks on the mantel, and a decorative Chinese umbrella hanging whimsically upside down from the ceiling completed the decor. Our hostess brought in the obligatory raisin bread and tea, and the women began to talk about their experiences: the fear of their sons getting caught, the loneliness and isolation of their situation, the certain knowledge of reprisal if they are caught.

Marie is a handsome, gray-haired mother of nine. She wore a skirt and sweater, stylish green boots and a matching green scarf around her neck, and, like the other women in the room, had just had her hair done in anticipation of a community party that evening. She sat on one end of the sofa and spoke in a soft, firm voice.

"I never thought it would happen to us," she said. "None of my kids had ever been in trouble before, and this one had a job and was going to work every day. I thought everything was just fine with him. I had no idea he was joyriding."

"Don't forget the wee touch of arson he got into," one of the women reminded her. Marie sighed and shook her head.

"Of course, the other kids knew about it before I did. They always do. I guess I was the last to know, and I didn't want to believe it. I would curse, then pray, then walk the streets alone at night. I didn't know where to turn and felt totally alone. I was so ashamed, and yet you want to stand up for them, despite the tears and the anger. In the end, I'm glad it was the police that caught him, not the other.

"He's in a youth detention center now. I think he'll be all right when he gets out. I really don't know what I would have done if I hadn't met these other women." She smiled at the others sitting around the room. "They all had the same troubles, they all knew what I was suffering. It was meeting them that saw me through."

Kathleen, the dynamic and articulate woman who founded the group, agreed. "We all suffered, but we suffered alone. This is a funny place. We tend to go about our own business and not interfere with each other. But finally I decided that it's happening to a lot of us, why not get together and at least share our experiences and sympathize with each other."

The only man in the room, the husband of our hostess, interrupted to explain the social situation to me, the prevalence of glue-sniffing among the very young children, the heavy drinking, the sense of futility. "You see, most of the kids in trouble now moved in here in the early nineteen seventies. They've seen everything: the violence, the killings and bombings. They have always been under great stress. Sure, we all have, but it was their whole childhood."

"Do the girls get into joyriding?" I asked.

"They don't; they sometimes have boyfriends who do, and they would try to protect them. Sometimes they might even go for a ride. But it's the boys that do it. It's their thing."

Apparently, it's an epidemic in the poor neighborhoods of West Belfast. When a car is stolen here now, the government reimburses the luckless owner. Otherwise, insurance companies would go broke.

One of the women in the group, a pretty, fragile-looking blonde with prominent blue eyes, had been sitting quietly in the corner of the room. She suddenly spoke up. There were tears in her eyes and her voice was shaky. "My son was shot while he was just sitting in that field. He wasn't doing anything, just sitting there, and the organization came along and shot him."

Kathleen interrupted her quickly. "We didn't come here to talk about that," she said emphatically, and changed the subject to tell me about the Car Project they have organized as an antidote to the joyriding. "The boys get old, broken-down cars and fix them up, then enter them in stock-car races," she explained. "They have a garage and a mechanic to show them what to do. It keeps them busy and, we hope, out of trouble." The Car Project was having a party that evening and I was invited. "Come and meet some of the lads," Kathleen urged. "You'll enjoy yourself."

It was raining when I left the house, and the wind felt cold and sharp after the warmth of the fire inside. Two young women passed by on the sidewalk opposite, pushing small baby carriages: the new generation of Twinbrook. Will their options be jobs or joyriding? I wondered, as I drove away. I'd been in Belfast less than a day, and my natural optimism was fading. A dog ran out into the street to chase my car. He gave up after a few listless barks and trotted back to his yard in the rain, head down, tail tucked in. He curled up on the small front stoop and watched me turn my car around in the street and drive away.

I spent the end of the afternoon getting to know the Falls Road, the main thoroughfare of working-class Catholic Belfast and the site of some of the bloodiest battles of the past decade. Except for sporadic outbreaks now, it is, on the surface at least, a quiet, seedy, poor thoroughfare. It should have been a short drive from Twinbrook to the Falls, but I got lost and made a detour that took me on a circular tour of the town before I found my way again. I meandered through the winding streets of Ladybrook, Andersonstown, Turf Lodge, and Ballymurphy. The poor streets of Belfast are dismal in their narrow sameness. Rows of tiny, crowded Victorian houses, attached and semi-detached, make long, straight rows down hundreds of small lanes and streets leading off main thoroughfares. Even in the sunshine the air is hazy with the smoke of coal fires. In the newer housing developments, the atmosphere is even more grim. Blocks of gray stucco flats, covered with graffiti, sit on rubble-strewn patches of unkempt lawns. The trash, the barbed-wire barricades, the boarded-up storefronts, and the endless slow procession of black taxis convey a depressing, funereal atmosphere to the commercial neighborhoods.

The army trucks that lumbered up and down the streets (seldom seen in the "good" neighborhoods) made me uneasy. Soldiers in combat gear with clear plastic visors over their faces stood on the backs of the trucks, their rifles pointed at the passing scene.

I finally found the Falls and parked my car by the side of the huge, barbed-wire-topped wall of the Royal Victoria Hospital, on the corner of the Falls Road and Grosvenor Road. The street was filled with young women pushing babies in carriages, often accompanied by their mothers. Mother-daughter relationships in Northern Ireland are intense; the females seem to have a secret bonding process that must be emotionally very satisfying for them, possibly exclusive of the male members of the family. The babies were beautiful — fat, rosy-cheeked, and smiling — but many of the young mothers looked thin and discontented: they walked on heels that were too high; their spiked punk hairdos — currently stylish in Belfast — were unflattering. Their plump, dowdy mothers looked more cheerful.

The street has a bereft air. Scars of past violence mar its exteriors, and its cramped shops are dark and ill-stocked. All the streetlights on the Falls are covered with heavy iron mesh. They have been broken over and over again, and now they are safe inside their metal cages. Every fourth storefront is boarded up, and crudely drawn graffiti covers the boards. I walked past a sweet shop, a few small grocery stores, butcher shops, a big, prosperous-looking filling station, pubs with dark, dank interiors. There is one relic of Victorian architecture on the street, the Beehive Pub, built in 1888. Despite its peeling paint and derelict condition, it is a handsome example of its era.

Older women, fat and double-chinned, stood together on corners, talking intently. Their faces crinkled with vivacity and animation; they talked with great energy, shifting their shopping bags from one hand to the other, their eyes roaming up and down the street as they conversed.

Farther down the street, I stopped in front of a wall covered with a mural depicting IRA women in military uniform, one with a hand uplifted in a defiant fist, the other holding an armalite rifle. The Falls Road is a largely republican neighborhood with strong IRA sympathies. The mural is a bit of propaganda that conveys the illusion that women are included in the organization. Someone had taken exception to it, however, and had thrown paint all over it. As I stood looking at it, two small boys passed by licking ice cream cones. I asked them who they thought had thrown paint at the picture.

They studied it for a few seconds, then responded almost in unison: "Brits." They went on their way, licking the melting ice cream.

The traffic on the street rumbled up and down the road in a steady stream; 90 percent of the cars are the black taxis that are used almost exclusively to transport people between the city center and West Belfast. They began operating here at a time when it was dangerous for a private car or bus to come in or out of the area. They are cheap and convenient and are one of the many businesses run by the IRA in Belfast. People say that the Protestant paramilitary organizations run the same business on the Shankill Road, the Protestant equivalent of the Falls.

At 3 P.M. the schools let out, and the Falls became a rushing river of girls in maroon uniforms, neat pleated skirts, little striped ties, white shirts, bare legs in ankle-length brown socks, maroon sweaters, matching blazers. Their sturdy, well-tailored uniforms contrasted with the poverty of the neighborhood. Obviously the parents here put great stock in the school uniforms and probably make a sacrifice to outfit each of their children.

Redheads and blondes and occasionally a dark-eyed, dark-haired little girl — all had the same animated faces of their grannies, none of the restless discontent of the young mothers. What happens to them on that route between schoolgirl and mother? Or is it that nothing happens, no dreams come true, that poverty and violence put a permanent scowl on their faces, and by the time of grannyhood the dreams have all been forgotten?

The girls walked in pairs and groups of three and four, laughing and talking, laden with books. I stopped a pair of them, a beauty with masses of tangerine-colored curls and freckles and lime-green eyes, and her taller pal, darker, with pale skin and deep-set blue eyes. I told them that I was writing a book about the women and girls here and could I please take their picture. They deflated with shyness. All their animation went, and they looked around frantically, anywhere but directly at me. They giggled helplessly, covered their faces with their hands, totally destroyed. I find that innocent shyness, typical of Irish children, infinitely appealing.

"Come on," I urged. "Just one quick picture." Their giggles made me laugh, and a woman standing nearby walked over to join us. She looked stern.

"Don't be silly, girls," she commanded with such authority that we all instantly shaped up and stopped smiling. I bet she was a teacher. The girls straightened up and stood quite stiffly, arms at their sides, while I snapped a few pictures. The woman drifted away, having put order into chaos.

"What do you want to do when you grow up?" I asked, putting the camera away. They stared at me with incredulity as if the possibility of growing up had never occurred to them. They consulted each other with a look, then one smiled and said: "I'd like to be a mum."

"I'd like to be a hairdresser like me sister," the other one ventured.

"How about a teacher?" I asked. "Or a nurse?"

They shook their heads.

"A doctor? An astronaut?"

They giggled.

As I walked on, one of them yelled after me: "A veterinarian!"

A veterinarian! Where did *that* come from in this poor, urban neighborhood? I waved back at them; their shyness was gone and their faces were creased again in smiles.

The longer I stayed on the Falls Road, the more I began to feel its special kind of down-at-the-heels charm, a sense of neighborhood, of kinship, of tribal loyalty; but the vitality of the street seemed to belong to the women. With the exception of one *very* talkative (maybe manic) shopkeeper, the men on the street looked impassive, almost dour; groups of them, mostly young, lounged on street corners. The skinheads and punks, dressed in macho black leather, stood out among the ordinary lads in jeans and tee shirts, the inevitable cigarette dangling from each mouth. There was an angry, defiant air to their stance, and they avoided eye contact. They are the statistical "unemployment rate" of Northern Ireland, bored, restless, ready for some action to prove their manhood. As long as they kill their day standing on street corners, paramilitary organizations have their potential recruitment.

A convoy of army trucks came down the street. No one seemed to notice them but me, the wide-eyed tourist. The soldiers standing on top were pointing their rifles, the trucks were moving swiftly, and the little girls in their maroon skirts and blazers ambled on home.

Shankill is to the Protestant community what the Falls is to the Catholics, a busy working-class thoroughfare. It was an extraordinarily warm, summery day, and everyone was out on the street in shirt-sleeves. Tattoos flashed on the muscled biceps of the young men. Mothers pushed carriages, couples walked arm in arm. There seemed to be as many Protestant babies there on the Shankill as there were Catholic babes on the Falls. Many men had dogs on leashes. There were older, cheerful-looking couples. It was midday on a Wednesday, a half-holiday in Belfast.

The shops are better stocked than those of the Falls. In fact, everything looks more prosperous here. Every other shop seems to be a butcher or a bakery, clean and inviting, and there are many churches between the shops. I stopped and bought things to take home for dinner. The food was cheap and everyone was pleasant, cheerful. Almost hyper. They were all in a holiday spirit brought on by the unusual weather. Biblical quotations and anti-Catholic graffiti are painted on walls and fences along the street.

An enormously fat woman passed me, chewing gum and showing off the tattoos on her huge white arms. She had little blond ringlets, like Orphan Annie, and many chins, and she was carrying a bouquet of yellow tulips in one hand and a Pekingese dog in the other. She looked cheerful, too. The traffic rumbled on in a steady stream. Although there were black taxis here, too, there were many more private cars than on the Falls.

I stopped a young mother and asked if I could take a picture of her baby in his carriage. He wasn't a particularly pretty baby, but he was smiling and very fat and had a winning smile. His mum was delighted and did a big wipe-up job on his face, which of course made him start to cry, but we waited and talked, and pretty soon he was smiling again. He was her first baby. She was seventeen and pregnant again.

"Are you happy about that?" I asked her.

"No," she said.

On down the street I passed a tattoo shop. I had a wild and, happily, fleeting impulse to go in and get a tattoo . . . someplace on me that wouldn't show. I gave up on the idea *only* because I'd been told it hurts like mad. But I'd love to come home with a Belfast tattoo that said "I love me mum"!

Small, red-brick houses line the narrow side streets that run off the Shankill. It's all very like the Falls, except you don't see the army trucks rumbling up and down the street like you do all the time over there. And the poor look poorer over there.

DERRY: MAY 1987

I'd been in Derry the previous summer and was making a return trip, driving up from Limerick. The road went through rich, fertile farmland. The spring fields were littered with yellow and white wildflowers, and grass shimmered under the cloudless sky. The sun's rays glinted off of the cylindrical metal milk cans that stood at every crossroads, waiting to be picked up by the dairy truck. Neat, whitewashed cottages sat sideways on sloping hillsides. New lambs leaped awkwardly over spongy tufts of grass, chasing their mothers' tails. The earth is at peace with itself here.

I arrived at the border crossing into Northern Ireland before noon and had the usual banter with the Irish guard. The road between the Irish and the British checkpoints is a no-man's land of several hundred yards. The day was so lovely I pulled my rented car over to the side of the road before I went through the British checkpoint so I could enjoy the view of the village church spire and the row of pastel-painted houses lined up on the riverbank.

It was a pretty, travel-poster scene. I took my camera and ambled down through tall grass to the edge of the river to take a few pictures and to feel the welcome sun on my face. Two gray and white ducks in the river paddled by and squawked when I skimmed a stone across the still surface of the water. I snapped my pictures and turned to retrace my steps to the car. For the first time in my life, I experienced a sensation of total disorientation. I hadn't been out of the car longer than three minutes, but the road was completely deserted. My car had disappeared. The side of the road was as empty as if an unseen hand had plunged out of the heavens, lifted up the car, and hidden it in the clouds. I turned back with a desperate glance at the Irish soldiers at their gate. They were busy talking with the passengers of a car just going through. No one was paying the slightest attention to me. I looked the other way down the road toward the British checkpoint. One car was on the road, moving slowly and traveling right down the center line. Oddly, no one seemed to be in it. It was a red Ford Fiesta. It was my car. I had forgotten to set the handbrake when I left it to take pictures. The road was on a very slight incline, and while my back was turned, the car began slowly rolling. Thank God, just at that moment there was not another car coming or going. It's a stupid thing to do in any circumstances, but there? Five days before, Lord Justice and Lady Gibson were blown up as their car crossed into Northern Ireland from the Republic. Someone within the IRA knew their route and a bomb had been planted in an abandoned car by the side of the road in no-man's land where they passed. It was exploded by remote control and both of them died instantly. And now I was letting an empty car roll toward the British checkpoint. It was too horrible to be real. Would they shoot me first, no questions asked, then blow up the car? Or would there be an international incident that would receive worldwide news coverage (there wasn't much happening in the world at that moment)? I might be interviewed from my hospital bed if I lived. My family would be humiliated. I would be considered unfit to be let out alone again.

As these thoughts were frantically telegraphing themselves to my consciousness, I was also running as fast as I could toward the car, and I could hear myself screaming, "Don't shoot! The brake is off!" My shoes fell off, and my bare feet pounded the warm cement surface. My car began to veer to the right, toward the sidewalk and the handrail that ran along the edge of the walk. Below that was a deep gorge: if the car hit the handrail with enough force, it would go through and drop twenty feet into the gorge. Did I have enough insurance for a total loss? The car bumped up over the curb, gently hit the rail, and stopped. There was just a broken headlight.

I opened the door and flung myself on the driver's seat, breathless, but so vastly, immensely, overwhelmingly relieved that I had not caused an international incident or been shot that I instantly vowed a litany of good deeds that I would perform with regularity for the rest of my life. It was like awakening from the worst nightmare and finding that you haven't really been thrown over a cliff tied down with concrete blocks.

After I retrieved my shoes, I drove slowly, sedately, toward the British gate. It was simply fantastic that no one on either side had seen the incident and that no other car had come through during my own car's solo flight down the middle of the road. By this time there were cars coming and going both ways.

A British soldier came out to look at my identification. I wondered if he could hear my heart beating and mistake it for a lambeg drum. He looked at my driver's license and then walked over and examined the broken headlight.

"Light's broken, Missus," he said laconically.

"Oh, I know it. Some fool ran into me in the parking lot in Donegal Town and didn't even have the courtesy to stop." Why in the world did I say that?

"You better get it fixed before nightfall."

"Right. I certainly will."

He waved me through.

I was free and alive. I was driving on a country road to Derry, the sun was still shining, and my nightmare was over. I began to smile, and then to laugh out loud. When you think of all that security . . .

Derry sits in tiers steeply banked up the hillside from the edge of the River Foyle, which runs through the center of the city, dividing it in half: Bogside and Waterside, Catholic and Protestant. Its spires and rooftops gleam in the summer sunset as one approaches it from the south. It is a unique town, with a character and atmosphere very much its own, unlike any other place in Northern Ireland — like a little city-state tucked away in a foreign land.

The first time I visited there was in 1978, and at that time so much violence had taken place in the preceding decade that it looked like a city at war. There were bombed-out houses and office buildings, bunkers on the streets, soldiers on foot and on Saracens, crowding its citizens off the public ways. This time, in the spring of 1987, it looked bright and bustling, and except for the ever-present truckloads of soldiers, it had repaired its physical wounds.

Straight rows of apple trees, white-blossomed and fragrant, line the road approaching the city. The sidewalks and streets were crowded with men and women: students, shoppers, workers, kids on bikes, young women with baby carriages. Babies, babies, more babies! The whole city looked like a nursery on an outing!

I found the Bogside, a warren of tiny, twisting, steep roads and lanes lined with neat row houses, snowy white lace curtains and shining brass knockers attesting to proud homemaking. Clusters of small children were playing in the empty streets or sitting in twos and threes on doorsteps. On corners, little girls fastened a rope to the top of a streetlamp and made a hoop seat on the end of the rope. They could then sit in the hoop and swing each other around and around the lamppost. They had a song that they sang while they swung, but when I approached them they were too shy to sing it for me.

There is something so tribal about the Bogside, so incestuous in its relationships, that even a stranger feels in some mysterious way "at home" there. I suppose otherwise you would feel instantly alienated. I felt engulfed as I drove into its narrow, closed-in streets, but the feeling was warm and friendly, not ominous or frightening.

Lilly McCafferty is a well-known and respected Bogside citizen. Pithy, witty, warm, and outspoken in her political views, she is loved by her family with the special passion that the Irish reserve for their mothers. I know one of her daughters, Nell, in Dublin. She is a gifted journalist and commentator on current affairs in Ireland, both North and South. Nell grew up in the Bogside, and her childhood memories are of the staunch camaraderie that surrounded the children in that enclave, but the images of her teenage years are of marches, confrontations, riots, shootings, firebombings, and civil disorder. Although she now lives in Dublin, her family (and, I suspect, her heart) are still in the Bogside.

Lilly and another daughter, Nuala, a secretary in the town government, live in a small row house where the key is always in the front door lock, a symbol of Bogside hospitality. When a stranger goes into the McCaffertys', sits down, and has tea, it is impossible for her to feel like a stranger for long. It is as if the first and second acts of friendship were performed off stage, and now it's the third act and strangers are effortlessly relating to each other in a way that usually takes many days or weeks to establish.

We sat down around a table in their small dining room while Lilly prepared a tea of rashers and eggs, toast and tea. Nuala had to eat in a hurry in order to attend a political meeting. Her mother's eyes twinkled behind her glasses as she teased Nuala about her political affiliation.

"Nuala belongs to a wee party. When she goes to a meeting, there'll be two members there: herself and the other one."

Anti-British feeling runs deep in Lilly McCafferty's heart, and nothing will ever change that. Despite her stories of wrenching poverty when she was young ("My mother died, and I had to help raise my brother and sister. We had to do that on two pounds ten a week"), she gives no credit to the British government for its generous welfare system that in recent decades has created a much better, healthier life for Derry citizens.

"Listen," she said, "that Mrs. Thatcher is a reptile of a woman, and you can quote me. Things are better now, but there is still massive unemployment. What's here for the children? Nothing. Nothing."

"Things are quieter now," Nuala said. "I can't believe it's been eighteen years since the Troubles started. There were barricades here. You had to be searched coming and going. You took it in your stride, but it was objectionable. I had a wee dog, I remember. It sat under my desk at work and didn't bother anybody. Once when we were being searched, my dog barked and all hell broke loose. I was arrested and taken to a detention center. They accused me of hitting the policewoman who had searched me — she was six feet tall and I'm four feet eight!

"We'd go to the cinema in those days and crawl home on our hands and knees to miss the bullets! People got used to it, I suppose, and took it all in their stride. Things are much better now. Women have come into their own. They got involved and realized that they had to speak up. They had to become the breadwinners. It gave them more independence."

Nell's view of this newly won independence is more jaded. "The situation in Derry removed the social structure of the neighborhoods. The women did become more independent, perhaps, but they also lost the structure which formed their behavior. With so many husbands and sons away in prison, they went wild. Unmarried pregnancies became common; lots of the women played around while their boyfriends or husbands were in prison. I remember once when Martin McGuinness [an IRA leader] came back to the Bogside to visit his mother. He saw what was going on in his old neighborhood, and he was horrified.

"He said, 'This fucking has got to stop!' And the women just laughed."

Lilly and women of her generation probably will never change or soften their views about the Troubles. But her daughter Nell has had second thoughts.

"One saw the need for an armed struggle then," she said. "There were injustices inflicted on the Catholic population. We had goals. The IRA had goals. But too many civilians have been killed. We're all war-weary."

Lilly was eager for me to meet as many women as I could while I was in Derry, and she went to her telephone directly to make a wee list for me. "Talk to them all, luv," she advised. "You'll hear a different story from each one."

Because I am an American woman, everyone in Derry assumed that I would be interested in meeting a fellow American who has made Derry her home and is an active member of Sinn Fein. So I went in search of Martha McClelland. So far as I know, she is the only American working full-time for the republican cause in Northern Ireland. Her small apartment is in a block of local authority (subsidized) flats in the Bogside, where much of the riots of the early 1970s took place. Although the sidewalk around the apartment building is littered with trash and its elevators and stairwells are covered with graffiti, the apartments are pleasant, all overlooking an interior courtyard.

A large, cheerfully enthusiastic woman, dressed informally in blue jeans and an open-necked pink shirt, Martha welcomed me cordially in an accent that sounded to me like an American imitating a Derry native, which made her easier for me to understand than those with an authentic Derry accent. (The real thing, spoken with pursed lips, makes everyone in Derry look as though they are about to kiss you, which is nice.) She had a motorcycle parked incongruously inside her tiny front hall, but her apartment was spotless and cozy. A big tabby cat was curled up on one chair, and potted ferns sat on tabletops. The lackadaisical attitude that most nationalist Irish women have toward housekeeping hadn't yet rubbed off on this adopted daughter of Northern Ireland.

Martha is a do-gooder from way back. She was involved in the civil rights movement and the anti-Vietnam demonstrations when she was growing up in San Jose, California. She earned a master's degree in the theology of liberation, and from American news coverage she became interested in the Troubles in Northern Ireland. When the National Council of Churches sponsored a group of Americans to visit Derry in 1973 and spend a summer working in a reconciliation program, she jumped at the chance.

"I stayed on after the summer was over," she explained, "and the following year I joined Sinn Fein."

I asked how she switched the pacifist politics of her anti-Vietnam days to the pro-violence stance of her political party now.

"My experiences here changed my attitude," she said. "I was arrested once at nine-thirty P.M. and kept overnight. It was part of an operation called 'screening': 'Round up forty people and we'll screen them,' they said. And then I saw small children being frisked on the streets. During 'Operation Motorman,' I saw the army come in here at four A.M. to occupy 'Free Derry' in tanks with revolving machine guns. I saw so much violence around me that I decided that counter-violence was the only way to fight it. Force is the only thing the British listen to."

She soon made her mark in Sinn Fein. Being a feminist, she railed at the lack of women in decision-making positions in the party. She realized that one of the reasons women stayed away was that they had children to mind at home. She began a campaign for Sinn Fein to provide child care at every meeting or rally so that young mothers would be free to attend. She worked for eight years as the press officer for the Derry Sinn Fein office and was eventually elected to the "Ard Comhairle" (national committee) of the party.

"There still aren't enough women in Sinn Fein," she admitted. "Party work takes so much time, and most women don't have the time to give. It's a working-class party, and women don't have anyone to do their work at home."

Martha married a local man in 1975, but they separated and eventually divorced. Sinn Fein has a liberal policy toward divorce, as it does toward contraception.

Although she worked when she first came to Derry, Martha lost her job some years ago, which entitles her to be on the dole, thereby freeing her to work full-time on her Sinn Fein duties. She has left the Ard Comhairle now and concentrates on community work, handling charges of rape and incest, housing complaints, and antisocial behavior. The fact that the British government provides housing and welfare to an American-born woman who is working in Northern Ireland for the violent overthrow of that government is an irony that Ms. McClelland — whatever her private views — didn't acknowledge to me.

As she talked, I had a feeling of déjà vu. I couldn't put my finger on it, but her words were very familiar. Weeks later I was alone one evening comparing notes on interviews. I reread my interview with a Sinn Fein woman in Belfast. The words were identical with those of Martha, even down to the same order. The Sinn Fein women have memorized their party line well.

Marlene Jefferson used to be the Lord Mayor of Derry. Her greatest disappointment was that her father didn't live to see her take office. Marlene is a moderate Unionist, open to change, compassionate about people's lives no matter where they come from. She is much loved and respected in Derry. I didn't meet many politicians like her in Northern Ireland, but I wish the country were full of them.

We sat in a restaurant on the outskirts of Derry one rainy, windy night and talked for hours. She's an animated woman, buxom and blond, with lively blue eyes and a pretty, cheerful face. Personal sorrow has not dimmed her vitality. Her daughter was widowed at twenty-three and is the mother of a deaf little girl.

Most of the people who came in and out of the restaurant knew her and stopped at our table to say hello.

"I can be a friend of someone despite his politics. But the sad thing here is that people who aren't in politics don't *know* you can be friends with people from other parties. There is nothing better than a good argument about politics! Isn't this new business about Gorbachev exciting, by the way? Now he has a forceful wife, and she's smart and well-educated.

"Anyway, I feel that these days people are just keeping their heads down and hoping that 'it' will all go away. I have been guilty of doing that myself, and then I hear things like the murder here the other day of the man who was sixty-three years old and getting a university degree. He was a shoemaker and he visited the prisons to teach the prisoners how to repair shoes. They shot him first, then put the bomb in the car. The police who came to investigate were also blown up. All because he visited prisoners. Then Tom Cook, a man killed at the Country Club. And Judge Gibson and his wife. You always think: Who next? Will they go after the man who delivers bread to prison? Milk? . . . So many decent people are disgusted and just don't want to know. The IRA are successful because there are so few and they have it down to a fine art now. They bring in the hit man, get him out quick, and the deed is done. It's very difficult to catch terrorists. I always feel that so many are covering up for them because they are afraid, but you can't lead your life that way! We are going to have a small country full of widows and children.

"Terrorists thrive on poverty and no jobs. Eventually we just take over our own fate and decide what we are going to do. You can't just bide time. Time is running out on us. There's no leadership now and no politics in the country at all. It's just gone flat.

"I worry so much about what the future holds for my children and my grandchildren. They could leave, but Jim [her husband] doesn't want them to. And you can't have all the good ones leave. This younger generation has been soured by politics. Why not? They haven't seen anything fruitful. They've grown up with bombs and bomb scares. We don't even *see* those trucks with the soldiers on them anymore; I only notice them if I'm on the motorway and get behind one, and then I think, 'Get well past, in case something should suddenly happen.' My sister was here visiting, and she thought it was very frightening, and it is an intrusion on your freedom, but you learn to live with it and it would be much worse if they weren't here."

I asked Marlene how the situation in Derry now affected her personally.

"Well, for instance, last week was Tom Cook's funeral. Every car in town was being checked and it was my grandson's birthday, so Jim and I headed over the bridge to take him his present. He was having his party in the park, so they set off with him and all his little friends in the car up the Strand to go over the New Bridge to the park. Meanwhile, my other daughter was coming over the Old Bridge to go to the party, but we were heading back to tell her not to come because of the traffic tie-up. So the *whole family* was caught in a three-hour traffic snarl, and eventually we all ended up at my house and we had his birthday party there. I had to get on the phone and call up all the friends' parents to say the boys were safe at our house. Well, it was a lovely Sunday afternoon and there you are. That's the country we live in.

"Even if the political parties got together tomorrow and started talking, it's not going to go away. Not for years to come. And what makes me so angry is: What's their cause? . . . Killing people, robbing banks, stealing a lot of money . . . Whenever the police do bring someone in, they never get the Godfather. The Godfather always seems to get off the hook. They say they never have enough information. I think they should bring back hanging. That's against my upbringing, but maybe they should just be removed altogether. When you get angry enough, your mind changes. You look at a young mother trying to bring up three kids. 'Oh, she's a police widow,' someone will say.

'She'll be well looked after.' Well, let me tell you, nothing in this world replaces a husband."

"What do you think about Ian Paisley?" I asked.

"Some people say he is a necessary evil at the moment. Not me. The man frightens me because I don't think you can mix politics and religion. But I think in the past six months he has begun to mellow. He is facing opposition in his party, which he never had before. I think he'll bow out in the next few years. Really, I always had great reservations about that man. He's a Jekyll and Hyde. He was so affable on television the other night, but just go to the record and read what he says. But he has an unbelievable following in Northern Ireland."

I told Marlene that I'd gone to hear Paisley preach and found the church half empty.

"Really! Now that's a surprise. Well, he hasn't produced the goods for the past couple of years. People are fickle. If they are looking for blood and thunder, they can look to [Peter] Robinson.

"Not enough women in Northern Ireland stand up and speak their mind. Mothers have a stronger influence on children than the father. The modern young mother has a conflict about going back to work, but I say: 'Now look. Do you need to go back to work for yourself? If you do, go! Don't feel guilty.' Nowadays, with all the modern conveniences, if you start in on your home Monday morning, you can finish by noon! There are so many bright young people striving to get on.

"I think Pat [Hume, John Hume's wife] should get involved in politics. She has great ability and she does all the groundwork. Berna McIvor, Hume's campaign manager, is another one. She should be in the forefront, not in the background. Ethel Smyth, the councillor from County Down, is quite strong; she got herself involved in rough politics, and I don't like taking to the streets. But at least she's doing something. It's hard to find women who are doing anything. Women in the Republic have come to the fore in the past ten years. It's really amazing. Women here just don't support each other. You find a bitchiness. I think it's just great what they have done in the South. Haughey [Prime Minister of the Republic of Ireland] has disgraced himself by not appointing one woman to the senate. I think it is despicable. They should go and picket. If the women don't make any buzz about it, they'll do it again."

I asked Marlene what her scenario for the future would be.

"I would like to see the moderate people get together — now this is only a pipe dream: let's sit down and put forward five or six points, then let's see what the differences are. First: jobs and the economy. Get the children involved in training programs. Agree on the type of policing you need here. And set up a government that would give fair representation. Leave the rest open. I wish we would have a very liberal candidate and a very conservative candidate and get people back into the way of voting on ideological lines rather than on symbols like flags and monuments and language. We are so entrenched in the past. The way forward is to treat history like history: don't do away with it, but change the celebrations. A friend of mine said recently: 'My son knows Protestants because we made an effort.' Well, when we grew up we didn't have to make the effort because we lived in a mixed area and there was no difference in us. Those days will never come again until you get children mixing at school. Segregated education is wrong. There is no way you can say it is right. But I will say that schools are mixing quietly here. People are making a conscious decision to send children to Protestant schools because they know they will get a place and will have smaller classes. Unless you see some things like that happening in the next five years, you can just forget about Northern Ireland."

Dodie McGuinness is a small, very pretty woman with short blond hair and pale blue eyes. She wears four gold rings on her fingers and a gold necklace. We sat across from each other at a desk in the stuffy, windowless back office of Sinn Fein. Separated from her husband, she has three young children, is active in Sinn Fein, and is a member of the Derry City Council. She is articulate and cool, and she didn't give me the "canned" answers of most of the other Sinn Fein women I'd met.

"I was born here in Derry and we went to live in Creggan [a huge housing development] when I was four. My family were nationalist but not political. One day I was standing at the top of the Strand Road, and there was a pub at the corner. I was watching a march from the island in the middle of the road, and I saw this drunken man stagger from the pub. The RUC grabbed him and threw him to the ground and started kicking him. That just stuck in my head. My own people never had trouble with the RUC, but that started me thinking. So I started going on the marches; you were told you were marching for housing, jobs, and votes, not against anything else. Just for the development of your community. Then one day I appeared on a television news show during the Battle of the Bogside, and when they saw my face on the telly, I lost my job as an auxiliary nurse at the hospital here. So my involvement grew from those events.

"In nineteen seventy-two, we [Sinn Fein] opened our first advice center for people who were harassed or arrested. It was open twenty-four hours a day. They had this 'screening' process in Creggan where they could lift you and question you for four hours, and everyone in Creggan went through that. And for those of us who worked in the center, it would have been a weekly, sometimes daily, occurrence.

"As time went on, we expanded our services and worked on people's social problems as well, and you develop a street awareness and a political awareness. My politics came from the street first, then I became associated with the political party. Women from the nationalist areas were involved in every aspect of this struggle, and they were harassed and jailed for anything. The women would stand behind their men here and they were always prepared to do that. In my community you could see the strength of women."

"What did your family think of your political involvement?" I asked.

"My mother is a strong woman. She would walk with five or six other women around Creggan at five in the morning, and if they heard the army coming they would rattle their bin lids. Although she is not a member of Sinn Fein, she supports the republican movement. My sisters are the same, although not as involved. They would picket and protest, but they would not get into politics. My mother fears for me, though, and always wants me to check in with her."

"Do you fear for yourself?"

"You don't fear for yourself because you are so wrapped up in it, but I think recently I have feared for myself because of threats towards councillors and prominent republicans from loyalists here. You see, here in Derry we haven't had much bother in that line, so we would be soft targets because we aren't as wary and cautious as we should be. We should probably take their threats more seriously."

"Have you served time in jail?"

Dodie gave me one of her rare smiles. "No, but not for want of trying. When they ran internment for women I was arrested. I was the first woman here to be arrested. They had six or seven girls from

Belfast. They flew me to Belfast, signed my internment papers, but at that stage the IRA here in Derry had captured a UDR [Ulster Defense Regiment] man, so they traded us. I think they bargained for my release against the UDR man's life, and they told the army that if they interned more women, they would shut down the town. I think it was probably more the pressure of that threat than the UDR man's life which made them let me go!

"I've been a councillor for two years. The term is for four. This is the first time that Sinn Fein has contested an election on the council here, and we won five seats. I'm the only Sinn Fein woman on the council. There are three SDLP [Social Democratic and Labour Party] women and two Unionist women."

"Are you a feminist?" I asked.

"I believe that women have their rights, but feminism here in Derry isn't very strong. I wouldn't say that I am a strong feminist, but I do think that women should be treated equal and not shoved into stereotyped roles, and should be allowed to develop. Within our organization in Derry I don't find any problems. Women are treated very fairly. At seventeen or eighteen I would never have thought I could be a councillor. Three years ago I wouldn't have believed it!"

"What made you decide to run?"

"We decided that we would run so many people from each area, and we went for the people who were well known and popular in those areas. I stood in the area where I was well known. I ended up topping the poll. It shocked me. It shocked the men in Sinn Fein, too! But it's a role that I can play now, because I see it as part of the whole struggle. We [Sinn Fein] had to get into politics, and the hunger strikes just brought us there quicker."

"Do you feel that you accomplish things as a councillor?"

"I get on well with people. What you find is that there is so much bureaucracy and cutbacks, you are restricted on what you can do. Councillors have powers for amenities and leisure. We say we bury the dead and sweep the streets. We don't have power for housing. We are involved now in discussions about having the councillors represented on the education boards, but we don't have social service powers."

"How many women are active in Sinn Fein in Derry?"

"We may have twelve in an election or a crisis who will work."

"Do women have a leadership role in the Sinn Fein party and make decisions guiding it?"

"Aye. Our government body discriminates positively in favor of women. There are fifteen seats, and one-third of them have to be women. Looking back at our party conference last year, the most controversial thing we discussed was abortion. We are very divided about it. When I said my family was nationalist, they are Catholic nationalists who have developed republicanism, and they are very strong in their church beliefs, so the abortion thing is hard for our party to deal with. I think the right to choose is just about ten years too advanced for Ireland, for any political party here, never mind just Sinn Fein. At least this year people thought about it and talked about it, so that was a victory of sorts. I personally think that if a woman wants an abortion, she should have the right to it."

"Is being a councillor a full-time job? Do you get paid for it?"

"We get paid for our meetings. I have three children, so I claim supplementary benefits."

"Derry women have a great network of family to help them out, don't they?"

"Aye. We do. If there is a problem, we are all together on it. My mother lives around the corner from me, and I wouldn't move any further from her. If one person on the street has a problem, everyone on the street pulls together. It's unbelievable for an outsider to watch it."

"Would everyone on your street be of your political persuasion?"

"I would say maybe half and half. But if my house gets raided, they are all there, standing outside the house to make sure there is no rough treatment."

"Does your house still get raided?"

"Aye. They take spasms and raid blocks of houses."

"What do they do in a raid?"

"The last one I had was at twenty minutes to seven one evening. I had to get the children ready for bed, and they came in and had to go through each room and through every single thing in each room. You're supposed to be able to go around with them so you can watch them. But if you have six of them upstairs searching, and six of them down, you can't be both places at once!"

"What do you think led you to Sinn Fein instead of the SDLP?"

"We're on the ground, working with ordinary working-class people."

"But when you belong to Sinn Fein, you have to justify the violence. If you belonged to the SDLP, you wouldn't have to advocate violence. How do you justify that within yourself?"

"I don't have any problems if I go back to the man I saw getting kicked around the street and all the events that were happening then [1969]. People have a right to defend themselves against that."

"What's the difference in the goals and aspirations of SDLP and Sinn Fein?"

"That's a fine line. Sinn Fein will support the IRA right to take arms and defend communities they represent because those communities couldn't exist otherwise. Now don't get me wrong. I don't want to see anybody die. I think death is a terrible thing. But under the circumstances that are here, it's going to happen. Civilian casualties are terrible and tragic, and I think the figures here in Derry have been low because we do try to be careful. That's the dividing line. At the end of the day, the SDLP goal is the same as ours."

"What do you think about the Anglo-Irish Agreement [AIA]?"

"It hasn't done anything except bolster the SDLP. The Americans and Europeans like it. If we get over the hurdle of the AIA, we'll be on the right road."

"What do you mean?"

"It's there. Although the loyalists reacted to it, its objective was to bolster the SDLP and to crush our political movement, and by crushing that, they would have presumed they would have crushed the support the IRA has. By crushing us, they would think the whole thing would collapse. That's what the AIA was all about. Our people think that because the loyalists reacted against it, there must be something in it for us. But it won't do anything for us. There are no jobs in it. Thirty million dollars from America is a lot of money, but a lot needs to be done."

"What would happen to you and to everyone else here who has no work and depends on Britain for their support if Britain walked out tomorrow?"

"First of all, if Britain went tomorrow, she couldn't go without making a financial commitment until Ireland stabilized itself. They have taken that much out of the country, they have to pay it back. The whole economic thing is hard, and we don't have a good, strong economic policy yet. We look at it every day and have strategy meetings, and I honestly don't understand it because I'm not that way. But Britain couldn't just walk away and leave people who have depended on state benefits. Everyone asks that question. It really wouldn't bother me. And it wouldn't bother most people in Sinn Fein. They know they will have to face it when it happens."

"Leaving the economy aside, how would your life change personally if you got what you wanted politically?"

"We would still be councillors. Still a small political party fighting for existence. Our movement is not strong in the twenty-six counties. A lot of work has to be done. So you keep your head down and you do the work."

"But if Britain left and you were united with the twenty-six counties, and Sinn Fein was just one more political party out of several, what difference would that make in your life? You would wake up and say, 'Right. We have achieved what we worked for. Okay, how is my life different than it was yesterday?'"

"You would know that the British are away, and you have to work to create what you have been fighting for. The goal we are working for is a life for our children so that they don't have to go through what we went through. Educating people to the system and how it works."

"How do you feel about the lack of support in the Republic for a united Ireland?"

"I think they have this fear: The Brits are away and the IRA will come down here and start in on the twenty-six counties. They fear that. They just don't want to be bothered. They are going to look for their best interest. The Prods in the Republic are treated as well as anyone else."

"They are sensitive now, after the divorce referendum failed." (A vote to legalize divorce in the Republic of Ireland was taken in 1986, but the proposal was defeated.)

"Aye. But you can see that breaking down. The Church doesn't try to run things like it used to."

"Are you Catholic?"

"Aye."

"In the last ten years a lot of republicans have left the Church and become more independent-minded."

"Aye. They have. I would go to Mass and take my children, but if they started a political speech from the altar, that's just not for me. They do it everywhere. They use what clout and control they have.

The younger generation coming up, they don't give a damn."

"Are you going to stay active politically?"

"Aye. I've been involved eighteen years. I won't stop now."

"Would you like to be the leader of the Sinn Fein party?"

At last, Dodie threw back her head and laughed aloud.

"You'll never see that happening! It would be an honor, of course, because of all the respect we have for one another. But you'll never see it happen."

The Way It Was

I thought our difficulties went back 400 years. Now I've been told 700.
— MARGARET THATCHER
February 1988

ALTHOUGH THE CURRENT ROUND of Troubles in Northern Ireland started in 1969, one has to go back 300 years to understand their origins. In the seventeenth century, Ulster was "planted" by Presbyterian Scots who were sent there by the British government to take over land owned by the native Irish. In case of invasion by the Spanish, the British thought these "Planters" would be more loyal to the Crown than the Irishmen, who never liked them anyway. The Irish clan chieftains fled the country, some to the continent, others to England, and a few to America. By 1703, only 5 percent of the land in Ulster remained in the hands of the Catholic Irish.

The newcomers spoke a different language, worshipped in a different religion, and were as prosperous as the natives were impoverished. The two traditions didn't blend well. The natives hated the newcomers for having usurped their land, and the newcomers feared and disdained the natives.

Throughout the seventeenth and eighteenth centuries, there were various (up)risings, massacres, rebellions, conflicts, and other acts of armed resistance to the state of affairs. Sometimes the natives massacred the Planters (as in the Rising of 1641), and sometimes the Planters killed the natives (such as the Cromwell Massacre of 1650). The overall score was heavily in favor of the Planters.

As prosperity grew among the Protestants in their corner of Ireland, the gulf between the northern and southern parts of the country intensified. Efforts on the part of Irish nationalists to establish home rule for Ireland brought this division into focus. The Protestant majority in the six northern counties were adamantly against home rule for Ireland and wanted their union with Great Britain to remain secure.

On Easter Monday, 1916, a small band of Irish patriots rose in rebellion against British troops in Dublin. Although the Rising, as it was called, was soon quelled, the subsequent execution of its leaders radicalized the nationalist population of the country to such an extent that the ensuing war for independence became inevitable. At the end of that war in 1921, the British government and the Irish rebels signed a treaty, giving independent-dominion status to the twenty-six counties in the southern part of Ireland and leaving six counties in the north (now known as Northern Ireland) as part of Great Britain. Many people in the South were unhappy with the terms of the treaty and so a civil war ensued, in which the anti-treaty faction lost.

The Unionist Party emerged as the monolithic Protestant majority party in the newly formed Northern Ireland. The regional government it formed enacted a series of measures designed to buttress the majority's advantages over the Catholic minority. The local government franchise excluded non-taxpayers from voting and gave owners of multiple properties more than one vote. Constituencies were gerrymandered to give Unionists the majority where in fact they didn't really have it. Housing was allocated to Unionist petitioners, and Catholics were put at the bottom of the list. The police force, the Royal Ulster Constabulary, was predominately Protestant. The 1930s saw severe economic problems in the North of Ireland, and unemployment never fell below 25 percent in that decade. For the first time in 100 years, the proud Belfast shipyards did not launch a ship, and the linen industry, long the stable employer of women in Belfast, began a long decline. The tight job market led to the formation of the Ulster Protestant League, which encouraged employers to hire only Protestants.

The economic depression of the 1930s gave way to the wartime boom and the relative prosperity of the 1950s. Sectarian tension lessened as jobs became more plentiful. The 1947 Education Act made secondary and third-level education free, thus enabling poor Catholics to receive equal educational opportunities for the first time. And so the 1960s began with more reason to hope for peace, prosperity, and reconciliation in Northern Ireland than at any time in its history. But this hopeful decade was to end in destruction, violence, and a rebirth of the sectarian hatreds that seem to thrive on fertile soil in Ulster. What happened in Northern Ireland in the next eighteen years is democratic Europe's saddest, most futile political fiasco. It is a drama of near success and bitter defeat, of high courage and faltering nerve, of misjudgments founded in ignorance and good policies gone wrong, of fanaticism and silliness. The winners up to now have been death, distrust, and hatred between fellow Christians. But in the summer of 1968, no nightmare could have foreshadowed the horror that was to engulf Northern Ireland in the coming decade.

That year, a group of young men and women, most but not all of them Catholics, founded the Northern Ireland Civil Rights Association (NICRA). Its aims were to end the political discrimination against Catholics. Like the civil rights movement in the United States, it sought to achieve its aims by peaceful demonstrations and marches. This was its platform:

1. One man, one vote. Before 1968, the voting laws stated that (1) voters had to be owners or tenants of a house, and in this category, only two people in a house could vote; (2) an owner had to have property worth ten pounds or over; (3) companies were entitled to appoint up to six votes for every ten pounds' value of the company; (4) voting districts were often gerrymandered to enable Unionist votes to overpower the minority. (Example: In 1966 there were 14,000 Catholic voters in Derry, 9,000 Protestants. There were 12 Protestants on the local council and 8 Catholics.
2. The repeal of the 1922 Special Powers Act, which gave the government the power to search without a warrant, arrest without a warrant, jail without a trial, deny trial by jury, and prohibit public assembly.
3. Fair housing allocation. (Example: Houses in Catholic housing developments in Dungannon had 42 square feet of space less than those of Protestants, although it is not a proven scientific fact that Catholics are smaller.)
4. Equal opportunity of employment. (Example: In the Belfast shipyards, with a work force of 10,000 people, 400 were Catholics.)

On August 24, 1968, four thousand civil rights activists gathered to march peacefully from Coalisland to Dungannon in County Tyrone, singing "We Shall Overcome." On October 5 they marched again, this time in Derry, a city strained by massive unemployment, unfair housing practices, and a gerrymandered local government. Mobs of undisciplined Orangemen attacked the marchers on the streets, and the police came rushing in . . . only to aid and abet the attackers! A lone Irish television cameraman stayed with the march, filming the RUC swooping down on the participants with batons flailing and water cannons flattening them against the sides of buildings. His film of the attack on the marchers publicized to the "outside world" for the first time what was going on in Northern Ireland. The British government didn't like what it saw. "If they claim to be English," Westminster responded, "why don't they act English?" The long descent down the ladder of political power began for Unionist politicians on the day of what became known as the Duke Street March in Derry.

The RUC, because of their behavior during and after the march, became the enemy of the Catholic population in the city from that day. The reaction to the march set off rioting and arson in the Bogside area of Derry. The citizens there felt totally unprotected by the legitimate police force and resolved to defend themselves. To this end, they formed the Derry Citizens' Action Committee.

For Eileen Doherty, whose house is in the middle of the Bogside, those days in 1968 were a traumatic time. The Troubles have victimized her family more ruthlessly than most, but she has survived, unbowed, angry, and still committed to republicanism and a united Ireland.

"Remember, we had to protect ourselves," Eileen said, talking about the October 1968 march as we sat in her small living room on a warm July afternoon in 1986. "The police poured in here. Many of them were drunk, and they smashed down doors, broke windows, frightened old people and children. Oh, it was a terrifying sight!"

The Doherty house became the headquarters of the Citizens' Action Committee, a cross-community group formed to orchestrate peaceful civil rights demonstrations. Eileen's husband, Paddy, was treasurer. John Hume was vice-chairman, and Ivan Cooper, a Protestant shirt-factory manager, was chairman. Eileen acted as quartermaster.

"We sent the younger kids off to relatives out of the city and barricaded the Bogside to keep the police out. We called it 'Free Derry,' and we held it for nine weeks."

I asked her if the women were on the front lines with the men during that time.

"No, the women didn't fight, but they made soup and sandwiches, gathered stones and broke up the pavements, then hauled the stones in wheelbarrows to the men in the Rosswell Flats, where they were holding the barricades. It was a community effort; without the women's help, the men couldn't have made it. Then the paramilitary took over, and the army came in."

"It sounds like the women did the hardest part of the job," I joked. "It takes more muscle to dig up pavements than it does to throw stones."

"We women have always had to work hard here," Eileen said. "Women are used to keeping the men because the shirt factories here employ mostly women. Hard work is nothing new to us.

"All through the early 'seventies, the fighting was going on, and it was very hard on the women. They backed up the men, but they also had to care for the children. Every day, every day, there would be a confrontation; once the women put a cordon across Francis Street [in the Bogside] and stopped the Saracens [British tanks] as they began to roll. CS gas [tear gas] was fired night and day. You could always smell it. Children would throw stones at the Saracens, and they would fire the CS gas back at them. Schoolchildren had their bookbags searched all the time. They would just grab their bags and empty them out on the streets.

"When the bigger boys were picked up by the army and taken off to the barracks in the Saracens, it was the women who always went with them. My son was brought up in it all and has seen it all. He was almost shot during Bloody Sunday, and he was arrested and held for four hours when he was thirteen. The IRA was the only thing we had protecting us then. I couldn't blame anyone for joining the IRA."

As we sat in Eileen's living room that day, she on her flowered sofa with a group picture of her thirteen children hanging on the wall behind her and I across from her on an easy chair with a sheepskin rug on the floor between us, the scenes she described seemed remote and unreal. Sounds of children playing and laughing drifted into the room; it was a warm late afternoon in Derry and the doors and windows of Bogside houses were open.

Still a handsome woman, with a widow's peak framing her face, Eileen was dressed in the usual Derry housewife style: slacks and a sweater, with comfortable sandals. The calm, patient good humor of a woman who has reared thirteen children was evident in her demeanor and style, but anguish clouded her face when we spoke of the past.

The Dohertys' son, Brendan, is in Long Kesh Prison for "possession [of firearms] and membership" in the IRA. His wife was five months pregnant when he was arrested twelve years ago; with Brendan due out in 1988, his son is like so many children of the Bogside who don't know what it is to have their father live in the same house. A Doherty son-in-law, Kevin Coyle, was shot dead by the IRA on suspicion of being a "supergrass," or informer. His wife was expecting their fourth child when he was killed.

"Didn't your son-in-law's murder weaken your support of the IRA?" I asked.

She sipped her tea before she answered, but her reply was straightforward and unhesitating. "Yes, I thought there should have been more thinking about that. They said he was giving information to the police, but it was an unjustified charge. He had been lifted [arrested] by the police and questioned, but he went straight to the IRA when he got out and told them about it."

"So can you justify all these killings?"

"No. Some, maybe. I couldn't justify them all. I used to think, when I saw the police doing such bad things to us: 'God, I wish I had a gun in me hands.' The IRA are no worse than the loyalists or the police."

"But you wouldn't defend *them*," I persisted.

"There'll never be peace in this country until the British let go. It's as simple as that. I want to see a united Ireland more than anything else, even if we have to pay a high price for it."

A daughter came in the front door then, carrying a new Doherty grandchild, and we got up to walk back to the kitchen and play with the baby. Eileen Doherty has given her life to caring for others — children, grandchildren, neighbors — but the elusive goal of a united Ireland takes precedence in her life over issues of life and death.

In Belfast, Queens University students began to mobilize themselves to support the civil rights movement. Two students there, Michael Farrell and Bernadette Devlin, founded the People's Democracy, and in January 1969, they led a march from Belfast to Derry. The eighty students taking part in the four-day march were stoned, heckled, and harassed all along the way. On the last day, when they reached Burntollet Bridge just outside Derry, they were badly beaten by a loyalist paramilitary force. They clung to their commitment to peaceful demonstrations, but that was perhaps the last time that the nationalists were to stand by and let their own people be bullied.

Dodie McGuinness, the Sinn Fein councillor in Derry, got her political baptism by fire at the Burntollet Bridge.

"Burntollet opened my eyes," she said. "I was fairly open-minded then and had a lot of Protestant friends, but I saw those beaten, bloody students being brought into the hospital, and it changed my attitude. I began to get involved in the marches and protests. I became more aware of things that were happening, of things going on around me. Eventually I was in the Battle of the Bogside. Everyone was behind the barricades then: grannies, kids, everyone. We were just trying to protect our own area from the RUC and the B-Specials."

Despite setbacks and sporadic violence, the determination and fortitude of the civil rights activists were beginning to pay off. Six days after the huge November 16 demonstration in Derry, Captain Terence O'Neill, the Prime Minister of Northern Ireland, announced a reform package that would replace the Derry municipal government with an appointed development commission; recommend a fair system of housing allocation to the local town councils; create an ombudsman to investigate citizens' grievances; establish a universal adult franchise, giving the vote to non–tax-paying citizens; and repeal various parts of the Special Powers Act.

These were major steps toward reform in Northern Ireland, and included many of the goals of the Civil Rights Association. They came about not by the use of violent force but by the peaceful coercion of mass demonstrations and a thoughtful, organized agenda. Even today, the IRA is unwilling to admit that it was peaceful demonstrations, not terrorist activities, that won these concessions.

The Derry municipal government set up a three-man committee made up of two Unionists and one nationalist to allocate houses. (In the past, the allocation had been the absolute right of the Unionist mayor.) But as so often happens in political situations where the downtrodden minority has been held in check for too long, the proposed reforms let loose long-repressed resentments. The Citizens' Action Committee was more or less defunct now, having achieved many of its aims. It was replaced by the far more militant, ominously titled Derry Citizens' Defense Association. Old republican veterans from the 1959–1962 campaign emerged as leaders of the organization, and they urged that armed barricades of the Bogside be erected as a defense against potential Protestant mobs.

The Unionists were beginning to feel that their backs were to the wall. Always inward-looking and sensitive to the point of paranoia about any initiative that might undermine their dominance, they reacted to the reform package with predictable provocation. On August 12, 1969, the Apprentice Boys marched in their annual commemoration of a siege mounted by Catholic James II in 1689. (As the Catholic Army tried to attack, young apprentice boys slammed shut the gates of the city, preventing the attack.)

The Bogside readied itself for an attack from the Orange marchers and set up barricades, but the inevitable happened: the marchers and the Bogsiders hurled epithets first, then stones, and finally the RUC smashed through the barricades, followed by the Orange mobs, and all hell broke loose. The undefended nationalist population in the Bogside fought to protect their homes and families from the attack.

For two days the area was under siege, the Bogsiders versus the Royal Ulster Constabulary. Over 1,000 casualties were treated at makeshift medical centers. The narrow, winding, hilly streets, lined with row upon row of tiny attached houses, were filled with the noxious fumes of tear gas. Protestant families who had lived peacefully in the area for years had to flee for their lives. Bernadette Devlin, who wanted to be a latter-day Joan of Arc of the Bogside, arrived to encourage the locals, but, as is always true in tightly closed Irish communities, she was regarded in Derry as something of a "blow-in," and her presence was not welcome.

John Hume, the spokesperson for the moderate Catholic civil rights people in Derry, had tried to send signals to the governments in both Dublin and London about the potential dangers of the march. His warnings went unheeded. Those two August days in Derry signaled the emergence of the more militant nationalists. Their message was clear: If the police won't protect us, we must protect ourselves. We can only protect ourselves by the use of force against force. Trust *us;* we will protect you, your loved ones, and your homes. The Irish Republican Army was reborn.

By the third day of the rioting in Derry, the British government withdrew the police from the Bogside and sent in the British Army. At 5 P.M., August 14, the men of the Prince of Wales Regiment marched smartly into town. The Catholic population of Derry regarded them as defenders against the hostility of the RUC and the unchecked aggression of militant loyalist mobs, and they cheered their arrival. The next day, 600 men of the Third Battalion, Light Infantry, moved into Belfast with fixed bayonets, ready to keep Catholics and Protestants from killing each other. As in Derry, Catholic neighborhoods in Belfast welcomed the arrival of the army. But their enthusiasm was short-lived, however, when it became evident that the troops were neither militarily trained nor psychologically equipped to deal with the kind of underground and subversive hostility that had bloomed into sectarian warfare in Derry and Belfast. The army's tactics soon turned out to be as crude and hostile as the RUC's. Their welcome turned sour, and the Bogside had a new enemy to face.

If anyone, either in Ireland or England, had prophesied then that the army would still be in Northern Ireland nineteen years later, he would have been thought mad. Lucy Faulkner, whose husband, Brian, was then Minister of Development in the Northern Ireland government, remembers that her immediate response to the decision to call in the army was negative. Years later, she recalled asking her husband how long he thought the army would have to stay.

"I remember it so vividly," she said. "We were in the bedroom, and he was bending down, tying his shoelaces. Without even looking up, he said, 'They'll be here a week. Or they'll be here as long as you and I live.'"

In retrospect, putting the British Army into Northern Ireland as a peacekeeping force seems one of the most bizarre decisions that England has ever made with regard to Ireland. Even though the suggestion of an impartial peace-keeping army, such as a United Nations force, was met with derision and ridicule from all factions in Northern Ireland, it is clear that one country's army — whose duty it is to protect the interests of that country — cannot go into a divided community and act impartially for both sides: they have to be "on" the side of the country they represent, and the British Army is obviously British. Their interests are Britain's. Who thought they could ever be impartial when it came to Unionists versus nationalists? Unionists are loyal to Britain, nationalists want to separate themselves from Britain.

By August 1971, Northern Ireland was on the verge of anarchy. The British Army could not contain the growing violence. Brian Faulkner, by now Prime Minister, decided that internment (arrest and detention on suspicion of terrorist activities without specific charges or public trial) was the only way of saving the country. On August 9, 1971, at 4:15 in the morning, three thousand British troops fanned out all over the province to arrest IRA suspects. Women took to the streets to act as lookouts. When they saw the army approaching, they banged their garbage can lids together in warning. "Republican tom-toms," Faulkner called the signals, "sending their tribal message across the city."

In his *Memoirs,* Faulkner says: "In Irish politics, you can do three things . . . the right thing, the wrong thing or nothing at all. I have always thought it better to do the wrong thing than nothing at all." In retrospect, internment was the wrong thing. He goes on: "I had expected a bitter reaction from some quarters to internment, but not on the scale which occurred, both on the streets and among nationalist politicians." In the seventy-two hours following the arrests — in which 363 suspects were "lifted," 2 of them Protestants — 30 people died in gun battles and bombings. Although there was a decline in the level of violence after internment, the emotional reaction against it far outweighed the immediate good it did, and it was a brilliantly effective propaganda tool for the IRA for years to follow.

Even today, people talk about the time of internment as if it had happened yesterday. One evening in January 1987, I sat in a house in West Belfast talking to a group of nationalist women who had gathered to tell me of their experiences living in the city and raising their families during that period. The small room where we met was hot and stuffy from a coal fire. Most of the women smoked cigarettes, as so many Northern Irish women do, so the room was soon hazy from their smoke. Despite the heat, most of the women sat with their winter coats on, as if they weren't too comfortable being there or might get up and leave at any minute.

Two women sitting at the end of the semicircle were laughing as I came into the room. One, with an appealing, deep-throated laugh, looked more Spanish than Irish, with large, dark eyes, black hair, and flaming rosy cheeks. A tall, gaunt blond woman was sitting next to her and nudged her after I had introduced myself to the group.

"Tell her about how they broke your door down, Ann, when you were pregnant."

Ann's smile faded as she began to talk.

"Well, I was asleep in my bed with my husband. It was August nineteen seventy-two. I remember it was a warm night and I was restless and couldn't sleep well, being as how I was pregnant with my fourth. I had finally fallen asleep and I heard this awful noise, bin lids banging away out in the street. I knew something was up. Then all of a sudden the whole room was filled with British soldiers. They had smashed the door open and had come trooping into the room. There must have been a dozen of them. They couldn't all fit into the room!" Ann's deep laugh interrupted her story. Her irrepressible humor, so inherent in Belfast women, broke through despite the traumatic event she was relating.

"They pulled my husband out of the bed. 'Get your trousers on!' they yelled. I coulda heard them without all the yelling. It's only a wee room. So my husband got his trousers on, and then they pulled him out of the room and leaned against the door so I couldn't get out and follow them. Sure, a bedroom is a very private place. They shouldn't have come bursting in there like that. They had broken down the front door to get in, and they pulled him out that way. The kids were all squealing and hollering and crying. 'Don't take my daddy,' they kept yelling.

"They took him away, and we didn't know at first where he had gone. They kept him in the Crumlin Jail for six months. They kept at him all the time: 'Your wife is back there with three kids,' they kept saying to him. 'You'd better tell us all you know.' He didn't have anything to tell. They went on and on like that, and then finally they sent him to Long Kesh.

"The Prods would stand outside our house on the street and sing 'Where's Your Daddy Gone?' or 'Are You Lonesome Tonight?' It would make your skin creep."

Another woman chimed in. "They always banged down the front

door and came rushing in at you. Someone in the family would have to go with them from room to room; they'd tear the place up if they didn't find what they were looking for. The children would all be up, screaming, and then we'd have to settle them down again, half the night's sleep gone, and get them ready for school the next morning. One night they came into our back garden. We had just dug up our potatoes, and they came in and tore up the garden. They said they saw the ground turned and thought we had planted a bomb. 'In our own garden?' I asked!"

Ann eventually got her husband back, and her kids are grown now. She isn't bitter about those bad years, but she has lost faith in politicians, in the "system."

"Prods are just the same as us. The only thing is, they have better jobs. One of my sons has gone to school in America. He'll get a chance there. You see, when fathers are employed, they put in a wee word for their sons, and then they have a chance to get a job. When they are always unemployed, they can't help their boys."

"My girl got eight O levels on her exams," the gaunt, blond woman said. "But my husband was in prison for fifteen years, so she's considered a security risk. Eight O levels and now she's working as a chambermaid in a hotel!"

"How's your husband doing?" one of the woman asked solicitously.

"Oh, *he*'s doing fine. It's me that's on the tranquilizers! Having him sit around the house all day, it drives me mad." She lit another cigarette and scowled at the floor.

I asked Ann if any other member of her family had a run-in with the police or army after her husband's internment.

"My son was beat up by the army, and he never bothered no one. But they denied they beat him, even though he was black and blue. 'What'd he do?' sez I. 'Beat himself up?' It's dumb of them to beat up on the kids for doin' nothing. If they ever once get a beatin' they'll join anything. I compare my life here with my life when I was a child. There's no democracy now."

Nineteen seventy-two was not a year to be proud of in Northern Ireland. Paramilitary groups paralyzed the country with bombings and murders. Everyone on all sides suffered from the vicious fallout: Catholic and Protestant, police and army, innocent victims, and the gunmen themselves.

The Northern Ireland Civil Rights Association in Derry had scheduled another demonstration to take place in the city on January 30. Although all marches had been banned in Northern Ireland since August of the previous year to avoid sectarian conflicts in the streets, the organizers decided to go ahead with their plans anyway. The marchers were stopped from entering the city center by the First Parachute Regiment of the British forces in Derry, and, apparently unprovoked, the British soldiers began firing on the unarmed crowd. Thirteen of the marchers were killed, many more injured. The anger and grief that swept across Derry that day was felt all over Ireland, and for the first time since the Troubles in the North began, Dubliners responded to the event with violence. On February 2, uncontrolled mobs pushed their way to the British Embassy on Merrion Square and burned it.

In Westminster, Bernadette Devlin, reacting in her typically forthright manner, punched the Home Secretary, Reginald Maudling, in the face when she felt he was lying about the events of Bloody Sunday.

Eglinton is a pretty little village just outside Derry. Berna McIvor went to live there just after she was married. She and her husband, Ivan, built their first home and had their five children there. Bright, active, and energetic, Berna taught school, was one of the few Catholic members of the Women's Institute, a founding member and president of the Credit Union, and choirmistress in her local church choir. Ivan was a successful businessman and pub owner. Life was happy, productive, and full.

And then the Troubles started, and by the early 1970s their pub had been bombed, their house shattered, threats made on their lives, incendiary devices thrown at their home. Their first response was to stick it out, not to be forced to leave because of terrorist attacks. Finally, though, they decided it just wasn't worth it. It wasn't fair to the children. So they sold their business and their home, and closed down twenty happy years, and left Eglinton for Derry, where they live now.

"It was a wonderful life," Berna remembered, as we sat in her new, spacious house in Derry. "Our neighbors and friends were Catholic and Protestant. The children loved Eglinton; sometimes nowadays I drive by there, and I think: 'How happy we were!'

"But when the Troubles began in 1969, we began having a very bad time. You see, we were prominent Catholics, in business and successful, so we were continually a target for loyalist terrorist groups. Fear permeated the atmosphere. Our pub was gutted by fire, and just a week after we reopened, it was blown up by a three-hundred-pound bomb. The house was damaged by that bomb as well. That was a devastating attack, although luckily no one was hurt, and Ivan wanted to leave right then and there. The next day as we were cleaning up, I looked around at all our friends and neighbors who were there with us, helping to clean. They were nearly all Protestants! Of course they were horrified at the terrorist attacks, but what could they do?

"The pub was blown up several times. After the three-hundred-pound bomb, Ivan put a sign on the door saying: 'Open for business tonight!' And we were! There wasn't a roof on the place, but luckily it didn't rain, and with the help of friends we had got the place cleaned up.

"Finally, though, we decided to go. I remember that day. Ivan had gone away on business and I had the weekend 'take' from the bar; I was in bed and had the money in the house and I didn't sleep at all that night, and I thought, 'Oh, God, it's just not worth it. I'm getting out.' That was a year after the big bomb. It was the waiting to be shot that finally got to us. It was leaving my house that I minded the most. It was lovely.

"I don't really know why we were singled out, because there were other Catholics in business there. Of course, I was in politics; I suppose I could have sat at home and been a quiet little housewife, but it wasn't in my nature. I was something of a pioneer, joining the Women's Institute, putting my girls in Brownies. And look at the treatment I got! But I'm not bitter. I think we made the right decision to leave Eglinton."

Berna is retired from teaching now. Her children are grown and all of them are living outside of Northern Ireland. She and her husband travel and enjoy their retirement, although Berna is still active in SDLP politics, acting as John Hume's campaign manager (or election agent, as they are called there). Blond and good-looking, she exudes the direct, friendly, humorous manner that I find so attractive in Northern Ireland women. She is forthright in her assessment of political life in the North.

"I'm not politically ambitious for myself," she told me straight off. "I don't want to run for political office, but I love politics and have always been involved in them. I had been riveted by politics in the

United States and by the civil rights movement there in the nineteen sixties. I began going on our own civil rights marches here when Ronan [her son] was only four months old. I would drive to the march with his carry cot in the back seat of the car. I was concerned about discrimination in this country, and the day the SDLP was founded, I joined! I was elected to the party executive committee, was party treasurer [the only woman to hold that post], and now serve as John's election agent."

I asked her what her duties as election agent were.

"I run the campaign," she said. "I do the administrative work and leave the candidate free to campaign and to deal with the media. John's stature as a politician continues to grow. The Unionists just don't have anyone like him, and he is thought as well of in Europe as he is here. I've had occasion to be in Europe, in Strasbourg, and in Brussels [at the European Parliament and the EEC, or Common Market], and he is held in very high standing there."

"Why would you not run for political office yourself?" I asked.

"I have the time, being retired and having reared my family, but there is no forum here except the local councils. We have a women's group now in the SDLP, headed by Angela Hegarty. But we were very cross at the last party meeting when women's issues were discussed because of the general lack of interest by both men and women. Nevertheless, when it comes to doing the donkey's work, the men want us! That's what we've been doing over the years. We run the elections.

"I just wonder: When will the day come when we have normal politics again, with a left and a right to choose from, instead of the politics we have here now? I heard our local Sinn Fein and trade union people talking on the radio the other day. The trade unionists on the Unionist side vote for conservative policies! It's a paradox.

"Jobs would go such a long way to solve our problems. Young married men want to work, want to have a job to go to and a house to come back home to. They want to work in the garden, go to the pub for a couple of pints, go home. Irish people really like to own their own wee home and have their own wee garden. The rest of Europe live in flats. They always have and they like it. But not Ireland. As it is, what do the young men here do? They have no jobs, no self-respect, so they hang about street corners all day."

"Are you happy with the Anglo-Irish Agreement?" I asked.

"I think it is the most important thing that has happened in my lifetime. It will take time for the results to filter through, but I'm older now, and I've learned to be patient!"

"What do you think will be those results?"

"Justice, equality, and reconciliation. Those are the three things this country needs to begin to move ahead. Of course, I was appalled at the results of the divorce referendum in the South. We were delivered a sharp kick in the teeth, and I think the Church was totally dishonest about it. Of course, now the loyalists can — and do — use it as a propaganda tool.

"Being an optimist helps facing the future in Northern Ireland. I wish the two sides had more communication. We're just not talking to each other now," she said, "and socially we don't mix anymore like we used to. There isn't integrated housing now. That's why we need some kind of Northern Assembly, so we could at least talk to each other.

"I'm worried, too, about the breakdown of family and social structures here. I wonder sometimes, as I listen to sermons at Mass, is the Church facing that? They know about it, of course, but they don't know what to do."

Since Berna spent much of her life as a schoolteacher, I was eager to hear her thoughts on integrated education.

"I have nothing against it if parents want it. I think it is sad to see children who play together when they are tiny get separated when it's time to go to school. I know people are trying to start integrated schools on a private basis, and I would encourage them. I just don't know what effect it will have, but certainly it would do no harm; I know people who live in Derry and they have never known a Protestant!

"But you have a big problem with the churches and integrated education. A big problem. A man in the DUP said to me the other day: 'I wouldn't be opposed to Protestant and Catholic children being educated together, as long as no Catholic taught them.'"

I asked Berna if she thought her life would have been very different if it hadn't been for the Troubles. If Ireland had been — I was about to say "a nice little country like Denmark," but she interrupted: "— Normal?

"Well, I don't think I would have done anything differently." She smiled. "I would have always been involved in politics. There are always injustices wherever you are, always things to fight."

On March 4, 1972, there was a horrifying bomb explosion in the Abercorn Restaurant in downtown Belfast. It was a pleasant day, and the restaurant was crowded with women and children who were out for an afternoon's shopping. Two women were killed and 130 were injured, some grotesquely maimed. Two of the shoppers that day were sisters, looking for one's wedding dress. Both of them lost both legs; the bride-to-be also lost one arm and an eye.

A total of 467 people were killed that year. Twenty-eight young women were tarred and feathered, a peculiarly disgusting punishment the IRA reserves for women who are known to have fraternized with British soldiers or Protestant men. The "offender" is tied to a lamppost, her hair shaved off, her skirt tied up over her head, and hot tar or oil poured over her body.

The day of the Abercorn Restaurant bombing, Barney O'Neill, a thirty-six-year-old RUC officer, was on duty at the Castlereagh RUC station in Belfast. He heard about the bombing and was worried about his wife, Eileen, and their two children, Brian and Ann. It was such a lovely day that he had an intimation that they might have decided to go downtown for a bit of shopping. When he phoned the house and got no answer, his worries magnified. Finally, after several tries, Eileen picked up the phone. She had just gone out for a few hours to do errands.

"He was more perturbed than I can ever remember his being," Eileen recalled. "As soon as I picked up the phone, he said: 'Oh, there was a terrible explosion at the Abercorn and I was afraid you and the children might have been there.'

"I said, 'Sure, Barney, I wouldn't have done that if I hadn't told you.' We always told each other where we would be.

"'I know,' he said, 'but I thought that you might have met up with some of your friends while you were out and decided to stop in at the Abercorn for coffee.' He was greatly relieved to find us all safely at home that day."

Although he was stationed in the control room of Castlereagh, Barney had to take turns with other policemen to do street patrol downtown. This was supposed to be an onerous job for the police in those violent days in Belfast, but Barney discovered that he actually enjoyed being back on foot patrol. He had done a turn on March 17 and had seen people he hadn't seen for years, shopkeepers and tradesmen. When he came home that evening, he told Eileen that he enjoyed it so much that if peace ever came to the city, he would ask for patrol duty again in the city center. When his turn came around again on March 20, he told Eileen and the children good-bye and set out enthusiastically.

Brian was home that day from school with tonsillitis; Eileen was in the midst of her household chores. She was standing in the kitchen, washing out a pair of socks at the sink, when she heard the radio news: "There was a serious explosion downtown at two minutes of twelve. Two RUC officers were among the fatally injured."

"I knew instantly it was Barney," Eileen said as we sat together on a velour sofa in her small sitting room fifteen years later. The O'Neills had just moved into their pretty new house in 1971.

"He would have known about the explosion well before it was announced over the radio, and knowing that I would be worried, he would have got word to me that he was all right. He always did that. So I just knew it was him.

"I rang the control room at headquarters and they knew about the explosion all right, but they couldn't say anything over the telephone. It was one P.M. by then, and I found out later that the delay had been caused by the fact that Barney, not being on regular patrol in town, couldn't be identified, and they had to send someone from headquarters to identify him.

"It was a car bomb, and he was just passing by. It was supposed to have been planted in a different street altogether, but the explanation was that they couldn't get the car parked in the street it was supposed to be in, so they left it in Donegal Street. They gave a warning to clear the area, but they gave it for the area the car was supposed to have been in. So hundreds of people were injured. Four dustbinmen, Barney, and another foot-patrol officer were killed. They were just in the wrong place at the wrong time.

"Well, when they couldn't tell me anything at the station, I just came out of the kitchen and sat down there in the front hall on the stairs waiting for someone to come and tell me. I remember thinking: When they walk in that door to tell me, please don't let me break down and be melodramatic! Be brave. Don't make a fool of yourself! And then I began to think: Maybe he is just injured. I can take care of him. I can nurse him back to health. [Eileen is a licensed nurse.] But he was killed outright and that was merciful. His injuries were so appalling . . ." Even now, fifteen years after his death, the memory of that day brought Eileen to tears again. Her strong, kind face crumpled at the telling, and we both sat quietly until she had gained control. I wished at that moment that I were not there, asking her to tell me, a stranger, this painful story. But I wanted to have a chance to tell Barney's story again.

"You see," Eileen continued, "he was such an active man and such a homemaker. He was always working around the house and had a hobby of making radios. He would have been left with no legs and only one arm, so even if he had lived and we would have had him, his life would have been a living hell. Oh, I would have nursed him. But what kind of a life would it have been for him? It was very selfish for me to have wanted him to live.

"So I sat on the stairs, with my head in my hands, thinking these thoughts and waiting for the knock on the door. They finally arrived, with a policewoman and the wife of another policeman who was my closest friend. They had gone to get her at her home to bring her along. I don't even remember telling Brian; I think one of the policemen went to his room and talked to him. I know that one of the teachers from school brought Ann home."

I asked Eileen if she and Barney had ever discussed his possible death, living as they did in a very precarious time.

"I suppose you never believe it will happen to you. We felt comparatively safe here, and things had been quieter. The only time we ever talked about it was when we went to a policeman's funeral who had been shot the year before, and Barney said to me: 'If anything happens to me, don't have a full police funeral. It puts the family in the background, and they should be the chief mourners.' So we tried to do that when his time came. He was buried in Antrim, in the family plot.

"The children had a hard time believing it was true. I think they denied it for a long time, and afterwards they suffered much childhood stress because of it. I think Ann especially missed her Daddy; she is the more practical of the two, like her Daddy was, and when she would fix something or do something, like putting the luggage rack on the car, she would always stand back and say: 'I think Daddy would have done it that way.'

"I tried to bring them up so they weren't bitter. Bitterness doesn't get you anywhere and I feel that you only change your own personality if you are bitter about anything. It's more logical to try to solve a problem or learn from it than just to sink into bitterness."

"Did you feel bitter yourself?"

"I just felt numb. Very numb. And I think had Barney's death seen the end of these Troubles, I wouldn't have felt that he died in vain."

I asked Eileen if she had ever thought about remarrying.

"No. Because I had had such a happy life with Barney. He was so good to me and the children that I would have felt no one could have come up to him! I had learned to live with his faults and he with mine. Oh, it has been a lonely life, raising children, keeping a home without a partner, and you miss out on all sorts of things that you can't do yourself.

"I tried to keep the children's life as normal as possible. We went picnicking and to the seaside. Brian was the more studious type; he didn't really try to play his father's role, but he missed him very much. It was a very vulnerable age for a boy to lose his father. I had to go back to nursing because my pension was too small, but fortunately I could drop the children off at school and then pick them up again at four P.M., and after that I never left them. I went back to work on a casual basis in July nineteen seventy-two, and in nineteen seventy-nine I got my own post. I love my work. I always loved nursing. Probably I wouldn't have gone back to it if Barney hadn't died. He always liked for me to be at home."

"Did you or the children get any counseling after Barney's death?" I asked. So many victims I have talked to in Northern Ireland have had to bear their grief alone, without support groups or counseling.

"No, we just got through it as best we could, although I had a wonderful friend, another policeman's wife, who was a huge support to me. But about three years afterwards, Maura Kiley's son was shot coming out of church. She felt so bitter afterwards and felt she couldn't talk to her husband and tell him all the things she was feeling about her son, so she had this idea of forming a self-help group for the innocent victims who had lost a loved one. We met every month and were able to give each other tremendous support. Things that I was feeling, the behavior of the children and so on . . . I discovered that others had the same experiences. We still meet about four or five times a year in each other's homes."

"Is it hard socially being a widow in Northern Ireland?"

"Well, I just don't do anything socially. If I go to a meeting, Maura comes and collects me because I don't like driving at night. I developed cataracts as a result of the trauma of Barney's death, and it's difficult for me to drive at night. Now just recently another friend has started to take me to some concerts and plays with her husband and her mother. But I wouldn't do that alone. It's too lonely.

"People sometimes say: 'Why do you stick it? Why don't you just pack up and get out?' But where are you going to go? How is a widow going to start a new life in a new place? That would be a stupid thing to do."

"How are the children now? Do you feel you were overprotective towards them because you had to raise them alone?"

"Yes, Ann was resentful of that. She was more outgoing and I worried about her. Brian was a homebird anyway and could always lose himself in a book. Unfortunately, Brian had a brain aneurysm five years ago. He has recovered now, but he lost his job while he was sick, so he is unemployed. He still lives here at home.

"Ann was married two years ago. She just lives about a mile from here, and she and her husband are happily fixing up their new home. She was married on Barney's and my wedding anniversary. She asked me if I would mind, and I said: 'No, do it.' I decided I wasn't going to be emotional over it. After all, life goes on."

Being the wife of a politician is not always an easy job. Obviously some women are more suited to it, enjoy the aura of excitement and glamour, and gain strength from being close to a center of power. For others, particularly private, less outgoing women, it is all one big headache. Often left to raise children alone, on call to make public appearances, they ride in their husband's wake rather than walking by his side, and as a result, resentments and antagonisms are created easily. Husbands and wives who make a success of their personal relationship in the political arena have to work hard at it.

Being the wife of a Northern Irish politician has not only those common strains. One also has to deal with firebombing, bullet spray, personal threats, physical attack, slander, and innuendo. Austin and Annita Currie, politician and politician's wife, have stood more often in the front line of the North's political violence than perhaps any other couple.

They live in a modern, handsome house just outside Dungannon, in County Tyrone. We knew Austin, a moderate nationalist politician, when we lived in Ireland; I had never met Annita but had heard many times of the terrible trials she and her family had gone through during the Troubles, particularly the vicious physical attack made on her in 1972 by members of the Ulster Volunteer Force, an illegal loyalist paramilitary organization.

I went to visit the Curries on a clear, cold January day in 1987. Dungannon seemed nondescript as I drove slowly around its small business area, without charm or interest to a traveler's eye. And it was strangely quiet, with none of the bustle and busy streets of many small Northern Irish towns. As I drove through the gates of the Curries' drive, I was horrified to see the big picture window in the front of the house smashed into a web of cracked glass. I had known about their past attacks, but were they still going on? Austin came out to meet me as I got out of the car, and after our first greetings, I pointed to the window. "What is that all about?" He grimaced and shrugged.

"They're at it again. They broke off one of the pillars on the gate and used it as a ramming rod to smash the windows. Fortunately, the windows are bullet-proof, so they only shattered."

Annita was waiting for us in the living room. Small and slim, with a lovely, soft voice that belies a very articulate, determined manner, she greeted me warmly as we sat down to talk. Austin perched on the arm of a chair.

"I know this is an interview with Annita," he said with a smile, "but I just want to go on record as saying one thing, then I'll leave you two. Simply this: I could never have done any of the things I have done if it hadn't been for Annita's support — moral, financial, and otherwise. That's all." He got up to leave but paused at the door and turned back. "And do you want me to build a fire?" We decided it was warm enough without one.

Austin Currie has been involved in political life in Northern Ireland since he was a student at Queens University in the heady days of the mid-1960s. Attractive, bright, and energetic, he was elected a Member of the Northern Ireland Parliament and was one of the founders of the SDLP. Annita remembers the night when she, Austin, and John Hume sat up in the Curries' kitchen half the night, the three of them deciding on the party's name, she typing out the party's constitution on her portable typewriter in the kitchen, finishing up exhilarated and exhausted at 3 A.M., and then retyping the documents for Austin to take to Stormont, the Northern Irish Parliament, the next day.

"It was all so exciting in those days," she remembered. "And then the euphoria of Sunningdale! We really thought we were on the right road. And now . . ." She looked at the shattered window of her living room. "I guess we've come full circle again. Unfortunately, this is about our third full circle!"

The early years of the Curries' marriage were circumscribed by Austin's political activities. Annita remembers the important events of those years by relating them to the births of their five children.

"In one sense, I am fortunate. Austin was already deeply committed to politics when I married him, so I knew what I was getting into. And my own father was a newspaper publisher in Omagh and had been a nationalist senator. So I came from a political background. Nevertheless, when you are a political family, your home is never private.

"I've always been his election agent, his secretary, typist, confidante . . . and his devil's advocate! In the early days, there was a marvelous sense of achievement. You saw barriers coming down, and you saw that you were part of those accomplishments. For instance, I went to the Domestic Science College in Belfast. You knew that out of the twenty-four places there each year, only three of them would be offered to Catholics. I was one of the three. Well, I didn't want to go to Domestic Science College, but it would have been unthinkable to turn down a place there. They were so coveted. Later on, I went back to school and did a degree in music, which is what I wanted in the first place. But in those days, you took what came along. It was just accepted that Catholics didn't get certain housing, didn't apply for certain jobs.

"Estelle, our oldest child, was born on the eve of the first civil rights march. Katrina, the second, was born a week after a bomb was exploded at our house. It blew in one of the walls of our bedroom and my obstetrician said: 'Well, Annita, if gelignite doesn't move that baby out, nothing will!'

"The third child was born just before internment was introduced, and I remember not having even a second to sit down and hold him with his bottle because the phone was ringing off the hook. Everyone wanted Austin. I often think, looking back, that all the quirks of that child's personality were due to the deprivations he suffered in those first six months of his life, when I had to prop-feed him just to see that he got a bottle!

"Young Austin was born the day that Sunningdale fell. Austin came down from Belfast to tell me about it just as I was being wheeled off to the hospital. I felt sorry for myself: other husbands would be at their wife's side at that moment, I thought, but politics comes first with Austin. It has taken me a long time to come to terms with that. Austin will disagree now, but I know that for a long part of our life, politics came first.

"Austin defied the party and wanted someone to take on the Provos [members of the Provisional IRA] in Fermanagh–South Tyrone when Bobby Sands stood." In April 1981, Bobby Sands, an IRA prisoner who was on a hunger strike, was put forward to stand in the election. He won, and held the post while in prison until he died on May 5. Currie had been prepared to run against Sands but the SDLP decided to stay out of the election, thinking that Noel Maguire would run. As it turned out, Maguire did not run and Currie lost the chance to win the seat.

The Curries had been targets for political militancy from the very beginning. As moderate nationalists who wouldn't espouse violence, they were under attack from the Provos. As Catholics, they were a natural target for loyalist extremists.

"At first, way back in 1969, it was just verbal abuse," Annita remembered. "Then it escalated. Shots were fired into the house. I remember once Austin got a phone call from a friend in a village a few miles up the road to say that he had overheard a conversation between some B-Specials that they were coming down to attack our house. I was expecting Katrina at the time, and Austin was away, so he got his brother to come and take us out of the house.

"'She's as stubborn as a mule,' he told his brother, 'but get her out of there even if you have to knock her over the head!' So we packed up and spent the night at Austin's mother's home. We came back the next day to find the house just riddled with bullets. So I went to the refugee camp at Gormanston, outside Dublin, and stayed there for quite a while, with women who had been evacuated from Armagh, Belfast, and other Northern Irish towns.

"That kind of thing went on intermittently. Then one night in nineteen seventy-two, when Austin was away in Cork at a political meeting, I had a knock on the door about three A.M. That wasn't so unusual in those days, because if a parent had a son arrested they would usually try to get Austin to make a representation on his behalf, because there were stories of a lot of prison brutality in those days. They would arrive at our door anytime in the middle of the day or night, so I wasn't unusually alarmed when the knock sounded at three A.M.

"I went to the door and called out: 'Who's there?' And a voice responded: 'Is Austin there?' I said: 'No, he's not at home.'

"Then the voice said: 'Oh, we've got to talk to you, Mrs. Currie. It's terribly important.' So I opened the door. There were three of them, and as soon as they came in, they produced the gun. First they ransacked the house, looking for Austin. When they finally became convinced he wasn't here, they were furious and took it out on me. Thankfully the three children were asleep in their beds, and they didn't bother them. But they battered the daylights out of me right here in this room. They hit me with their fists, then threw me on the floor and kicked me. Then they ripped open my housecoat and carved 'UVF' across my breasts with a knife. The only thing they didn't do was rape me. I suppose I have that to be thankful for. At some point, I passed out and Estelle, who was four then, woke up and heard the noise. When she appeared at the living room door, that stopped them and they left."

"Were they drunk?" I asked.

"No, they weren't drunk." She smiled ruefully. "Just mean.

"Anyway, after that the police decided that we needed a permanent guard on the house, so they built a little watchhouse in the garden. Then, of course, the Provos decided that they should have a go at our police guard, so they would wait outside our gate until the guards changed their shift, and then spray the gate with bullets. These windows were out more often than in, with bullet holes in them. The children got so used to it that every time they heard a strange noise, they would come running to me and say: 'Mummy, is it time to lie down, cover our heads, and say three Hail Marys?'

"So that was our situation in the early 'seventies. We were caught between two stools. The Provos wanted the police who guarded us, and the extreme loyalists wanted us! One of the policemen was shot in the leg while he was here, and then we had the horrendous experience of one policeman shooting the other one right here while they were cleaning their guns. He died a few days later, and of course that was blamed on us by the Protestant community here, and it's still thrown up at us. Not that they thought we had done it, but that it was our fault that the police had to be here at all. In those days, anything that happened to a police patrol within a radius of two or three miles from here was blamed on us. It just finally became an intolerable situation and we decided that we would rather go back to our old way of living, without guards, dangerous as it was, and we installed security measures — bullet-proof glass and all that sort of thing."

I asked Annita if anyone had ever been caught in connection with the attack on her, or any of the other attacks.

"No, no one has been caught or charged, ever. I got a lot of sympathy from the moderate Protestants, of course, and sympathy from the South, but it has taken me years to get over it. When Austin is away, I still require sleeping pills. And now this business . . ." — she pointed to the newly shattered window — "it has brought it all back again. It really is so depressing. Things had been quiet and we had settled down into an almost normal life. We had just completed an extension of the house, which we had worked so hard and saved so long to do, and we were really proud of it. And after this attack, I was really depressed, feeling like it is starting all over again."

"Annita," I said, "don't you feel very bitter about having been the target of all these awful things?"

"Yes. I do. I long for normality." Her voice was very low and she sounded profoundly sad as she said this. But then she smiled again. "On the other hand, we have lived with it so long now that I think if we ever did return to a normal life, we might both end up in a mental hospital. We wouldn't know what to do!"

"With hindsight, would you have packed up and left if you had known how bad it was going to be, or how long it would last?"

"Oh, yes! Look, if someone said to you today: Next week you are going to be living in a siege situation, with searchlights on your house, bullet-proof windows, a husband carrying firearms, a telephone link with the local police station, your children victimized at school . . . well, you could never do that. But it builds up slowly. There have been many, many times when I was feeling low and depressed and I *begged* Austin to go, but he always said no. He feels that he has a commitment and a responsibility to try to do something and a role to play in it. It has taken me a long, long time to come to terms with that. I felt bitter that I didn't have the lifestyle I thought I ought to have. I would listen to people at work talking about things they had just bought, or holidays they were planning — other working wives — and here I am using my salary to pay the mortgage and other necessities. And I felt sorry for the children, too, because they are caught between two stools. Kids in Belfast and Derry have various voluntary groups who see the problems that those children are living with and take them away from time to time to get them out of the environment. But because of who Austin is, we don't have that advantage.

"For a few years, we took them camping in France in the summer, and it was only then that we began to realize the pressures we were all under. I would suddenly realize that everything felt normal, and then, a few days before it was time to return, you could feel the tension coming back. I remember in the early years of the Troubles, when things were really at their worst, and I was at my lowest, crying my eyes out as we would come through the border — literally sitting in the car in hysterics because I had to come back, and I didn't want to.

"But having a job and a career now has done a tremendous amount of good for me in that way. It has given me a whole life, which is totally different and separate from politics. And I just don't have time to get depressed!"

Annita went back to school and did a degree in music, which had always been her first love, and then, in 1976 ("when there were no jobs for politicians!"), she went to work. She is now a music center organizer, in charge of all the music in the schools in her area, which total 150, both Catholic and Protestant.

"The fact that I am who I am has never interfered in my job; no principal or teacher has ever shown antagonism. I go into schools in the most right-wing Protestant areas and I am accepted. I think everyone is just practical about it. I am the one who can provide them with the equipment and staff they need. You know, most of the people in Northern Ireland are levelheaded and will go the way that is best for them, particularly when it comes to questions of education.

"Some of the things that we've gone through here have almost been forgotten now. Although Austin is only in his forties, he has been in politics for so long that he is looked upon as one of the older generation of politicians, and some of the children growing up now wouldn't remember his part in the struggle to bring them the rights they have. I see job and educational opportunities for my children that are much greater than Austin or I had, and I know he is partly responsible for that. It isn't true that things haven't changed: many, many things have changed here in the past fifteen years.

"We're blessed with our children. They are very good, loving, and obedient. In a lot of ways we have so much to be thankful for. If things had been more normal here, if we had had a hefty salary and could have given our kids much more material things, we would have been facing a lot of the problems that parents of our age group are facing with their kids now — opting out of school, daughters pregnant, facing the drug scene. But because we couldn't afford to socialize, couldn't go out at night, couldn't get babysitters even if we wanted to go out occasionally, we are a stronger family unit, so it's not all negative. As we lived through it, I don't think we saw what the positive sides were going to be.

"I think we've come through the worst of it now."

In March 1972, British Prime Minister Edward Heath, fed up with the troubles in his angry little province, suspended Stormont, the Northern Ireland Parliament, withdrew responsibility for the province from the Home Secretary, and created a new Secretary of State for Northern Ireland. When the Parliament adjourned at 4:15, March 28, it was thought that the adjournment would last at least a year. In fact, it was never to meet again. If Ulstermen couldn't govern themselves, England would, once again, have to show them how. Heath then orchestrated the Sunningdale Agreement in 1973, a "power-sharing" government in which Catholics and Protestants both had a voice in cabinet affairs. It lasted five months before it was destroyed by a loyalist-backed countrywide strike. Its failure was one of the saddest events in the history of modern Ireland.

It began on Thursday, December 6, 1973, a blustery, cold day all over the British Isles, when the most senior politicians and civil servants from Northern Ireland, the Irish Republic, and Westminster convened at the Civil Service College in Sunningdale, England. The Northern Irish Catholic community was represented by leaders of the SDLP. Leaders of the official Unionists represented the Protestants. The groundwork for the meeting had been done in the previous four months, with Northern Irish politicians working with Willy Whitelaw, the imaginative and genial British Secretary of State for Northern Ireland.

For four days and nights, working around the clock, the politicians and their staff put the finishing touches on a new agreement for governing Northern Ireland. It was named the Sunningdale Agreement after its birthplace, and it created an Assembly with a "Power-Sharing Executive," a board composed of six Unionists, four SDLP members, and one Alliance member. It was a major victory for the moderate, nonviolent nationalist population of Northern Ireland and proved without question that a faction of the recalcitrant Unionist leadership was, at last, entering a new age of fair play and equal representation.

The men involved in the creation of the agreement flew back to Belfast, Dublin, and London at the end of the fourth grueling day, exhausted but elated and optimistic, hopeful that for the first time in its short parliamentary history, a new and equitable era was beginning for Northern Ireland. And from January 1, 1974, when the Power-Sharing Executive took office, until May 29 the same year, the Protestant majority and the Catholic minority were fairly represented in Northern Ireland. Somewhat to the astonishment of both sides, the politicians learned to know and respect each other, and they worked well together. Alas, they misjudged the suspicion, fear, and bigotry of the extreme loyalist Protestants in their country. Where they looked upon their parliamentary creation as a fair and equal process of governing their divided country, the extreme loyalists looked upon their accomplishment as treacherous disloyalty. Shared power, by Catholics and Protestants, was simply not on their agenda, and they would not stand idly by and watch the erosion of the supremacy by which they defined themselves. Their reaction to the establishment of the Power-Sharing Executive was simple: destroy it. After due consultation in different sectors, it was decided that a countrywide strike would cripple and ultimately undermine the new government.

On Wednesday, May 15, the strike began. It was led by a relatively new working-class Protestant organization called the Ulster Workers' Council, whose members felt betrayed by the moderate (and mostly land-owning, middle-class) Unionists. With the backing of many Protestant paramilitary organizations, they set up barricades and roamed the streets armed with sticks and cudgels, threatening and intimidating anyone who tried to go to work. Thousands of employees at Harland and Wolff's, the huge Belfast shipyard, were told at lunchtime that any cars left in the parking lot after lunch would be burned. The British Army, which was still responsible for security in Northern Ireland, according to the terms of the Sunningdale Agreement, seemed impotent, unable to cope with the growing chaos. What started as a "strike" was rapidly turning into the overthrow of a legitimate government.

Finally, when the strikers were threatening the shutdown of the major power stations, the government had to decide whether to try to negotiate with the strikers or hold out. Brian Faulkner, the Prime Minister, wanted to attempt negotiations, but John Hume, of the SDLP, was adamant against any negotiation. He felt if they held out long enough, the strike would fail and the people would see what chaos had been created. Perhaps he knew, better than Faulkner, the futility of negotiation with the extremists. When untreated sewage began seeping up through manhole covers throughout the city as the strike continued, Hume held firm: "I'll sit here until there is shit flowing up Royal Avenue and then the people will realise what these people [the strike leaders] are about and then we'll see who wins."

In the end, the strikers won. Although the majority on the Executive felt that dialogue between the government and the strike leaders should take place, Merlyn Rees, the Secretary of State for Northern Ireland who had replaced Willy Whitelaw, would not agree to negotiation. By midafternoon of May 29, the government was terminated. It was the end of a short-lived, courageous experiment in governing. For the men who had been personally involved, it was a heartbreaking failure, but they walked away from it with newfound trust on both sides. With hindsight, the government should have stood up to the strikers, perhaps calling in United Nations Peace-Keeping Forces when the British Army proved unable to provide security. It was also a victim of partisan politics: Heath's Conservative government had fallen in February, and the new Labor government at Westminster was not eager to salvage what had been one of Heath's political creations. That will be forever a black mark on Harold Wilson's government.

The Sunningdale Agreement did leave a legacy to Northern Ireland, however. It proved that it was possible for both sides to work together for the mutual welfare of their country, that old wounds could be forgiven and the future, not the past, be a guiding force. In a letter he wrote to Reginald Magee a few weeks before he died, Lord Faulkner said, "If we had [succeeded,] the rewards for Ulster would have been beyond our brightest expectations. There would have been strong support for our Government from virtually every country in the world . . . Terrorism could not have flourished on this island."

I talked about the failure of Sunningdale in 1986 with Bríd Rogers of the SDLP.

"The irony is," she said, "that quite a number of middle-class Unionists in this area — granted I don't meet that many — now take the view: 'Oh, if only we had accepted Sunningdale!' There's a journalist in Portadown, a fairly typical middle-class Unionist, and he takes that view. So I said to him the other day: 'Well, for all your sakes, I hope that in fifteen years' time you aren't saying: 'Oh, if only we had accepted the Anglo-Irish Agreement!' Surely they should begin to think about that."

"Wasn't it sad that Merlyn Rees didn't have more foresight, or more courage, or whatever it would have taken to have stood up to the strikers?" I asked.

"Merlyn Rees was wishy-washy from the very beginning. He was. It's just his nature," Bríd said. "If we had had the luck to have Willy Whitelaw then, things might have been very different."

"Unionists now think Brian Faulkner was a traitor because he was willing to give a little."

Bríd smiled. "They still say that, do they? You see, if only they knew it, Brian Faulkner was the man who could have saved them from themselves. They just can't see that."

Three from Bunbeg

For there is no friend like a sister,
In calm or stormy weather . . .
To lift one if one totters down
To strengthen whilst one stands.
— CHRISTINA ROSSETTI

THERE'S A SMALL, whitewashed village on the northwest edge of County Donegal called Bunbeg. Although it is in the province of Ulster, it is not a part of the political entity of Northern Ireland. It's very far from anywhere, and the roads that lead to it climb over mountains, swerve around bogs, and hug the sea. The beaches around Bunbeg are wide and glorious, and on rare sunny summer days tourists flock there. On a map of Ireland Bunbeg is colored pink because it's in the "Gaeltacht," an area where people still speak the Irish language.

On the southern edge of the village there are two pretty whitewashed houses not far from each other. Three of the women who have grown up in those houses have had their lives shifted dramatically because of the political turmoil that erupted in Northern Ireland in the 1970s. One made the change in her life by a conscious choice: she saw physical force eroding the political process in her community, and she chose to participate in that process as it was evolving in Northern Ireland. She has never swerved from her course.

The other two, sisters, became victims of political forces over which they had no control. They spent a decade of their lives in a prison cell. None of the three is "typical" of any woman in Northern Ireland. In fact, their lives — as politician and as prisoners — are uniquely atypical, but they would not be who they are today without the political eruptions of Northern Ireland.

* * *

For the Gillespie family in Bunbeg, 1961 was not a good year. The eldest son of the family, Sean, was in Mountjoy Prison in Dublin for republican activities. Mr. Gillespie had lost his job, and economic prospects in Donegal were bleak. He decided he would have to immigrate to England in order to find work and support his family. With a heavy heart and not much sense of adventure, Mrs. Gillespie followed her husband to Manchester. Two of the other boys, Liam and Joe, were already there with their father. The two youngest girls, Ann and Eileen, accompanied their mother. They spoke no English; they had grown up speaking Irish at home and school. It was hard to break their ties with Bunbeg entirely. They kept the family home there, hoping that one day they would return to live by the sea in their own small village.

Ann and Eileen were, by Manchester standards, naïve country bumpkins. They had lived a very sheltered life in Donegal. At nine and twelve years old, their life experiences had been limited to the simple ways of a small Irish town, which wasn't much different in the 1950s from what it had been for the past hundred years. But both girls were quick and bright, and by the time they had finished elementary school at the Loretta Convent and started high school, they had assimilated their new culture. But their hearts were still in Bunbeg, and together with their mother they made the long trip home every summer: by boat to Belfast, bus across Northern Ireland to Derry, and then the lovely, winding mountain road across Donegal to the western coast. Anticipation of summer days in Bunbeg made the long, wet winters of Manchester more bearable.

The girls grew into very pretty young women, each one typical of an "Irish beauty": Eileen taller and slim with thick red hair and wide-set green eyes, Ann smaller and more fragile, with jet-black hair and violet eyes. Both of them have soft, pale Irish skin. When they finished high school, Ann spent several years modeling. Eileen trained as a nurse at the Manchester Royal Infirmary and worked there after she received her diploma. Ann eventually left her modeling career and went to work as a receptionist at the same hospital.

Like most Irish families, the Gillespies were extremely close. They depended on each other for emotional support, for fun, and for company. Although the girls were popular and had dates, they considered the family the core of their lives. Their close family bonds were made even stronger by a feeling of being somewhat alien in a foreign land.

In 1969, when the Troubles started in Northern Ireland, the Gillespie family was not closely involved with the Irish political community in England. Their family sentiment was strongly nationalist: Mrs. Gillespie had had two sisters in Cumann na mBan, the female arm of Sinn Fein, and Sean had briefly become involved in the flurry of IRA activities in Ireland in the 1950s. But for Ann and Eileen, the problems of Northern Ireland seemed remote. They occasionally attended Sinn Fein functions in Manchester, more for the social side than from a deep political commitment. They participated in fund drives to raise money for prisoners' families, and they periodically marched in demonstrations protesting army and police activity in Northern Ireland.

When the IRA stepped up their bombing campaign in England in the early 1970s, relationships between the English and Irish there became strained. All Irish were suspect, whatever their political leanings. And those with strongly nationalist backgrounds — which would certainly include Irish speakers from Donegal — were soon on the local police hit list. As the bombings continued, the police were under tremendous pressure from the government to find suspects and prosecute them. Plainclothes policemen would mingle in the crowds at demonstrations and photograph participants. Homes like the Gillespies' were routinely raided by the police during this period.

"They would come storming in around two or three A.M.," Ann remembered. "If they had a search warrant they never produced one. Some would come rushing in the back door, others through the front, so it was chaotic. Sometimes as many as twenty would come in at once, and although someone from the house was supposed to be with them at all times while they searched, it was impossible. There were too many of them. They raided our house so often we got used to it and would say to them: 'Oh, hurry up and get on with it!' The thing I resented was that it upset my parents so much. One of them roughed up my mother once, totally uncalled-for.

"They liked to come in in the early hours of the mornings so the neighbors couldn't see them. There were lots of newspaper articles in those days about how the Irish people in England were suffering police harassment, so they didn't want to draw attention to themselves. Given the climate of that time, what finally happened to us isn't surprising."

What happened to them was that they were convicted of being part of a general conspiracy to set off explosives in the United Kingdom and were sentenced to fifteen years in prison, starting in March 1975. Ann was twenty-six, Eileen twenty-three. They served ten years of their sentence in Durham Prison, the full term minus maximum remission for good behavior. At the time of their trial, they were known in the press as "Sisters of Terror" or "The Semi-detached Brigade."

It was a gloriously clear, sunny day when I drove from Derry to Bunbeg, right across the width of Donegal. It was a deserted and beautiful drive, which dipped into lush green glens, passed over flat bogland, and skirted cold, gray lakes. For miles at a stretch there was not a passing car, and seldom a house. Lonely herds of sheep and cattle grazed on rough, hilly terrain looking forlorn, as if they belonged to no one. As I approached Bunbeg, a covey of white seagulls plunged and rose, their hoarse cry announcing the nearby sea.

The Gillespie cottage is the middle house of a row of three whitewashed cottages sitting on a windswept knoll. Various other family members live in the houses on either side. Bright red geraniums spilled out over pots on the floor of the red-tiled foyer; both sisters were at the door to greet me as I walked up the path from my car.

These are the "Sisters of Terror"? I wondered to myself as we shook hands. They are both strikingly pretty, Ann, the serious, dominant talker, Eileen, smiling often, seeing the funnier side of life. Both girls were dressed casually in jeans and sweaters and looked far younger than women in their late thirties. It was as if that decade in prison had simply washed by them, leaving them untouched, and they were beginning adult life now.

"The first time I thought we were in trouble," Ann began, "was on Easter Saturday, nineteen seventy-four. I had gone into the village to go to Confession and to bring Mommy some cream for the trifle she was making for dinner on Easter Sunday. And I wanted to pick up the Easter eggs I had ordered from the pastry shop. When I left the house, Mommy was stuffing the turkey and I said: 'I'll be back in an hour.'

"So off I went, and I was in the pastry shop when the police came in. They said to me: 'We've got a car outside, come along quietly.' I had no idea what the charges were or what they wanted. They took me home, and on the way they told me they had found a gun in our house.

"'That's ridiculous!' I said. 'You lads are always searching our house. Why would we try to hide a gun there?'

"Anyway, they had been searching the house while I had been at the shop, and they said they found this gun. Mommy said later that it was very strange: they came into the house and went straight down the basement and came straight back up again with the gun in their hand. We knew they had planted it there."

Ann was taken to the police station and charged with possession [of firearms]. She told them over and over that she didn't know anything about the gun. Finally, they released her on her own bail and told her to appear on Tuesday in the city center police station. She had sent for a lawyer, and when she was released, he warned her: "Keep out of their way. The next time it won't be so easy."

Ann laughed, recalling his warning. "I was so naïve! I said: 'Next time! What do you mean, next time!'

"'Well,' he said, 'a lot of things have been happening around here and nobody has been arrested yet. They are pretty desperate. They need to make an arrest, and you are an easy target from now on.'

"After that I was followed everywhere I went. Eileen had come back from Ireland, where she had been on a short holiday when I was arrested, and the two of us would make little detours, turn corners, retrace our steps . . . just for the fun of it, to see them follow us. Even then, I think we were still treating it as something of a joke."

"Why," I asked, "did they pick you as a target? Did you know anyone who was suspect?"

"There was a man who had been arrested and convicted, and he admitted to being guilty. I had probably met him three times in my life and that would have been in a group at a dance. We didn't know anybody else who was involved."

"So then, what happened?"

Eileen took over the story. "Our brother Owen had a new car and was looking for a place to garage it while he was in Ireland. He had met this fellow who said his sister had a spare garage and she might rent it. It was only a few streets from where we lived. So on Saturday, a week after Ann had been arrested for possession, we were going to a shopping center, and on the way I said to Ann: 'Let's stop at that fellow's house with the garage and see if we can rent it for Owen.'

"His sister let us in; she said the brother was out but would be back soon, so we went into the living room with her to wait. She had three small children and we just sat there, chatting and playing with the children. She was an Irish girl from Tipperary, sort of a fat, dumb blonde.

"Pretty soon, not more than fifteen minutes, the brother came in, but he went straight upstairs and didn't come in the living room. The sister got up and yelled up to him: 'There's two girls here to see you about the garage,' and he yelled back down: 'Tell them to come up.'

"So we went up, and he was in a bedroom. There was another fellow sitting on the bed, but he had his back to us and didn't turn around or speak. We both stood in the threshold of the door.

"'You're Ownie's sisters, is that right?' he asked.

"We said we were and were looking for a place to garage his car. Just at that moment — nothing more had been said — there was this huge explosion and the room was filled instantly with smoke. We couldn't breathe and we couldn't see. I can't tell you how bad it was. We thought we were suffocating."

"The bomb was in the very room you were in?" I asked.

"We have no idea. We've tried and tried to work that out. You see, from the time we walked into that house until the time the bomb exploded was no more than twenty minutes. And while we were talking about the car we weren't really noticing what the fellow on the bed was doing, if anything. Then there was this dense, thick, black smoke and you couldn't see anything."

"I tried to find Eileen," Ann interrupted. "I kept saying: 'I must find Eileen.' I was crawling around the room on my hands and knees, choking and calling to her. Finally I found her up against the opposite wall, where the force of the explosion had thrown her. I dragged her across the floor — I remember bumping into the bed — and got her to a window and just literally threw her out. From the second floor."

"I landed in the garden," Eileen said. "I just sat there, shouting for Ann to jump. I could hear myself screaming: 'Jump, Ann, jump!' and I couldn't figure out why she didn't."

"Would you believe that the belt of my raincoat got caught somehow on the windowsill and I was stuck! I kept pulling and pulling at it. Finally, it came loose and I jumped, and landed on the roof of the coal shed. Neither of us was hurt in the jump."

"We were all singed and black and covered with soot," Eileen said. "And we were obviously in shock. But I remember we ran back into the front door of the house to see if the woman and the babies were all right. The woman was hysterical. She threw the baby at me and ran to call the fire brigade. When she returned, she became quite hostile. 'Get out of here,' she kept screaming at us."

Eileen laughed. "Yes, first she tries to kill us and then she throws us out of the house. Anyway, we were in a state of shock, or we would have stayed there 'til the fire brigade and the police came. Instead, when she told us to get out, we just left. A neighbor had come out and Ann said to her: 'Please go help the woman in that house.' She remembered us and testified later at our trial."

"We ran down the street, headed for home, and at the bottom of the street we saw the fellow from the house. He was standing by a van, and he grabbed Eileen as we approached and pushed her into the van. 'You drive,' he said, and then pushed me in behind her, in the back. The other man, the one who had been sitting on the bed, was lying down there, very, very badly burned and in severe pain. I mean, he must have been sitting on the bloody bomb, his injuries was so severe. I knew instantly that he must get to a hospital or he would die. But the other guy kept directing Eileen: 'Turn here, turn there.' I had no idea where we were headed. We finally stopped in Salford, the next district, and we all went into a little council house there, where a woman was waiting for us. I said to her that we had to get this man to hospital immediately. Eileen cut the hair away from the burns on his face, then we tried to wash ourselves a bit at the kitchen sink. All we really wanted to do was to get away from there, and we did it as soon as we could. We took a bus back to our village. We must have looked pretty funny, with our singed hair and blacked clothes, but no one said anything."

"Maybe they thought we were chimney sweeps," Eileen added.

"We got home and just ran in the door and straight upstairs," Ann recalled. "We didn't want Mommy to see us in that state. We bathed, and then went down. It was time to drive Mommy to work — she worked a few hours each evening as a receptionist in the hospital."

I interrupted. "Didn't your mother notice the cuts on your hands?"

"No," Eileen said. "She didn't notice.

"Then we drove to my brother's house in Cheshire and told him the story. His first reaction was fury; he wanted to go find those two guys and kill them for putting our lives in danger. When he calmed down, he told us we should go immediately to the authorities and tell them everything. But Eileen thought we should try to get out of the country."

"With everything that had gone on in the past few months, I knew we didn't stand a chance," Eileen explained. "I wanted to leave right then and there. And we should have."

"I know," Ann sighed. "It was my stupid fault. I kept delaying us. We should have headed for the nearest airport or boat and been out of the country that night. But no, I was stupid and kept saying: 'Oh, what will happen to Mommy and Daddy? What will they do to them? I thought, even then, that if we went to the police and explained everything to them, they would listen. And all Eileen kept saying was: 'They'll send us to prison, that's what they'll do!'"

"I finally persuaded Ann that we must leave," Eileen said, "even though my brother and his wife were against it. But still . . . more delays. We sent them back to our house to get us some clothes. Imagine! Thinking that was important! And we were driving our own car, an old Escort, and Ann said: 'I'm worrying about the fan belt in that car, so when you go home, get Ownie's car and bring it back to us.' Can you believe that we were practically on our way to prison, and we were worrying about fan belts?

"Anyway, we were finally on our way. We thought that if we drove through the night to Holyhead, in Wales, we would be there in time for the early morning sailing. And then we'd be home in Ireland and safe. There were no extradition laws at that time.

"We were a bit too early for the boat, so we stopped for a while at a lay-by, across from a roadside cafe called Chef's. Well, we got to the docks, and I went in to buy two tickets, and we got in the long queue to get to the boat. And just to show you how relentlessly stupid we were, we saw that there was a checkpoint up ahead and cars were being stopped, and we didn't even have the sense to get a story ready. Ann said to the policeman: 'We're going to Ireland to see our grandmother,' and I said, at the same time: 'We're going to Ireland to see our aunt!' We don't even have a grandmother! But, to our amazement, they just waved us on through.

"We approached the ramp, and I turned to Ann and said: 'We've made it!' We were actually on the ramp, ready to board the boat. And at that very second, I looked in the rearview mirror and I saw them coming. I said to Ann: 'That's it. I see them coming. We're finished.'

"They came up to the car, motioned for us to stop, and said: 'Excuse me, Madam. Would you mind to put the car into reverse and back down. We've a few questions we want to ask you.' They were very nice.

"I looked at Ann again and said: 'We're goners.'"

"Did you say that right in front of the policeman?" I asked incredulously.

"She did," Ann said. "And she was right.

"They took us into a big shed and began to question us. It went on and on and on. The Welsh police were very nice, I'll say that for them. But the Manchester police were there and they were brutal. They tried to strip us, but we fought back. Finally, they put us in a car and drove us back to Manchester. On the way, they kept saying things like: 'You girls are finished! It will be a long, long time before you see daylight again. Look, we know you didn't actually do it, but you know who did do it.' They would go on and on like this. They were trying to scare us."

"Trying!" Eileen said. "They succeeded! We were petrified."

"They were the same police who used to come to the house and search it. We knew them all. We even had nicknames for them. So we tried to joke them along. But they weren't in for jokes!"

"But why," I asked, "didn't you tell them who did it? Just explain it all right then?"

"We didn't know who those guys were. We had never seen them before in our lives. But can you imagine me starting to tell you a story about going upstairs in some strange house and there was a guy sitting on a bed and he never turned around and then there was an explosion! Our story was so stupid, even though it was true, they never would have believed us.

"We got back to Manchester; it was about midnight now, and they took us to a jail and dragged us along these corridors. They wanted to put us in a police lineup for identification. Can you imagine what we looked like by now? Sick, scared, bedraggled, nothing to eat for hours, and here was this line of immaculately dressed young women, calmly standing there. I said: 'You're not going to drag us in there. Look at us! What kind of a fair identification is that?' You see, we were still telling them that we didn't know anything about it."

"I was sick," Ann said. "I had an ulcer and it was acting up because

I hadn't eaten all day. But Eileen was so strong!" She smiled at her sister. "She kept demanding dry toast and milk for me."

"When we refused to go into the lineup, one of the policewomen assaulted me," Eileen said. "She caught me in the forehead, but I'm pretty strong, and I got her up against the wall. Then she asked the policemen to help her, but they wouldn't! Finally, they didn't put us in the lineup. They just brought the woman out and she identified us."

"What woman?"

"The sister."

"But why didn't they make her tell where her brother and the other guy were?"

"She didn't know.

"So they stripped us then, right down to nothing, and made us cover ourselves with a blanket, and the interrogation started. They separated us for that."

"What was the point in stripping you and making you sit in a blanket?"

"Humiliation. Dehumanization. How can you keep face when you are sitting there with no clothes on, trying to tug the blanket around you to keep it on?"

But before the interrogation began, Eileen demanded to make one phone call. "I've seen it on television," she kept shouting at them, "and I know my rights!"

"Eileen," I said, "it sounds like you are the tougher of the two."

"When someone gets tough with me, I get strong. If someone pushes me, I get stronger. And stay strong. Also, Ann was sick, and I was very worried about her."

"Were you both really scared at this point, or did it all seem like a bad movie?"

"At this point it would have been so easy to just lie down and die. They kept asking the same questions, over and over, and I kept slumping down on the desk, falling asleep. They would thump on the desk, I would wake up, and they'd keep at it. We were still denying everything. After a whole night of interrogation, I finally asked them if they would mind very much if Ann and I could go home for a good sleep, a bath, and then come back. They looked at me as if to say: 'What have we got here?'"

"Did they give you anything to eat?" I asked.

"No. Nothing. They wouldn't even let us go to the bathroom."

"What did you do?"

"Strangely enough, we didn't even need to. I didn't think about it. And I wasn't hungry, either," Eileen said.

"On Monday, a woman from the Police Women's Union came to look at us. We had been there since Saturday. She asked the women who were guarding us: 'When did they have their tea?' When she found out we had had nothing to eat at all, she just went into a frenzy! She went absolutely mad! 'You can't do this to people,' she screamed. 'Go to the canteen and get them food. Now!' They told her the canteen was closed. 'I'll go myself,' she roared, and she did. She cooked us eggs and beans, and then she made the guards give us some clothes to wear." Eileen began to giggle. "You should have seen me. They first gave me an old dirty nightie to put on. It was too short, so they gave me another one to put on top of it. That's it. No shoes. No comb or brush. We hadn't had a wash in three days. We were raving beauties!"

Ann took over. "The worst part was that they didn't let us see each other, and their system was to tell each of us that the other had said this or that. They kept saying we weren't cooperating. Finally, a policeman got up to hit me, but another one dragged him out of the room. 'Keep him away from me,' I remember shouting. 'He looks like a madman.' Finally I said to them: 'If I make a statement, will you let me see Eileen?' They agreed. They also let me make a phone call to my mother, so I could have her ring our lawyer. Then I got to see Eileen, although they wouldn't let us talk to each other in Irish. I could tell she was all right, so we both said: 'Hang in there.' It did us a world of good to see each other.

"Then the lawyer came, and I made my 'statement,' which is I told them just what we have told you, about being in the house and the bomb going off. The police said: 'But where are the men? The ones in the room?'

"I said I didn't know. So they looked at me and said: 'Is that it?' I said yes, that was all I knew. And they were furious. Just livid. They just couldn't believe that that was all I had to tell them."

"What did they do?" I asked.

"That was it, really. They took us to another center and kept us overnight, and we appeared the following day in court and were charged. We were put in the Risley Remand Centre and kept there in isolation for eleven months while we awaited trial. They finally set the date of the trial: February 3, 1975. It lasted four weeks. The jury deliberated for three hours before they came up with their verdict. Guilty. The judge spoke briefly to each of us, and then sentenced us: fifteen years' imprisonment. We made only one request: that we be allowed to spend the time in prison together. "*Giorraionn beirt bothar,*" as they say in Irish, which means 'two shorten a road.' Our request was granted." Fifteen years. Ann was twenty-six, Eileen twenty-three.

We sat in silence for a few minutes in the small, sunlit living room of their Bunbeg house. I was in a big, comfortable overstuffed chair; they sat side by side across the room from me, in small, straight-backed chairs. As they told their story, they often looked at each other for corroboration, each nodding in agreement or smiling together over a memory.

Ann broke the silence, jumping up from her chair. "You must be starved," she said. "Let me bring you some tea." She left the room and returned in minutes with a tray laden with tea and ham sandwiches. While I ate, the women told me about their new profession. They have become interior decorators, redoing homes, offices, and hotels in their area.

"We work hard at it," Eileen said, "but we love it. There aren't any decorators in this area, so it is an open field. But there also isn't much money here, so we have to scramble for jobs." They make the long trip to Dublin periodically to shop in the wholesale fabric centers. They also take in children in the summer months from other parts of Ireland to live with them and practice their Irish. All the Gillespies still speak Irish in their homes.

Eileen is married now to a local man, Hugh McGee. Ann is living in the family home with her mother. Their father died just three months before they were released from prison, and it is still a source of grief and bitterness that they were not allowed home for his funeral. The burying of the dead is a sacred ritual in Ireland. Various Irish politicians and church officials intervened in their behalf; one local politician even offered to sit in their cell as a "hostage" while they made the brief trip home, but all their pleas were denied.

I asked the women about their boyfriends; both had serious relationships at the time of their arrest. Were the young men supportive?

"Oh, yes. They were. They wrote often, even though they couldn't come to see us. We're the ones that broke it up. We didn't think it was fair to them to keep them waiting so long."

"How did they accept that?"

"Well, from the stories we heard from home, they took it very badly. They started drinking heavily and so on. I must say, we weren't too sympathetic with those stories. We felt like we were the ones having the hard time!"

"Have you seen them since?"

"Yes. They live here and they're married now."

I picked up my pen and notepad again. "Tell me what remand is, and what it's like there."

"It's no-man's land," Ann said. "It's where you wait until your trial comes up. Our remand center was in Warrington. It was a fifty-mile drive for my parents to make each day."

"They could visit you?"

"Every day but Sundays. They never missed."

"Did you get to be with each other during remand?"

"No. That was the hardest part of all. We were in isolation, and for the first four months the only time we saw each other was when we were taken to court or during our exercise period. And on our birthdays they allowed us to spend some time together. We couldn't even see our parents together when they came. In retrospect, we were treated badly as remand prisoners. There are certain rights which we were entitled to, but we just didn't know about them."

"For instance?"

"We were allowed one set of clothes and no more. We had to wear prison shoes, which were men's shoes and about twenty sizes too big. No knitting or sewing. We were in isolation cells with a bed six inches off the ground, a wooden chair, a tiny wooden table, and we spent all day there. We could get books from the prison library and that's all we did. We went through two or three books a day. They finally had to relent and get books from the outside for us.

"Finally the prison doctors could see that we were in failing health. We had lost weight — that wasn't hard to do, the food was diabolical! — my nose would often bleed and I had dizzy spells. But when we were together we tried harder to eat. They didn't want anything to happen to us. Our trial had caused a lot of publicity, and they knew they couldn't afford anything happening, so finally the doctors persuaded the Home Office to allow us a few hours together each day."

That, they are convinced, was their lifeline. It sustained them through the emotional roller-coaster of prison life. They gave each other hope when despair overcame one or the other.

"It was us against them," Eileen remembered. "And in the end, we won. But there were hard, dark times. If, when we were first sentenced, we had any idea that we would in fact have to serve the whole term, I don't think we would have survived. You live on hope in prison. You think every day that some miracle will happen and you will be freed. We never once believed, until near the end, that we would end up serving the full term, minus our allotted time off for good behavior."

"What about the two men? And the sister whose house was blown up? What happened to all of them?"

"The fellow who was so badly burned was taken to hospital, and of course they caught him there and he was arrested just a few days after we were," Eileen said. "In fact, he was remanded in the same prison as Ann and I, because when we were taken back and forth to court he would be in the same van, but he never spoke to us. He recovered from his wounds. He got exactly the same sentence we did, and he's out now, living in Ireland."

"Do you ever see him?"

"Never! We wouldn't want to."

"And the other one? The brother?"

"They didn't catch him for four more months, and then for a bombing in Birmingham. He got eighteen years. It was he who was manufacturing the bombs. Apparently the sister knew what was going on all the time."

"What happened to her?"

"Nothing," Ann said. "She gave state's evidence. But I don't blame her, really, or hold any grudge against her. She's a poor, uneducated thing . . . a wee slut, really. She was living in that house, trying to raise her children while her husband, a Pakistani, was doing seven years in prison for rape. We didn't find that out 'til afterwards! But as Eileen said: 'If the police approached you and scared the hell out of you and threatened you with prison, and you had three small children, wouldn't you say anything they wanted you to? And they may have offered her money. Certainly they relocated her after the trial in another council house. She gave evidence against her brother as well as us."

"What did she say at the trial?"

"First of all, it was the way she said it. You could tell in a second that she had been primed. When we talked to her for that brief period in her house, it was clear that she was uneducated, dumb. She couldn't have known the words she used at the trial. She had been rehearsed, and she had a year to learn her lines! For instance, she said that we had been in the house before, that we had known her brother. There would have been no conviction without her testimony, so it was very important to the police that they get her to testify."

"So the two men in the bedroom were Provos and had made the bomb?"

"I don't know what they were. They must have been. I never want to see or hear about them again."

The room had begun to grow dim as the sun slanted away from the windows. It was time for me to leave.

"Can we meet again?" I asked, gathering up my things.

We made a date to meet the next time I was in Ireland. They walked me out to my car, and I snapped a picture of them standing side by side by the wall of their house, smiling, laughing, clowning for the camera. The "Sisters of Terror" waved a friendly good-bye as I backed my car down the rocky, rutted lane onto the main road.

It was almost a year before I returned to Donegal to see the Gillespie sisters again. We met on a Sunday afternoon in a small hotel in Letterkenny, halfway between Bunbeg and Derry, where I was staying. We greeted each other like old friends this time; we were all three more relaxed. After we'd caught up on family news, I took up where we left off the previous July.

The two women served their sentence in a high-security prison in Durham, England.

"Although we couldn't share a cell, because we were classified as Category-A [high-risk] prisoners, we were together for most of the day. The worst adjustment we had to make was learning to live with the other prisoners. I just couldn't believe that I was going to have to live with this type of person. I didn't know they existed. Their moral standards, their hygiene . . . they didn't have any. Their vocabulary, conversation, general knowledge . . . everything was totally alien to anything we had ever known. It took us literally years to adjust to that. We didn't even know what lesbians were, much less how to handle their overtures!

"Most of the English women prisoners were the real scum. They were childbeaters, murderers, and so on. If we visited with any prisoners, it was the foreigners, the Americans, Malaysians, and the Chinese, who were in for drug charges. They were a much better class of person.

"And then the rampages! They would rush into the dining room and pull all the plates and cutlery off the table, get in fights, abuse themselves. One poor soul who had murdered her son hung herself. It was just awful. In the beginning we were stunned by it all. The strange thing is how it becomes familiar, and after a while you hardly notice.

"We would go down to breakfast and maybe two women would be tearing the hair out of each other. At eight in the morning!"

"They would fight a lot?"

"They would chop themselves to bits, especially the lesbians if they were emotionally upset. If they had a relationship, either on the outside or in prison, and it had gone sour, they would get a blade and cut themselves up."

I asked if the women formed relationships with each other in prison.

"Oh, all the time. It was encouraged. If they were involved with each other, they wouldn't give the screws [guards] hassle. And of course some of the screws had relationships with the prisoners. There were very, very few straight marriages among the screws. Almost all of them were divorced, alcoholics, or lesbians. Or all three!"

"Did the prison officers ever make overtures to you?" I asked the women.

There was a long pause before either answered. Finally Ann said: "The situation in prison is so awful it is hard to believe. The only way Eileen and I could cope with it was to laugh at it. Therefore we have a really weird outlook on it."

Eileen continued. "If it was a soap opera, you couldn't believe it. We turned it all into laughter, because we couldn't have stood it straight. For instance, they all knew that I am a nurse, so they always came to me when they started cutting themselves up. One night, there was a girl in cell seven, and she had gotten a letter from her outside lover saying she had gone off with someone else — a man! Even worse! So she started to slash her chest. And just at the same time, on the same floor, another girl, a junkie, was slashing her wrist to the bone so she could get out and into hospital. Fortunately, because she was such a bad junkie, she had very little blood. And then downstairs on the next landing, in cell number one, another girl was cutting her throat.

"Now I was watching a movie at the time; there was a nurse on duty, a big, fat, lazy thing, who plods downstairs and says to me: 'You take the one in the shower because I think she's the worst.' By this time the place is covered in blood. So I go down to the one in the shower and try to get the broken glass off her, which she is using to cut herself. She was very unstable, God love her, and I had tried to be friendly with her —"

"Was this the one who had gotten the letter from her lover?" I interrupted.

"No. This one heard the commotion from upstairs and decided that those two were getting more attention than she was and that if she just cut herself up a little, she'd get some attention, too.

"Then a screw, an Irish girl named Kelly, rushed in and grabbed the girl, and the girl slashed Kelly's thumb from one side to the other. More blood. Finally, the male screws were called and they came in and grabbed this girl — she was stark naked — and pulled her downstairs by her hair. By then there was so much commotion all the other girls were locked in their cells except for Ann and me, who were left to do the mopping up. (Remember that Ann and I are "the most dangerous prisoners" in the jail and we aren't allowed the freedom of the prison like some of the others . . . but when there is a dangerous situation like that, with all of them going crazy at once, what do they do? They lock up all the 'safe' ones and let the two 'dangerous' sisters help.)

"Anyway, the deputy governor comes in and sees us mopping up all the blood and asks a screw: 'What are these two girls doing out of their cells?' And the screw answers: 'Because they are the only two sane people around here, that's why.' So the deputy says: 'Well, you will have to take the responsibility.'

"'I bloody well will,' she says, 'because I can't cope without them.'

"So then we go downstairs and make supper for all thirty-odd women and serve it to them in their cells. But the women were all angry because usually they were allowed to take a flask of hot water to their cells at night in case they wanted to make coffee, but because of the uproar on this night, they didn't have their flasks, so each time we would approach a cell with a supper tray, they would let fly at us with a shoe or a flask or a book! The male screws went around with us, and if they got hit by a flying object, they would burst into the cell, grab the offender, and drag her by her hair down to the punishment block. I mean, it's just crazy.

"Other nights, they would all start ringing their alarm bells, banging on the doors, and we would go around to see what they wanted . . . maybe Librium, maybe valium. This is prison life. You get to the stage where it just becomes a part of everyday living. You can't believe that you would get to that point. Once we saw a prisoner start to cut herself up and I just leaned over and said to Ann: 'Look, there's some bitch trying to kill herself again.'

"Another time, we went into the washroom and there was a girl lying on the floor with a plastic bag over her head. I turned to Ann and said: 'Oh, my God, here we go again.' It became a way of life. Once, when one girl tried to kill herself and failed, I said to a screw: 'For God's sake, why don't you teach them how to do it properly, if they're going to do it.' You can see these women, most of them, were psychiatric cases and should have been in a hospital, not a prison."

Ann added: "The only thing that really frightened me was when they set the place on fire. That terrified me. And they used to do it all the time. I knew if there was ever a fire that got out of control, we couldn't get out of there.

"The only decent women in prison — and this sounds funny — were the pushers. I mean, they were more intelligent and usually came from a middle-class background. You could at least have a conversation with them."

"Were there drugs in prison?" I asked.

"Oh, yes. Smuggled in all the time. One girl's mother smuggled them in to her. There are a lot of women who didn't do drugs on the outside and come in and become addicts while they are in prison. Drink was freely passed around, too. But I hate drugs, and I used to destroy them if I ever found them, flush them down the toilet."

"How did you pass the days?" I asked. "What was your routine?"

"Up at seven forty-five A.M. We could wash in our cells, but we had no toilets, so we had to use plastic pots, which we then had to carry down the corridors to empty. Just at the time, they would bring us breakfast. You can imagine how appetizing that was, with thirty-eight women walking down the hall to empty their pots! I never, never got used to that. I trained myself not to have to use my pot until after breakfast.

"During the day we worked sewing mailbags or scrubbing the landings. We had lunch, exercise periods, and then evening tea. After that we could chat, wash, and go to bed at eight o'clock, listen to the radio, read the papers, and write letters. It was really the letters that we received that kept us going. We received mailbags full; lots of them were from America, from people who had read about us and wrote to encourage us and sympathize. We could only write three letters a week, so we wrote to our family and never got to answer those letters. But they meant so much to us. Please say that in your book!"

"We had each other to talk with, to laugh with," Eileen said, and clearly their humor, their zest for life, and their own self-esteem made their captive years bearable. "We would sometimes be scrubbing the floors together and just fall over our buckets laughing." Eileen smiled at the memory. "I would say to Ann: 'Is this for real? Is this us?' And sometimes, with luck, that would strike us funny and we would laugh. It made the screws mad to see us laughing, but in some ways it made them respect us. 'Why are you laughing?' they would ask. 'Why aren't you crying?' Well, we cried plenty, but not where they could see us."

"One of the things I minded," Ann said, "was that we weren't supposed to speak Irish together. At least, that was the rule. I think it was later rescinded. But we did anyway. We would call the screws bad names in Irish to their faces, and that helped cheer us up enormously! But there was no doubt that we were treated worse than other prisoners because we were Irish. For instance, when we had menstrual cramps, they wouldn't give us aspirin, although they always gave it to the others.

"Another really bad thing was the strip-searching. Every time we received visitors, we had to be taken to a small cubicle, take all our clothes off, and be visibly searched by female screws. No internal searches were made, but it was humiliating, especially since most of the screws were lesbian. That somehow made it worse for us. The only thing you could do in self-defense was to stare them down. I hated it," Eileen remembered.

"We were allowed to go to Mass on Sundays, and a priest visited often with us. It was a great help and comfort to us," Ann said.

I asked the women if they are deeply religious.

Eileen smiled. "Well, I guess you could say we've got this thing going with God. The visits from the priest were very important to us, especially in the first few years we were in prison. You know, it's trendy now for people in the IRA not to practice their religion. I disagree with them. We fought for hundreds of years to be allowed to practice our religion, and now we are throwing it away ourselves. They are so far left that the Church has no part in their lives."

"When you first went to prison," I asked, "did you really think you were in for fifteen years?"

"Never! We expected every day we would go home. We didn't realize at first that prisoners live from appeal to appeal. If you sat down and thought you were going to do nine years, four months in prison, you couldn't. The life of a prisoner revolves around hope. You would always know when one of the girls was going up for appeal, and when she got a 'knock-down,' it would be a disaster that night. She would always do something crazy and disrupt the whole wing. I guess, deep down, we knew we would do a long time, but we always hoped and hoped that it would be cut short."

There were very, very bad times, tailspins when the sisters had to draw on every reserve of emotional stamina they had to get through days and weeks of depression, sleeplessness, and despair. There were months when only valium would ease the pain. And then, finally, August 1983.

"It had been leaked to the press that we were about to be released," Ann said. "The Home Office was very annoyed about that, so they arranged for us to be released a week early, and leave the prison in the middle of the night, so the press couldn't interview us. So when the actual evening came, we went to bed as usual, as if nothing was going to happen. No farewell parties, because we had been warned not to tell the other women we were going. We were to be 'awakened' at three A.M., but do you think we slept? Only one prisoner, an Italian woman in on a drug charge, guessed that we were going. She came in and hugged and kissed us good-bye.

"We were taken to a reception area, changed into 'outside' clothes, and signed our release forms. Eileen scratched something on the wall of the reception room while we waited, a little 'farewell remark,' she said."

"What was it?" My curiosity was piqued.

Eileen just smiled. "I'll never tell. Just a little parting message for the whole lot of them," she said and giggled.

"And then, at four A.M., they told us to walk through the gates. We never looked back. My brother, sister-in-law, and their two children were in their car outside the gates, waiting for us. We hugged them, got into the car, and drove away."

"What did you feel like? Numb? Hugely emotional?"

"We were crying as we walked through the gates, but we were numb, too. We went home with my brother, to his house in Cheshire. They had saved bottles of champagne over the years for our release. My brother has a civil-engineering firm and hires lots of people from home. They started coming in to see us. Our lawyer and his wife arrived. Neighbors, friends. We had given my sister-in-law a list of things we wanted to eat, and she had it all there. I remember the chocolate gateau! I guess the very first thing we did when we got there was to go upstairs and take a long, leisurely bath, and then put on all the new, lovely underwear she had bought for us. And perfume. And high heels! We wobbled on them!"

Eileen chimed in: "And we kept opening doors, walking through them, shutting them, and opening them again. We just couldn't do that enough times. Then we went outside, to a little park across the street where they had children's swing sets. We got on the swings, and I can still remember what that felt like, seeing the sky come nearer and then recede as the swing went back and forth. I think that was the first time that I really felt — really knew — that I was free! 'I'm free,' I kept thinking. 'I can see the sky anytime I want to!'

"Then some friends of my brother gave us a ride on his motorbike. That was fun, just to drive freely along the road. Finally it was time to leave for the airport. We were taking a ten A.M. plane to Dublin.

"I thought there would be family and friends to meet us at the airport when we arrived. But when we got off the plane, there were hundreds and hundreds of people there. The press, television, well-wishers, family, friends. We were literally mobbed. People were pressing gifts on us, flowers and boxes of chocolates. We had to have a police escort to help us get out of the airport. And then, on the way home, all along the route there were crowds of people at each town: Bundoran, Ballyshannon, Liskenny, Kilcara. There were banners and bands and, after dark, bonfires in each town. They were all welcoming us home.

"Finally we got to Bunbeg. There were thousands and thousands of people at the crossroads in Bunbeg. Nine bands were playing, and the sky was lit with bonfires. Honestly, I didn't know there were so many people in Ireland! Even a woman from America flew over to welcome us home. I didn't know her, we just shook hands at the welcoming reception and I never saw her again."

For months after their return, all of Ireland welcomed the Gillespie sisters home. Visitors came in streams to the little white cottage on the knoll overlooking the sea. Gifts — china, flowers, lobsters, salmon, and cakes — filled the house to overflowing. The girls put prison behind them forever, never once corresponding with anyone there, not even the one kind prison official who had tried to make life a little easier for them. They wanted not one remembrance of those years.

The two women think that prison has made them vastly different people. They feel stronger for having lived through the experience. Eileen thinks that she appreciates all the good things of life now more than she ever did and doesn't let small worries bother her. Perhaps Ann has suffered more from their ordeal and has traces of bitterness from it that Eileen seems to have escaped.

"I must admit that the first year I came out, it was like being born again," Ann said. "Everything was beautiful, and I went around saying: 'This is a beautiful world, and people just don't appreciate it.' But now, I don't know. There are times when I think: 'Was it worth it? Are the people of Ireland worth the sacrifice people are making on their behalf?' I am angry with the people of Ireland as a whole. I think there are people who allow us to be railroaded into choices that are not right for our country. This is a recent feeling with me."

"What is it you are angry about?" I asked her.

"I am angry about people being so neglectful towards the situation in the North. People in Southern Ireland don't give a damn. We are so crazy here about helping black countries; we are so concerned about what's happening in South Africa, Ethiopia, El Salvador, Nicaragua . . . and we have worse happening in our own country. Do they want to know? They do not. What kind of people are we that will tolerate this at their own front door and will go out the back and help anyone else?"

"But it's been going on so long," Eileen said, looking at Ann with concern in her face.

"No, I will not accept that," Ann said. "We are a caring, loving people where other countries are concerned, and we do not care two ha'pennies about own country. And it has such a long, sad history. So many people over so many generations have given so much for so little."

"What would you like to see the people in Ireland do?" I asked Ann.

"I would like to see them stand up and say: 'This is our country and it is too small to be divided. We can live in peace. Together we can be great.' But we have always been divided, and a divided country won't achieve anything. We are one of the best races of people — really caring and compassionate. Catholic or Protestant, we are not bad or evil, but there is a blindness where politics is concerned. I think the government has pandered too long to the British government. I know that economically we have to depend on neighboring countries, but they shouldn't be allowed to dictate to us. I don't trust the government, either party. I don't think they are strong enough to stand up to the British government. It has taken them too long to wake up to the fact of prisoners languishing unfairly in British jails, and then only because someone embarrassed them about it. I am very critical too of the Irish Embassy in England, because it does not take care of the Irish people there. The ambassador's duty in a foreign country is to look after his own people; the embassy staff never once visited an Irish prisoner. The Americans came all the time to look after their own in prison in England, to give them legal help and so on.

"The Irish Embassy wouldn't even write on behalf of an Irish prisoner, criminal or political. All it was doing, it seems, was selling passports!! Now we have Irish T.D.'s [representatives] taking the credit for reopening the Birmingham prisoner case [six Irishmen convicted of a bombing in Birmingham in August 1975], when credit should go to people like Sister Sarah, a nun in England who did so much for Irish prisoners there."

"So you feel very embittered?"

"Yes. I feel angry. We all thought the Anglo-Irish Agreement would come up with something, but it hasn't. I think finally everyone — the

Irish, the British, and the Unionists — will have to talk to the IRA. They can't just go on ignoring them. They won't go away."

"What are your sympathies now with Sinn Fein and the Irish Republican movement?" I asked Ann.

"First, I am a Catholic nationalist. I love my religion and my country equally. I totally agree with the aims of Sinn Fein that a united Ireland is the only way we will live in peace. Some of the people they call terrorists have strong feelings. They aren't lunatics or madmen. We visited Northern Ireland and we saw a lot of homes where the men were in prison and the wives had left them or they couldn't get back together. Only a very few prisoners' families have managed to stay intact. That really had a disillusioning effect on us. We met a few of the ex-prisoners, and they are so sad. They have no get-up-and-go. Who do you blame? Maybe two out of ten get it together again. The person you remembered going in is not the person who is going to come out to you. And there is no rehabilitation for Irish political prisoners. None.

"I don't know. Of late, I get this lonely type of feeling. A lot of prison has come back to me now, like a delayed reaction. And I often think: What does the future hold?"

Eileen looked at her sister sadly as she spoke of her disillusionment.

"Nothing has been achieved," Ann said. "Nothing has been changed."

Bríd Rodgers grew up in another pretty white house in Bunbeg. She left there when she was eighteen to go to school in Dublin.

"When I was at university, I used to hear the students from Northern Ireland complain about injustice and inequality; I had never experienced anything like that in Donegal, and I thought they were just whining. Little did I know!" After she finished school, Bríd married a young Donegal dentist with a practice in Lurgan, County Armagh, and came to live in Northern Ireland for the first time in the early 1960s.

"When I saw the situation here firsthand, I was shocked. I knew then what those students had been complaining about. I began doing behind-the-scenes work at home, collecting data and information for the Campaign for Social Justice. We knew that if we were going to complain about the way Catholics were discriminated against, we couldn't just sit back and moan. We had to compile facts. So I would prepare data on housing and employment statistics to back up our complaints. When the civil rights movement started here in nineteen sixty-eight, I had four small children under seven, so I couldn't do much. Nevertheless, when the first meeting was held here in Lurgan, my husband and I went along to it, just to support the idea.

"It never occurred to me then to get deeply involved in politics. I thought I was too busy at home . . . I *was* too busy! Anyway, at this meeting a very prominent local man got up and started making a rip-roaring, beat-the-drum republican speech. You know, all the old verbal republican stuff. Well, it annoyed me intensely because the civil rights movement wasn't about that sort of thing at all. I kept whispering to my husband how angry I was, and he finally whispered back: 'Well, then, get up and say so!'

"I had never spoken at a public meeting in my life, and my knees were knocking, but I really didn't want to sit and let this man have the floor with that kind of nonsense, so I got up and said what I thought of his speech. I said that the civil rights movement was about getting rights for Catholics, not about whether you were orange or green, and that Unionists could participate in it if they so wished. Those who had waved flags and made emotive speeches over the years had changed nothing. They might well have encouraged young men to resort to violence. That same violence, in turn, whilst increasing the sectarian hatreds and compounding existing divisions, had served merely to keep the spotlight from resting on the underlying injustices and inequalities.

"The next day two members of the committee landed on my doorstep to ask if I would consider serving with them. I really had to think about it, but my husband said: 'Get involved. I'll do my share at home.' So I became their public-relations officer, then I was co-opted onto the Northern Ireland Civil Rights Association Executive [council]. And that's how I began. I really never had any intention of getting into politics!"

Bríd Rodgers is one of the few women in Northern Ireland who has had the commitment and the staying power to remain active in political life throughout the past two decades. She became a member of the Social Democratic and Labour Party shortly after its formation and served on its executive council, as vice-chairman, chairman, and finally as general secretary. In 1983, the Irish Taoiseach (prime minister), Garret FitzGerald, appointed her a Northern Ireland senator to the Irish Daíl (parliament). She remained a senator until the Irish elections of 1987.

A tall, slim, attractive woman with short brown hair and blue eyes, Bríd retained her commitment to nonviolent politics throughout the troubled 1970s and 1980s while others despaired of a political settlement or turned to violence. "We aren't a country like South Africa," she said. "People looking for justice and equality for Catholics in Northern Ireland have a political route open to them. It is slow, difficult, often frustrating. I am totally convinced it is the *only* way to progress."

As we sat talking in the living room of her handsome, spacious home on the outskirts of Lurgan, she was periodically interrupted by phone calls from the media asking about the situation in neighboring Portadown, where the July 12 Orange Order parade was expected to cause trouble. After one such call, Bríd said to me: "It has always been the custom in Portadown for the RUC to escort provocative, coat-trailing loyalist marches through nationalist areas of the town. In these circumstances the police were clearly perceived to be supporting the assertion of Unionist domination and supremacy. This has served to compound Catholic mistrust of the police. As a result, although most Catholics are sick of the IRA and recognize the suffering caused to themselves as well as to Protestants by the activities of the IRA, fears of attack from loyalist paramilitaries (and many innocent Catholics have been murdered or maimed in the Portadown area) leave Catholics open to exploitation by the IRA, who, despite their failure to protect anyone in the past, still manage to present themselves as the 'defenders' of the Catholics should the need arise.

"In precisely the same way, the loyalist response to the civil rights movement through attacks on peaceful demonstrations, attacks on Catholic homes, and sectarian murder of Catholics led to real fear in nationalist areas. This fear was cleverly exploited by the IRA. Defense committees were set up and grew in strength. These became totally controlled by IRA elements. Defense soon turned to attack. Innocent civilians, both Catholic and Protestant, eventually became the victims.

"From the very foundation of the party, the SDLP has set its face against violence as a means to our ultimate goal of unity and reconciliation between Irish people. We use the political process to achieve reform and equality, and it has been working, slowly but surely. A sizable majority, indeed an increasing one, support and prefer our approach.

"Anyway, the civil rights movement finally broke up into disarray," Bríd explained. "Other, smaller minority movements began to use it for their own ends, and it became like the Peace Movement: it splintered into conflicting objectives. But we had managed to put the international spotlight on the North, showing it as a place where there were grave injustices, and where the system was corrupt. We had also drawn some concessions from the O'Neill government — under pressure. Things really were beginning to happen. But it seems to be the fate of all mass movements in Ireland that they get taken over by small groups.

"I began to realize that no organization would be effective unless it was a political one, which had policies and objectives and strategy which couldn't be taken over by another movement. Having been excluded from political participation for so long, we were all newcomers to the political process, and had never had a properly organized nationalist party. So I was delighted — really excited — when the SDLP was formed in nineteen seventy. But I was pregnant again! I couldn't even go to the inaugural meeting of the SDLP here in Lurgan. I remember that John Hume [the leader of the party] rang me up that night to ask why I hadn't been there, and I said: "Because I'm about to have a baby!'

"A year later some issue arose — I don't even remember what it was now — but I remember thinking that the party wasn't doing anything about it, so I wrote John Hume a letter complaining, and he wrote back just one line: 'What are *you* doing about it?' That was it. I joined the party — my sixth child was three months old at the time — and I've never looked back. But I couldn't have done it at all without my husband's help and support, although it hasn't always been easy for him. He's taken on a lot more domestic chores than most Irish husbands ever would!"

Bríd suddenly looked at her watch and realized it was time to drive to the airport in Belfast, where she was to see her sister off to America. So we got in the car and continued our conversation as she drove through heavy traffic on the forty-minute trip to Belfast. Her fourteen-year-old son, Antoin, a veteran "political child," came along for the ride.

"Were there many women working with you in the party in those days?" I asked.

"Not many. And most of them were secretary of the branch, never chairman. As you know, the secretary does all the donkey work! I think I was elected to the executive because I had come up through the civil rights movement. In nineteen seventy-eight I ran as chairman against Sean Farren, a great friend of mine, and a feminist! I was chairman from 'seventy-eight to 'eighty. I thought two years of that was enough. You have to go to conferences in Europe and always be on call for staffing problems, political problems. I thought it was unfair for my family; I had six children at that stage, the youngest one six. But then the general secretary of the party suddenly died, and the new appointment didn't work out, so I was asked to take over in a temporary, part-time, voluntary capacity. Well, you know what 'part time' always means. I was often there all day, until late at night. I'd end up on the phone to my husband at three P.M., 'Can you get someone to pick up the kids?' I finally took it over as a permanent, full-time job; at least then I had a salary and could afford to hire a housekeeper."

Her fourteen-year-old chimed in from the back seat at this point: "Yes, that was a good thing. We were all getting tired of hamburgers." Bríd laughed. "My husband is marvelous about helping me take care of the children and the house, but he isn't a very good cook. Hamburgers are his specialty!"

"So you stayed on as general secretary until you were appointed to the Irish senate?"

"Right."

"Where are all the other women?"

She smiled ruefully. "Well, partly it's because we nationalists had no tradition in politics here in the North, so we lacked confidence and political skills. This is true for the men as well as for the women. But then on top of that, there's a very deeply rooted feeling here that women should run the home and defer to men's opinions on public affairs. That's almost a universal feeling here, despite lip service that some men might give you.

"Women can take back-seat political jobs, indeed very often they do much dedicated organizational work behind the scenes. They are not expected to take on leadership roles and are not generally encouraged to do so by the men. Because of the traditional view of women's role, not only among men but to some extent among women themselves, such encouragement and support for women's real participation at the higher levels is vital. For my own part, I have to admit that, apart from my own local organization, and apart from my husband, who was always very supportive, I can think of only two men who positively encouraged me in my political career. Neither of these were members of my own party.

"The lack of women's participation is due also in great measure to the fact that so many of them have family commitments and are not free to give the time necessary to politics. I'm afraid that most Irish husbands would simply not tolerate it! Come to think of it, it must be the same all over the world. Politics everywhere is male-dominated.

"Also, the churches here so dominate everyone's life, and they are obviously male-oriented. They have a very conservative, traditional attitude towards women."

Leading members of the SDLP are often in the United States, giving lectures, attending seminars, visiting Congress. I asked Bríd if she had ever made a political junket to the States.

"I'm not really interested in junkets as such. At the same time, now that I think of it, I've never been given the chance to refuse. I don't like to be away from my family if I can help it. Involvement in politics takes you away so much that you are glad to spend any free time you get at home.

"Just the same, given my long involvement right through from the Campaign for Social Justice in 1965, the civil rights movement, and the SDLP, I would have welcomed the opportunity of lecturing in the States and visiting Congress."

She maneuvered the car expertly into a parking space at the airport, and we headed for the terminal. We were stopped in the airport for a search by the security guards, a gesture so taken for granted by Bríd that she kept on talking as she lifted her arms in the air while a female guard ran her hands over her body.

"Despite all our hard work, I think the polarization between the Catholics and Protestants is worse now. Escalation of violence from all sides has seen to this. The Unionist middle class will say: 'Oh, things were fine, and we were beginning to come together in the late nineteen sixties,' and I guess on the surface that was beginning to happen, but you know you never could have established a real coming together of the people so long as you had the basic anomalies and the injustices. It was a surface, middle-class effort. But discrimination affects all sections of the Catholic community, and that was bound to boil over. I think the polarization is more . . . in some strange way . . . more honest now. Certainly more evident. You see, there was always polarization in this town and many other towns. You had Catholic and Protestant housing estates for a number of reasons, but one of the reasons was for gerrymandering the votes. You had to lump a lot of Catholics together and Protestants together so that you could gerrymander the wards.

"In a sense, Protestants feel that they have to maintain their solidarity and their dominance in order to remain secure, and Catholics of course have always felt aggrieved because they have always been second-class citizens, and that has caused polarization. Now the Protestants don't accept the idea of the Anglo-Irish Agreement: they think it will do them harm; but I think eventually they will come to see that it is only intended to bring nationalists, or Catholics, up to their level, and that will be good for both communities. Because if Catholics would only lose their sense of grievance, it would create a new atmosphere. A young lad in Portadown said to me the other day that he had been in the IRA and had got out and was quite disillusioned about it because he sees now how they lead young people astray and how they exploit them, but I would have thought that he was still a very 'united Ireland' person, so I was surprised to hear him go on: 'We don't want a united Ireland in a hurry. What we really want is fair play. Then the united Ireland thing will take care of itself, one way or another.' He would have nothing to do with the Provos now. You see, I think that if we were united, the nationalists here would identify with the government in the South. But the loyalists wouldn't. So that's why I'm for a federal state here, with the North still separate. Also, I think that the Anglo-Irish Agreement has definitely hurt the IRA. It has effectively removed their very *raison d'être.* They have always claimed that the only way to achieve a united Ireland was by violence. In the Agreement, the British government has solemnly undertaken to introduce and support legislation to give effect to Irish unity if in the future a majority of the people of Northern Ireland clearly wish for and formally consent to it. That means that the achievement of Irish unity is now very clearly a matter of those who desire it persuading those who do not. Furthermore, the presence of the Joint Secretariat [made up of representatives of the Irish and British governments] in the North and the commitment to achievement of equal status for nationalists are already beginning to deal with the grievances which they have exploited for their own ends. Changes in emergency legislation, repeal of the Flags and Emblems Act, and proposals for stronger and more effective anti-discrimination laws are already under way."

Bríd went off with Antoin to say good-bye to her sister. I stood in the long cafeteria line to get us tea and biscuits. The cafeteria was crowded, and by the time I had balanced the teapot, cups, milk and sugar, plus a plate of biscuits onto a tray and found an empty table, Bríd was back.

"I got there just in time," she said breathlessly as she sat down. "That's yet another one of the problems of politics versus family: you try to squeeze everything in and end up doing it all on the run."

While she caught her breath and poured a cup of tea, I asked her about school integration in Northern Ireland. It has always seemed to me as an outsider that integrated education could help overcome the sectarian divide in Ulster — although certainly forced integration in the United States did not miraculously solve our racial problems.

"I'm not opposed to school integration. I think people should have it if they want it, but I do wonder if it would help as much as people think it would. The only thing that will end sectarianism is a political situation which allows all people to feel equal at the end of the day; when both communities see themselves standing on equal footing, you will get rid of the sectarian division.

"The problem with the integrated-schools idea is that they are preaching to the converted. At the moment, people who want to participate in integrated schools and who have worked very hard towards establishing them are in fact people who already see themselves as socially integrated. Some years ago it was fashionable, particularly for Unionist politicians, to attack separate Catholic schooling as one of the root causes of sectarianism. I felt strongly that their perception of 'integrated' education was one of Catholics attending 'their' schools, conforming to their ethos and absorbing their culture. I have noted that their enthusiasm for 'integrated education' has waned considerably since the idea of accommodating both cultures has been promoted by the new integrated-schools proponents."

"If there had been an integrated school in Lurgan, would you have sent your kids there?" I asked her.

"No. Because I want my kids to have a Catholic education. They have emerged from the Catholic education system with open, independent, and tolerant attitudes. My eldest girl went to UCD [University College Dublin], and she is a petroleum engineer who lives in England. Her friends there are of all religious persuasions. My other daughter is doing her Ph.D. in Cambridge University; her Northern Ireland friends there are mostly Protestant. And so on. But I'll say this: If there had been an integrated school here, and I had sent them to it, others might very well be saying now, 'Those kids are the way they are because they went to an integrated school'! Who knows?"

We stopped on the way home in Moira, a village in County Down, to buy groceries for her dinner. Moira is a lovely little village, often the winner of the "Tidy Town" contest; its somber, gray stone houses and shops are enlivened by colorful window boxes streaming with ivy and red and white geraniums. Today, as we parked on the Main Street, the town was bedecked with the red and white Unionist flags and banners for the July 12 celebrations.

Bríd picked out some meat for their dinner and a quiche for our lunch. Back on the street I snapped pictures of the village while she shopped for fruits and vegetables.

As we turned into the Rodgers's driveway back in Lurgan, I complimented Bríd on the lovely July-blooming roses lining the drive. "Never have time for gardening now," she muttered as she switched the engine off. A television crew was already there, waiting to do an interview about the planned march on the twelfth. One of Bríd's sons met her at the door with phone messages to return. We piled the groceries in the kitchen as an older, college-age son appeared with a school problem he wanted to discuss with his mother. She didn't think that such an important issue should be discussed on short notice. The phone rang, and, as if on cue, the doorbell rang. A man appeared at the kitchen door with a paintbrush in his hand.

"Could I have a word with you, Mrs. Rodgers?" he asked. He was painting the front door and needed guidance about color. Antoin had been carsick on the way back from the airport and still looked slightly green. As he was foraging in the refrigerator, Bríd advised him not to eat anything for a while. The television crew appeared, wanting to get started.

Bríd looked at me helplessly. "The quiche . . . ," she began, and we both laughed. "Go!" I said. As I slipped out the door and headed for my car, I heard the first question as the television interview began:

"Do you think the RUC will be able to provide protection to Catholic homes if the march gets out of hand?"

Today's Revolutionaries

The more ancient the abuse, the more sacred it is.

— *VOLTAIRE*

WORKING-CLASS WOMEN in Northern Ireland don't sit around nursing ancient wounds or quoting statistics of Cromwell's dirty deeds. They live in the present out of necessity. They have to have a baby in two weeks, change a diaper in five minutes, get a meal on the table in one hour, get to the shops before closing, give Granny her medicine in thirty minutes, get a child to bed in two hours, get a teenager out of bed in ten minutes. If they have a job outside their homes, the present bears down on them even more insistently. So when they talk about the Troubles, they only throw in a little history and a little bitterness to hold up the family honor, so to speak. Their time frame is now, their concern is care: they have to make the weekly visits to prison, to worry about the son gone in the night, to hide the runaway lover, and they have to do all that quietly without public complaint. That would be letting their side down. If they complained too loudly, too publicly, they would be punished for that, one way or another, psychologically or physically.

Perhaps the most poignant victim of the Troubles in Northern Ireland is the mother. Portrayed through Irish history as the martyr and virgin (she may be a mother of twelve, but she is still thought of as sexless), she is both queen and victim, loved and used, a symbol of sacrifice and suffering.

I met the relative of a Provo in Northern Ireland recently, a very kind and gentle woman who is ceaselessly worried about the effects of this man's paramilitary activities on his mother. Although the family are all republicans, none supports the armed conflict. The other siblings are angry; his girlfriend is about to give him up; but his mother protects him, rationalizes, spoils, worries, and downs a bottle of valium a week. The others call him "the fucking rat." The mother thinks he is wonderful, only a wee bit misguided. If he just wouldn't kill people, he'd be a fine lad altogether.

"Oh, he's his mother's darling, all right," the relative said bitterly. "You know how an Irish mother has to be subservient to a man? Well, Sean's [not his real name] mother has chosen to be his lackey, and he allows her to do that. He promotes that. It's his role in the house as the eldest son. He does it in subtle, emotional ways. He tests her all the time: How loyal will she be? How much will she forgive?

"He has been in trouble with the police since he was sixteen. Criminal trouble. But he could rape, plunder, steal, and murder, and at the end of the day he is still her darling son and therefore she will stand by him. He really is a bad egg. Their house was raided last week. Again. I told her to get rid of him. There are three younger siblings living at home. I tell her that she is putting them in danger, that they are being pulled into all of this. The police will get tired of coming here looking for him and one day they'll just take one of the others. I don't give a shit about what happens to Sean, but I'll be damned if I'll sit here and let any one of the others be some kind of sacrificial lamb for him because of her misguided sense of loyalty to him.

"'He cares about our safety,' his mother says, but I know he doesn't care a shit about anyone but himself.

"Now if he had any political commitment for what he was doing, I would find it much easier to support him. I would even be sympathetic, maybe. But no, there's no politics to it. He is only playing the macho Irishman, the do-or-die murderer, who spends all his money on drink. Well, his mother finally got him out of the house because it became so unbearable. But he still drops in at all hours of the night and morning. And when I say to her: 'Get him out!' she says: 'I'm just doing a wee bit of washing for him' or 'He's only coming to Sunday dinner.'

"He was arrested a few months ago and taken to Castlereagh [a jail in Belfast where IRA suspects are often taken for interrogation] for three days. One of the children phoned me up and said: 'Please come over. Sean's been arrested and Mum's in a bad way.' So I went over and there she is, knocking back valium as if it's going out of fashion. So I have to take charge and be responsible for everyone. I phoned up Castlereagh, and then phoned a lawyer. I promised her that we would take him some clean clothes. That calmed her down; she could go do his laundry! If she can work for him, she's happy!

"This shit of a man is her hero. This is a man who might die for Ireland! Jesus Christ!

"I don't know how much longer that family can all take it. I think his girlfriend is going to ditch him soon. Maybe she already has. She doesn't like it. He always looks exhausted. He's on the run all the time, and never eats properly. He's always angry. He can't define his involvement with the IRA in political terms, it's always about his anger, his frustration, his hatred. He desperately wants to be macho and male. He wants to flex his muscles as a man, and he sees what he is doing as a way of expressing his manhood. That's where he and I start to argue. I think that is sick."

I asked if that was a common trait among the Provos, to use their political activities as a way of expressing manhood.

"Not among the older ones. I think experience makes them wise up very quickly, and then you realize that there has to be an easier way of expressing your manhood than to put your life on the line every day! Sean is twenty-five, still a young man, but I know also that he has changed. The bravado he used to have is eroded. I think the last time we had a conversation he was obviously having great difficulty with his conscience."

"Has he killed people?"

"Yes. And I think that is beginning to gnaw a little bit. But he's not going to stop. I'm only glad that he's not doing it callously, in the sense that he never gives it a thought. That it preys on his mind now. That he doesn't like taking life. Because I would worry that it becomes this bravado thing . . . you get out there with a gun and you shoot your manhood off. And you lose your conscience. But he has a conscience. I know it, and it troubles him a good deal. That's why he looks so ill. He can't sleep. But I know he will continue. I suppose he thinks he is right."

"But you said he doesn't have any political interest in what he is doing."

"No, it's just emotional."

"Is he high up in the organization?"

"No, he's a foot soldier."

"But he's never been caught?"

"He's been pulled in a few times.

"His mother has tried to talk to him from time to time. She is overcome with her maternal instinct: 'This is my beloved son, and I can never deny him no matter what he does.'

"I think she needs to take a colder, more distant stand with him, because as long as she is always there for him to fall back on and for her to nurture, he will never stand on his own two feet and deal with his own conscience."

"Do you think a lot of young men — the foot soldiers, as you call them — if their mothers or their families said they wouldn't go along with what they are doing and said, 'Don't come home to us,' that it would erode the whole movement?"

"No, I don't think so, because there are a lot of cases where I've seen that happen. I've also seen people who have been involved who don't even come from a Catholic background, so they have never had that support, but it doesn't seem to make any difference."

"You mean there are Protestant Provos?"

"Yes."

"I didn't know that. I don't understand that experience at all. That really makes me think that they are in it for the excitement."

"No, I think they are highly politicized people. They are the ones that can quote history and give you all the ideology. They are political at a very sophisticated level. I think they see injustice for what it is, and they don't want to be a part of it. Of course, there aren't many of them!"

"How does Sean manage to stay out of prison?" He has never had a conviction, although he has been lifted several times.

"I honestly don't know. Either he is clever at covering his ass, which I find hard to believe, since he isn't clever at anything, or else he is lucky, but of course his luck won't hold out forever."

"Aside from his political activities, is he good? Can that be separated?"

"He's no bloody angel. Oh, his mother sees tenderness and kindness in him that no one else sees. When he's in good form, he can be very charming and very gregarious and sociable. He can talk to anyone on the street, have a good rapport and be very funny. But he is basically insensitive and uncaring. It's a great burden to his mother, and that's where my anger really comes from, when I see what it has done to her. I worry about her using so much valium. She is so gentle and she abhors violence of any kind. She never smacked her children like so many other mothers do. Oh, she has a tongue like a razor blade! But she would never lift a hand."

"Would most of the people in your neighborhood, even if they don't believe in the IRA, support the men who are involved? Protect them, the way Sean's mother does?"

"She doesn't believe in the IRA. But yes, most would support them, I guess. Some won't. Some refuse to be involved."

"Would they be punished for that?"

"If you look at it from the IRA viewpoint, it's better to have someone totally committed than someone who feels very bad about it and is pressurized about it. On a day-to-day level, people would not necessarily espouse the IRA, but they would feel that they had need for an organization that is tough about representing them and isn't prepared to take any shit. An organization that is tough and will lay down the law. For them, in my area, the only ones who will do that are the IRA. When there is a physical manifestation of unrest, like a street riot, then yes, the people will protect the rioters. To go farther than that in terms of protection requires a degree of commitment that some people just don't feel they can give, because of the jeopardy it puts them and their families in. But on a day-to-day level, they accept that the IRA is their representative.

"Or take the joyriders, for instance. When the IRA gets involved in something like that, they are trying to punish petty criminals for their antisocial behavior. Sometimes the rest of the community, whose kids are not involved in joyriding, ask the IRA to do something about it."

"So what's in Sean's future?"

"He won't quit. I know that. I suppose he will stay in it until he burns out or is killed. Or put in prison. That's the endgame for most of them."

"And then what about his mother?"

"That's what I'm afraid of. I don't know if she could survive that."

"These men, who cause so much heartache for their families — how do they justify that?"

She smiled a sad, lifeless smile. "You know how it goes," she said: "'. . . But on the cause must go, Amidst joy or weal or woe, Till we've made our isle a nation free and grand.' Well, that's all the justification they need."

Women in Northern Ireland who are connected with the republican movement will tell you proudly what their role has been. They feel that they are on equal footing with the men, involved in equally dangerous assignments, well able to carry them out. They have served their time in prison, gone on hunger strikes, participated in the "dirty protests" in prison (adding menstrual blood to the general mess of feces and urine spread on prison walls), and in the case of Maire Drumm, one of Ireland's most ardent IRA female members, served temporarily as Sinn Fein president while other officers were in prison.

Sinn Fein accepted women into their organization as equals at their annual Ard Fheis (party convention) in 1972. Sean MacStiofain, past chief of staff of the Provisionals, said of IRA women: "In the early seventies, a selected number of suitable women were taken into the IRA and trained. Some of the best shots I ever knew were women. So were the best intelligence officers in Belfast. From that time women were admitted on a basis of full equality with men, as in the Israeli, Chinese, and other armed forces." (Sean MacStiofain, *Revolutionary in Ireland*, p. 218.)

By 1972, women were actively involved in terrorist activities: three women dressed as nuns robbed an Allied Irish Bank; a seventeen-year-old girl was killed while trying to assemble a bomb; two teenage girls were charged with attempted murder of a soldier; three women were detained at Heathrow Airport in connection with two car-bomb explosions in London in which one person was killed and 180 injured. It became a long, dreary litany of women and violence. Dr. Bridget Dugdale, the daughter of a British millionaire, with her Provo boyfriend, Eddie Gallagher, broke into "Russborough House," the elegant Georgian mansion in County Wicklow belonging to Sir Alfred and Lady Beit, and stole 8 million pounds' worth of paintings, including ones by Goya, Rubens, Vermeer, and Gainsborough. (The pictures were later all found.)

Republican women had a particularly "feminine" terrorist activity: they would hide a bomb under a baby (usually someone else's baby) in its carriage and pass through army checkpoints. The soldiers were unwilling to lift out a small baby, look through its diapers, blankets, bottles, and all the other accoutrements, so they would often let the woman and baby pass. The "mother" would then lift out the baby, make a run for it, and the bomb would go off. It was very effective while it worked.

Republican women were also frequent victims of the violence in the North. In 1976, Maire Drumm, whom Merlyn Rees, Secretary of State for Northern Ireland, had once described as the "Madame Lafarge of the movement," entered the Mater Hospital in Belfast for eye surgery. Three gunmen dressed as doctors broke into her hospital room and shot her dead. She was given full military honors by the IRA at her funeral. Dr. Miriam Daly, another republican activist and a member of the National H-Block Committee (people who worked for political status for the political prisoners in the Maze Prison), was shot dead in her home in Andersonstown, in West Belfast. The population of Armagh Prison for Women in Ireland, where female political prisoners were incarcerated, grew by the month.

The best-known woman in Northern Ireland, Bernadette Devlin McAliskey, was shot and seriously wounded in her own home in 1981. Private Margaret Hearst, a UDR member, was killed in her mobile home in Armagh in 1977. In 1987, a female victim was Mary McGlinchey, whose husband, Dominic, is one of the leaders of INLA, the Irish National Liberation Army. She was shot in her home while bathing her young sons.

Throughout their participation in terrorist activities, the isolated events that republican women instigated are notable for their innovative horror and for not being in keeping with Irish puritanical tradition. Women in Northern Ireland are just as repressed about their sexuality as they are in the Republic of Ireland. Both Catholic and Protestant women in the North have told me hilarious yet poignant stories of their first explorations into sexual experiences. Their male partners were just as ignorant as they were, and the results were often comical, bizarre, and obviously unsatisfying. Older women, married and mothers, often complain that their husbands don't have the sexual drive or interest that they would like them to have. "He only does it on his birthday," one of them moaned. "We've been married six years. We have six children. Guess when they were born?" Another friend was laughing about her wedding night activities. "Were you a virgin?" I asked her. "How would I know?" she answered.

It was out of the national character, therefore, when four IRA women decided to lure four British soldiers to their death by using sex as their come-on. It was in the early months of the army's posting in Northern Ireland, and their defenses were not so acute as they should have been. They certainly had been told not to fraternize with republican women, but boys will be boys. This particular group of women picked them up in a pub with promises of a long evening of fun and games. There were three enlisted men, one officer. They felt safe in numbers; they would not have gone off with a woman alone.

When they arrived at one of the women's flat on the Antrim Road in Belfast, they chatted and had a few drinks, and one of the women suggested group sex in the bedroom. To prove their intent, the women stripped. What could be dangerous about a naked woman? Where could she hide a weapon? So the soldiers joined them. Just as they were at the point of no return, the women's accomplice jumped out of a wardrobe in the room where she had been hiding, took aim, fired, and killed all four soldiers.

Besides having to hear of the tragedy of their sons' and loved ones' deaths, the families also had to hear of the obscene manner in which they died: soldiers not on the field of battle, but felled by a ruse used from the beginning of time. IRA women used the ploy several more times, but it finally backfired; even the most ardent republicans on the Falls Road did not approve of women using their sexuality to fight for the cause of Ireland's freedom. Killing was okay; sex was out. It soon ceased to be a respectable form of murder, and the women turned to more mundane, less exciting methods: bombing and shooting.

"I want to meet some women who are playing leadership roles in the IRA today," I explained over the telephone. This was the third man at the other end of a phone line in Belfast who didn't seem to understand what I wanted. There was a pause.

"We haven't always been happy with what journalists write," he said, hesitating.

"Why don't you put me in touch with some of the women and let them decide," I answered testily. "Why are you making the decision for them?"

He gave me an address in West Belfast and told me he would have two young women just out of prison there for me to interview. He didn't say anything about leadership roles.

I had to watch the house numbers carefully to find the address. The wind was howling and a heavy rain gusting as I ran across the almost deserted wide street and into the tiny shop where I had been directed to appear. Scraps of paper sodden with the rain lined the walk and the gutters. It was an ugly, desolate block, poverty was evident, and the boarded-up storefronts signaled the incipient violence that lurks around every corner of West Belfast, quiet one minute, ready to flare up the next.

Given the derelict atmosphere of the block, I was surprised to find the shop I entered looking so clean and neat. It appeared to be a combination bookshop and curio store. Republican literature, newspapers, flags, emblems, tie pins were laid out neatly on open shelves. The store was empty when I entered, but a woman was sitting in a tiny office in the back. She didn't even look up as she heard me come in, but said loudly: "Go around the corner. Second door on the left. They're expecting you." The second door on the left was covered by a large metal cage, the kind you see all over Belfast. The door of the cage lets you enter an enclosed metal cell. Once the outer door is closed behind you, you can then enter the building. It keeps out bombs and riffraff. The doorbell was high up above the door, out of the reach of curious children. I had to ring it twice before it was answered. An old man with rheumy eyes and a rusty black jacket wordlessly let me in, locking the cage door behind me. He looked more like the sweep-up man in a poor pub than a terrorist. We entered a tiny, dirty anteroom where three young men stood silently smoking. All three were short, stocky, sullen, and unsmiling. You could say they looked like thugs, or you could say they looked like three unemployed, bored youths. They eyed me without interest. A bicycle was chained to a filing cabinet, and there wasn't space for anyone or anything else in the tiny room. The paint on the walls was chipped and peeling; cigarette butts littered the floor.

The old man motioned for me to follow him out of the anteroom and into another dark and dingy room where three more old men sat on wooden benches, smoking and muttering among themselves. I settled down on what looked to be an old banquette; the room might once have been a cheap, dreary pub, the kind of dismal, lifeless place that may only exist in Northern Irish towns and cities. The wall on one side of the room was covered with a crude mural of a typical Provo scene: a soldier prone, holding a machine gun. None of the men here looked like the soldier in the mural.

I tried to overhear the old men's conversation, it seemed so conspiratorial. Were they planning a bombing? A murder? A kneecapping? I watched them out of the corner of my eye and strained to hear; it soon became obvious that they were wondering if they could fix a broken refrigerator that was standing in one corner of the room. The discussion took a long time. One of them finally got up and prodded the refrigerator a few times, opened and shut its door, and sat down again. Clearly, it was beyond them. They all three lit another cigarette and settled into silence.

The outer door opened again, and two men were ushered in and sat down beside me on the banquette. They were clearly not Irish or American; from the cut of their drab, gray, ill-fitting clothes and cloth caps they looked Eastern European. They too spoke together in low tones, in a language I couldn't identify. I tried to open a conversation with a tentative smile and hello, but they didn't respond.

At last a cheerful, bustling young man came into the room, smiling, and apologized for keeping us all waiting. I stood, thinking I was "first" in line, but he said he was sorry, he'd have to see the two men first, so off they all went, and I settled back onto my hard, dirty seat, waiting again. Not for long this time. The man returned and said to follow him, that the "girls" were there now, ready to talk to me.

We went back through the little anteroom; the three musketeers were still there, smoking, saying nothing, leaning against the wall. Would they be there all day? Were they waiting for an assignment? Were they just in out of the rain? Up a narrow flight of stairs, past a tiny office where I saw the two male visitors sitting at a desk, down a small, dark hallway, through a door (which was locked behind me), across another room, out the door, locked behind me again (was this done for show, or were they serious?). After three rooms, and three locked doors, we entered a cluttered office where two young women sat waiting. A couple of desks, four little wooden chairs, and a filing cabinet filled the room.

The women were unsmiling and solemn as they shook hands and introduced themselves. Sile and Pauline, in their late twenties, were just out of a decade of prison.

The man perched against one of the desks and began to question me about the purpose of the interview. Was I writing a book or magazine article? What else had I written? Why was I interested in Northern Ireland? His questions were friendly and unaggressive, but it bothered me that he was doing the questioning. I finally said: "I'm really here to interview these two women. They should decide whether or not they want to do the interview. Why are you making that decision for them?"

"Right," he said, seeming relieved, and immediately left the room, locking the door behind him. The two young women sat silently. I turned to Pauline, who was plump and healthy-looking. Her jeans strained against her stomach, and her sweater was too tight. She was either fat and out of shape or pregnant. Her pretty, freckled face was impassive, but her wide-set blue eyes were sad. She looked vulnerable, like someone who would cry very easily. She definitely did not have the self-confident air of a leader about her.

"What were you in prison for?" I began, taking out my notebook and pen. They did not want me to use a tape recorder.

"I was in for seven years on a bombing charge," she answered. Her voice was so soft I had trouble understanding her. "The worst part of prison was the strip-searching. That's the part I hated the most."

Strip-searching is a big, emotional issue right now within the Provo propaganda campaign. They are using it quite effectively to enlist the sympathy and support of women's groups who would not ordinarily be sympathetic to their organization. Pauline clearly had been co-opted to give me her views on it.

"All women prisoners in Northern Ireland are strip-searched every time they enter or leave their prison compound, like when they are going to meet a visitor, or taken to court on remand, or visiting the infirmary. You have to stand in a closed-off cubicle, take off all your clothes, and hand them out to two screws."

"Are the screws women or men?" I asked. She seemed surprised, perhaps shocked, at the question.

"Women. Women guards. We call them screws. We have to stand there without our clothes on and turn around, and they inspect us."

"Do they do an internal search? Or do they touch you?"

"No. They just look at us. It's humiliating.

"I knew one women prisoner, and she was having a miscarriage. She was hemorrhaging, and on her way to hospital, and they stopped her and strip-searched her while she was bleeding. That's harassment."

"What did you bomb?" I asked, changing the subject.

"I'd rather not say," she replied.

The other woman, Sile (which is the Irish spelling for Sheila), had remained silent during Pauline's monologue about strip-searching. She had risen from her chair and leaned against the back wall of the room, so that when she began to speak, I had to turn around and look up at her the whole time. She began to talk, softly and urgently, in a steady, disconcerting monotone. Much of what she said sounded very much like it had been memorized. Unlike Pauline, she was small and thin, but with well-proportioned, fine bones and large, dark brown eyes. Except for the dark circles under her eyes and her unhealthy pallor, she would have been a very pretty young woman. The unsmiling intensity of her personality was palpable in the room and made a strange contrast with the informality of stylish cotton pants, shirt, and sleeveless sweater. She talked without pause, stopping only if I interrupted her to ask a question, or to lick her lower lip in a nervous gesture. Her face never changed expression, and no flicker of warmth entered her eyes or her voice. It was a chilling experience. I have never met anyone whose emotional valve was so tightly closed.

"I grew up in Short Stand," she began. "It's a republican neighborhood in East Belfast, a Catholic ghetto surrounded by a Protestant, middle-class area near the shipyards. My mother died when I was eight years old; my family wasn't political and my father never allowed 'subversive talk,' as he called it, in the house. I think he knew what would be in store for us if we got involved politically, and he was afraid for us.

"Unlike most Catholics in the area, he had regular work in the shipyards, so we were never badly off. Two of my brothers went off to England to work, but my other brother got involved politically. Then our house used to be raided at night by British soldiers. I was about eleven then, and I would be so frightened. They would burst in the front door, rush in, and make me get out of bed and go stand outside. Then they would tear the house up. They left it in shambles. I think it was then that I began to question the system and to read books to find the answers. My father begged and begged me not to get involved, but I was finally convinced, and I joined the organization.

The one thing which really did radicalize me was the shooting of a six-year-old boy in the Divis Flats by a British soldier."

"How," I asked her, "does the death of the child in the Divis Flats in any way validate similar kinds of IRA murders, where innocent women and children had been killed, such as the Le Mons bombing [where the IRA planted a bomb in a restaurant in County Down, killing twelve and injuring twenty-three], or the blowing up of Lord Mountbatten's fishing boat, where a local teenage boy was killed, as well as Mountbatten and members of his family?"

"Our goals are valid and just," she replied immediately. "And therefore anything we do is justified, even murder."

"What are *your* goals?" I asked. "Not the party line, just what you want for Ireland and for yourself."

"A united, socialist, thirty-two-county Ireland, with the British out, and a return to Irish traditions, culture, and language. I want to be able to go down the street and say my name in Irish, for instance. If I was stopped on the street now by a policeman, and he asked me my name, and I told him" — she repeated her full name in Gaelic — "I could be arrested for 'speaking Irish.'"

"Has that ever happened to you?" I asked.

"No."

"Is it likely to?"

"It could."

"That seems like a very, very small item on the agenda of Northern Ireland's problems," I said, "despite all the historic symbolism.

"What about the role of women in your vision of a new Ireland?" I asked Sile. "They haven't done too well in the old Ireland."

"Sinn Fein is the only party in Ireland with a feminist slate," she retorted. "And that slate includes provisions for both contraception and abortion. Women have a real voice in Sinn Fein politics. Women in Northern Ireland gained a sense of independence when their men were put in prison and they had to run their own households for the first time. They had to make decisions about their homes and their children that they had never done before, and they found out that they could do this perfectly well. Republican men accepted this new role for women and respected them for it."

I asked Sile what she thought would happen to the already fragile economy of Northern Ireland if the British government were to withdraw, taking with it all the generous government subsidies that prop up a welfare state with high unemployment.

"What would you do if you were suddenly without welfare payments, free education, dental care, medical care, food subsidies, community services . . . ?" (In an economic overview of Northern Ireland in 1986, the *Financial Times* stated that the total public expenditure in Northern Ireland currently works out at £2,700 per person, or £8,700 per household, 36 percent of which comes from the U.K. Exchequer.)

Her doctrinaire defense didn't slacken, but her answers had much less conviction and she was clearly on shaky territory. "We'll find a way. There's been some talk [and at this point, the tiniest shadow of a smile played around her mouth, but not her eyes] of finding gold here, or maybe lignite. But we can make the things we need for ourselves. We would sever our connection with the EEC [the Common Market] and ban all foreign imports. We'd be totally dependent on ourselves."

A timid knock sounded on the door, and Sile moved over to unlock it. A very old woman stood outside. She glanced warily at us, then whispered to Sile: "I've come for the cigarettes." She looked and sounded so conspiratorial that I was convinced that "cigarettes" was a code for something much more sinister, but Pauline pulled open a large box on the desk and drew out several packs of cigarettes and gave them, wordlessly, to the old woman. She stuffed them into a deep pocket and disappeared down the dark, gloomy hallway. The door was shut and locked again, and Sile took up her sentry post, standing against the wall, arms folded, stern expression intact.

"Do you think the rest of Ireland will agree to your vision of its future?" I asked.

"It makes no difference to me if the government is here in Belfast or in Dublin. It can be anywhere. We're the only political party in Ireland with branches in the North and the South, anyway. We'll be one country, united. That's our goal."

"And do you think there is a role in that government for you? For all the women in your party who are eager to serve?"

"I do."

"In what capacity?"

"We'll have to wait and see."

My allotted time had run out, and it was clear that the two women were eager to end the interview. I shut my notebook and smiled at Sile but didn't receive the slightest flicker of response.

"What did you go to prison for?" I asked her.

"I'd rather not say."

"How long do you plan to stay active in your organization?"

"'Til we win."

In 1976, when she was nineteen years old, Mairead (pronounced Ma-raid) Farrell, a Belfast girl from Andersonstown, was sentenced to fourteen years in prison for possession of explosives and membership in the IRA. She was sent to Armagh Prison for Women, a forbidding, nineteenth-century granite jail in the center of Armagh Town. Before 1969, there were seldom more than a dozen women in the prison, and those who were there were often using it as a hostel until they could find housing. After 1969, its population grew steadily as Irish women joined the armed struggle. Bernadette Devlin carried out her constituency work as a member of the British Parliament from her cell in Armagh, where she spent six months for participating in riots in Derry.

Mairead served ten years of her sentence and was released in September 1986. By then Armagh had closed its doors forever and the few remaining women prisoners had been transferred to a new, modern facility in Magheraberry, just outside Belfast. But the name of the Armagh Prison will remain sacred in Irish republican lore as the place where women involved in the armed struggle for Irish unification won their place as heroines in the organization.

I was late for our appointment and was running up the street to the friend's house where I was staying when I saw a pretty, brown-haired girl standing on his stoop, ringing the doorbell. She was small and slim, and she looked like a Queens University student in her denim jacket, jeans, and white tennis shoes. She had a long, red muffler wound around her neck and matching red mittens. It was a frosty winter day, despite the sunshine. I reached the house, breathless, just as she was turning to leave, and I apologized for nearly missing her. Her manner was cool and reserved, and in the bright sun her freckled face was pale. Ten years behind prison walls give a woman a certain translucent pallor that I was beginning to recognize. She must have been thirty, but she looked twenty.

"Let's go have lunch around the corner," I suggested. We found a table in the back of Welcome, a local Chinese restaurant, and I turned on my tape recorder as soon as we had ordered. Mairead's voice was so soft I was afraid the background noise in the restaurant would drown it out, so I urged her to speak more loudly. When she dutifully raised her voice, we both looked nervously at the next table to see if there was any reaction to our extraordinary luncheon conversation. Talk of bombings, prison life, no-wash protests, and strip-searching seemed grotesquely out of place in this quiet Chinese restaurant, *even* in Belfast, where conservatively dressed businessmen were lunching, and soft wind chimes tinkled in the background.

"I grew up in Belfast," Mairead began. "My family are republicans and we always were politically aware. They weren't always in agreement with me, but they believe, like I do, in a united Ireland. As I was growing up, I saw the curfew the British imposed on the Falls Road, I saw soldiers coming into our neighborhood, into our homes. I saw the violence. I saw discrimination all around me. I lived in a ghetto, and I came to believe that something had to be done. Passive resistance wasn't the way forward. It doesn't work."

Mairead's way forward was to become active in the IRA armed struggle. In 1976, she was arrested for planting a bomb in Conway's Hotel in Belfast. One of her two male companions was caught and arrested with her; the other was shot dead while trying to escape. She had only been released from prison a few months when I met her for lunch, hence the prison pallor, but she was already back in the organization, still as committed, maybe more so, to the cause of Ireland's unity, to the end of British occupation, to her vision of a fair and equal society for everyone. "I would bomb or kill again in a minute if called upon to do so," she said.

"No one told me to go out and plant a bomb. I did it because of my own ideology. They didn't pay me to do it. I didn't have a grudge against the Conway Hotel. It was simply a target which I thought would help us pursue our goals. We want people's support, but we don't want power. We want to change this country, not just for our small lot. We want to change the whole country for everyone."

"Just for my own curiosity," I interrupted her, "how do you plant a bomb?"

She smiled for the first time. "I'm not going to give away my secrets."

"But innocent civilians get killed as you pursue your goals," I said.

"It very seldom happens. We don't want it to happen. It's our own people, after all. Life is sacred."

"How can you say some lives are sacred but not other lives? How do you distinguish?"

"I'm not saying that." Mairead waited until the waiter had put our plates down, then leaned across the table, speaking with a low intensity. "I'm talking about a war. You have to understand that this is a war. We try very hard to insure that innocent civilians don't get killed. We try that to the best of our ability."

I pursued the point. "But they do get killed. Over and over."

"Well, we deeply regret it. I know it happens. But it happens on both sides. It's the casualties of war. The British have murdered our people. When you think of how long they have been here . . . from the very beginning they have murdered so many people. Those are the only methods the British know. At the end of the day, though, they will have to sit down and talk."

"Why do Catholic nationalists here who don't believe in violence and paramilitary activity think they have made progress?" I asked.

"I don't think they believe that. I think they know the Anglo-Irish Agreement is a joke. I mean, what is it? It's a joke. It's a joke! That's all."

"All those years you spent in prison — the no-wash protest and the hunger strike — was it worth it? Did you accomplish anything?"

"Of course. I was the first prisoner to arrive at Armagh for a political crime and not receive political status. Before nineteen seventy-six, all the political prisoners there lived in a special section of the prison set aside for them, and they didn't have to participate in regular prison life. I had to go in as a regular criminal, and all my comrades that followed me in were in the same category. So we refused to do our prison jobs. For every day that we refused to work, we lost a day's remission. Finally, there were thirty-two of us on work protest. We organized ourselves; I was the Wing O.C. [Officer in Command]. We were strong and determined, and we gave each other support.

"We continued the work protest until nineteen eighty. Then things got much worse." [In 1979, the first woman prison officer of Armagh was shot dead as she left the prison grounds.]

"They began to punish us by not letting us use our toilets. We had to use pots in our cells and they would overflow. So to protest that, we went on a no-wash campaign. They tried to get us off that by locking us up for twenty-three hours a day, only letting us out for one hour of exercise."

"What was the point of the no-wash protest?" I asked. The same technique was used by male prisoners in Long Kesh, and I always thought it was one of the most bizarre political protests I had ever heard of.

"We were forced into it. We had been locked up for four years and we felt that we needed more publicity. The only way we could get it was to escalate our protest. It was either that or a hunger strike, and we had to try a no-wash protest first. A hunger strike, after all, is the end, it's death. So we excreted in our cells and smeared it on our walls; there wasn't anything else to do with it. You are in your cell twenty-three hours a day and you have to live with it. Putting it on the wall is the best way."

"Did you wash yourself during your dirty protest?" I asked Mairead.

"No."

"For over a year you didn't wash your hands, your face, your body, or brush your teeth?"

"No."

"What did you do about your periods?"

"I used Tampax because I felt that kept me as clean as possible."

"And you didn't get sick?"

"No."

Other women in Armagh during the dirty protest would disagree with Mairead about the illness and debilitation caused by the unsanitary conditions that they inflicted on themselves. Liz Lagrua, an Englishwoman who lived in Belfast and was a member of Women Against Imperialism, a feminist group in Northern Ireland, served a brief term in Armagh.

"Cystitis was common. Some had skin disease of the head that couldn't be treated unless they washed their hair. . . . There was vomit and diarrhea in all our cells and dust accumulating from the shedding skin. Flies buzzed everywhere, dying in orgies on the shit and the uneaten food. Creatures with wings, like fleas, used to jump out of the po [toilet pots] and we discovered it was woodworm." (Nell McCafferty, *The Armagh Women,* p. 15.)

Mairead admitted there was massive weight loss among the protesting prisoners. "We had to go get our food and bring it in our cells and eat it there. Only one person could go at a time, so if you were the last, your food was freezing cold, but it was always so bad anyway that didn't matter. Stew, rice, and porridge. Always cold. I used to try to talk to my comrades through the cell doors as I went for my food, and the screws hated that. They would drag me away and not let me get my food.

"There were two of us to a cell. Luckily, I got along well with my cellmate and we are still very close. We organized ourselves in the cells. During the day we couldn't really do anything, but at night when the screws went off, we would communicate by yelling out our doors, studying Irish together, and making up games. We'd tell stories to keep up everyone's morale. We were in stripped cells with two beds; we had to make up our own entertainment. We would sing songs and each tell her life's story."

The women would say the Rosary each night in prison and recite other prayers in Irish. They were allowed out of their cells for an hour each Sunday to attend Mass, and that was a great time for exchanging news and gossip gleaned from outside visitors. While she was in prison, Mairead took extension courses and prepared herself for university admission.

Father Raymond Murray, a Catholic priest in Armagh, served for many years as the chaplain to the women in prison there. When I visited him in Armagh, he spoke with affection for and admiration of the women prisoners and of the sacrifice they were making for a cause they believed in. I said I had to disagree, that I thought it was sad and pointless for a young woman like Mairead to be back in the organization, perhaps risking her life again in an armed struggle when a nonviolent, political path was open to her.

"You don't understand these women's lives," Father Murray retorted. "You can't understand how they feel, always being second-class citizens in their own country."

"I understand perfectly," I replied. "It's something like being a woman in the Catholic Church, a second-class citizen in one's own religion."

We didn't continue on that line of conversation.

Father Murray had arranged my introduction to Mairead, and I asked her about him.

"He's brilliant," she replied. (*Brilliant* in Northern Ireland is not used the way we would use the word; it means "wonderful" rather than "intellectually gifted.") "He was so good to me the whole time I was there. I could talk to him about anything. All the women liked him."

"Are you a practicing Catholic?" I asked Mairead.

"Yes."

"And you don't have any difficulty reconciling your religion with your political beliefs?"

"No."

In December 1980, Mairead and two other prison inmates decided to go on a hunger strike, continuing their effort to be given political status as prisoners.

"We had a lot of discussion about it among ourselves. The republican movement didn't want us to die. They were against a hunger strike. British propaganda tried to make out that we were forced to go on the hunger strikes by the IRA, but you can't force someone to go on a hunger strike. You can't force someone to die. In fact, they tried to get us not to go on the strike. But we felt like we were in hell anyway. Death would be a release. We were on it nineteen days and had really deteriorated. When we received word that the hunger strikes had ended in Long Kesh, we thought things had developed, that we had got some of our demands, but in the end it turned out there was nothing gained. We didn't participate in the second hunger strike. There were so few of us by then, and all our efforts had gone into the first strike. On March first, we went off the no-wash protest, so that all publicity would focus on the men in the second hunger strike.

"In nineteen eighty-two, a new prison governor arrived and he had a lot of new psychological weapons to try out on us. He was determined that we would conform, and that's when he introduced strip-searching. We were brought down to this area all alone and put into a wee cubicle. Then someone would say: 'Strip naked!' If you refused, you would be thrown down on the floor and forcibly stripped. And you are so vulnerable. You have to stand there with all your clothes off, and they stand there looking at you, passing remarks like 'You're too fat,' or 'You're too thin,' and then they search you and slowly walk all around you. You just have to keep telling yourself what they are trying to do, that they are trying to humiliate you. You just have to keep that in your head."

Mairead was released in September 1986. Her mother and father and her brothers came to prison to take her home. "I was very sad about leaving my comrades behind," she said, remembering that day. "We were very close, they were like a family to me. Leaving them behind was an awful thing to do."

"Do you think things are better now than they were a decade ago? Is there more equality for Catholics in the North now?"

"No, I don't see any difference. The economic situation is frightening. How many people are working? I hardly know anyone who works."

"People get government subsidies. What would you replace those with if you weren't getting them from the British government?" I asked.

"Well, we'd have our own economic policies, of course. Naturally. We would also expect some sort of payment from Britain for what they have done to us over the years."

"Do you really think they would do that? Give you some massive payment and just leave?"

"Well, I suppose not, but we will just have to see. But I mean, we would have our own economic policies. Look at the amount of money that is going out of the country. And nothing is coming into the country. That's what we would change. Why, millions upon millions are going out each year. That's why unemployment is so bad. Multinationals will have to be dealt with, too. Vast changes will be made. In the South as well as the northwest counties."

"How do you deal with the fact that many people in the South say they don't want to be united with the North?"

"Do they say that? I didn't know that."

"Well, they do."

"Those polls show that the vast majority want to be reunited."

"But they are very worried about their own economic conditions."

"Really? I thought they were doing great."

I couldn't tell if she was serious or funny.

"Tell me about something that I find very hard to understand," I asked her. "Why do you threaten your own people all the time if they don't do what you want them to do?"

"Like what?"

"You know. To vote in a certain way. To pay someone off. To take the law in your own hands."

"We don't do those things. We don't need to use those tactics. The IRA needs support, yes. If we didn't have the support of the people we wouldn't exist. But we don't have to do those things to get our support."

"Well, nationalists who live in housing estates, for instance: they say they are being pressured over and over again."

"To do what?"

"To give someone money. To loan their car, to vote in a certain way."

"I definitely wouldn't agree with that."

"But they say it. You must know that."

"I don't know it. I can't answer that. People . . . if they don't want to do something, they don't do it."

We had long since finished our lunch and the restaurant had emptied. Our waiter was hovering over us, eyeing the tape recorder and clearly wishing that we would clear out. Our "welcome" was over. As we were waiting for the change from the bill, I tried one more question, although Mairead had clearly been angered by my questions about IRA tactics.

"What," I asked, "if the miracle you want happens tomorrow and you achieve a united Ireland. What role do you see for yourself?"

"In the first place, we would have to be elected. We would go to the people."

"But you have a very small percentage of the vote."

"Well, we may not be up to SDLP, but we are bigger than Alliance. We'll have to work hard."

I offered to drive her home, and as we walked toward my car, we talked about the role of women in the organization. She agreed with me that they have few leadership roles, but she said that doesn't bother her. "We are all dedicated to the same cause," she said.

We drove up the Falls Road towards Andersonstown, where Mairead lives with her family. She was quiet on the way home. We stopped at a block near her house and she jumped out, thanking me for the lunch and asking me to send her a copy of the book. She went swinging off in the direction of her house, her red scarf blowing out in the wind. Small, determined, angry, ready to sacrifice her life or anyone else's to her cause, ready for whatever comes her way.

I talked about Mairead to another friend, a woman whose loyalty to republicanism is just as ardent, but whose commitment to violence has diminished as each year's horror stories are related.

"I understand where she comes from," my friend said. "A complete frustration from a lack of a political process. A feeling of anger and frustration from years of repression. She looks around, just out of jail after all these years, and what does she see? Things haven't changed! They are still unemployed, still living in shitty houses. Still being denied access to power structures. Nothing has changed as far as she is concerned! So, if they [the British government] can't be talked into giving power over, they have to be bombed into giving it over. I believe that is a valid opinion for her to hold. It's not my opinion; mine would be more diluted. But it is valid for her. Work within the political structure? Are you crazy? There isn't any political structure for her."

The last time I saw Mairead Farrell was on that bright January day in 1987. A year later, on March 8, 1988, Mairead, thirty-one years old, was shot dead on a street in Gibraltar by the Special Air Services, a plainclothes, counterterrorist arm of the British Army. She was with two other IRA members who were killed by the SAS. The three of them were allegedly in Gibraltar on a terrorist mission. Her body was flown back to Ireland and she was buried on St. Patrick's Day in Belfast. As her graveside funeral services were taking place, a deranged loyalist supporter plunged into the crowd of mourners, shooting at random and throwing hand grenades. Three of the mourners were killed instantly and many more were seriously wounded.

The Troubled Majority

True patriotism doesn't exclude the patriotism of others.
— QUEEN ELIZABETH II

THERE SEEMS TO BE an unspoken law in Northern Ireland that a good Protestant woman will not have an opinion on public issues. If she is bold enough to do so, she will at least have the decency to keep it to herself. Unionist women become active at the community level and often are elected to their local council, but they don't go much further than that. As Ethel Smyth, a Unionist councillor in County Down, said, "If you want a seat in Parliament, forget it. That's a men's club. They think you're all right for local politics, but for anything better, forget it. If you hung an orange sash around a donkey's neck, they'd vote for him over you."

The most sensible, compassionate, and realistic voice I heard among Unionist women was that of Lucy Faulkner, the widow of Brian Faulkner, the last Prime Minister of Northern Ireland. Widowed when her husband was killed in a fall from his horse in 1977, she lives in a small cottage on the grounds of her family home. A son and his wife and children live in the big house where she raised her own family. Once a brilliant horsewoman herself, she doesn't ride anymore, although horses still graze on the rolling green pastures that surround her house. After her husband's death, she was appointed a governor of the BBC in Northern Ireland and served on that prestigious board for a seven-year term.

The countryside around the Faulkner land is quiet and peaceful now; the police guards, sentry posts, and intrusive protection necessary for a major politician in the North during the turbulent 'seventies are gone. The brilliant winter sunshine had faded by the time I reached Lucy's house on a late winter afternoon. We sat down by a fire in the living room, and I was made instantly welcome and comfortable. A big Labrador and a small cairn terrier lay sleeping at our feet, exhausted by an illicit all-night run over the countryside, chasing rabbits. A friend of Lucy's who works for the BBC came for dinner, and the three of us talked about Northern Ireland politics and the country's future.

As a political wife, Lucy has seen the turbulent decades of the 'fifties, 'sixties, and 'seventies from the vantage point of her husband's career. He had been active in politics since 1949, when he won his first election to the Northern Ireland Parliament from his constituency in East Down. The growing prosperity of Northern Ireland throughout the 'fifties and 'sixties owed much to Faulkner's astute business sense. He served as Minister of Commerce, Minister of Development, and finally, in March 1971, as Prime Minister until March 1972, when British Prime Minister Heath suspended the Stormont Parliament and imposed direct rule from Westminster on Northern Ireland. During the brief, hopeful days of the Power-Sharing Executive, he served as Chief Executive, a post he held for only five months, until the Executive collapsed under pressure of a general strike throughout the country. In describing that time, Faulkner said it was "[my] proudest moment to be able to chair such an Executive, and it is my main regret that it was brought to a premature end. . . . I shall grieve till my dying day that we did not succeed." (Brian Faulkner, *Memoirs of a Statesman*, p. 278.)

I asked Lucy what he said to her the night the Executive fell.

"He was not an emotional man," she said. "He was, above all, a pragmatist. He accepted reality. But I remember his coming home that night, exhausted, and saying, 'We will never see self-government in Northern Ireland again in my lifetime.' And of course he was proved right on that score." He was killed on March 3, 1977. The previous August he had retired from political life.

Faulkner had the reputation in the 'sixties of being a hard-nosed Unionist, unyielding, and unwilling to compromise with the nationalist community.

"It was fashionable then to be a 'liberal' Unionist," Lucy said. "In those days, many of our Unionist friends thought Brian was too conservative. Nowadays, it's fashionable to be 'extreme,' and some of the same people who criticized Brian in the 'sixties felt that he had become a 'traitor' to Unionism when he supported and participated in the Power-Sharing Executive. They have never forgiven him for that."

Very few politicians change their fundamental views about public issues, and this is particularly true in Northern Ireland among Unionists, where political ties are so intertwined with one's cultural and religious heritage. But Brian Faulkner was, as his wife described him, a pragmatist, willing to do what "worked," and as he saw the Power-Sharing Executive begin to work, he was able to adjust his long-held attitudes and move with the times. It is a great tragedy for Northern Ireland that Unionist politicians of his calibre don't seem to exist today.

Lucy's political views are very much like her husband's were, and she, unlike so many Unionist women I met, is able to view the situation in Northern Ireland today and form her judgments in an objective manner. She was one of a small number of prominent Unionists who signed a public declaration of support of the Anglo-Irish Agreement (although she told me two years after the Agreement went into effect that she was disappointed that better security in the North — one of the Agreement's goals — had not evolved).

"I'm not a feminist, I guess," Lucy laughed when I questioned her about her attitudes toward liberated women. "I think marriage should be a partnership, but someone has to take care of the children! It hasn't been part of our tradition for women to be active in political life. But that's changing too, and for the better."

When she went out of the room to check on dinner, her guest said to me: "Lucy is so modest about her own abilities. I think she was the best politician in the family: she had a better-developed political sense, and her judgments always proved to be right. In another place and another age, she could have been Prime Minister!"

Some of the old neighbors and friends of the Faulkners, Unionist families for generations who feel that Brian Faulkner betrayed them by his participation in the Power-Sharing Executive, are not discreet about their feelings. On her side, Lucy is far more compassionate and forgives them their critical and sometimes unkind attitude.

"Why bother with them?" I asked.

"Because," she replied simply and eloquently, "they are my people." Tribalism exists in Northern Ireland on every level, including the most sophisticated.

At the end of a tiny country road in another part of the County, Mary Sandford and her husband, Sandy, live in a big gray stone house overlooking Strangford Lough. Lucy Faulkner had encouraged me to meet them. "You will get a straight, unbiased view from Mary," she had said. "She thinks for herself, and that's rare enough around here!"

Mary was standing in the doorway as I drove up the narrow lane. Tall and slim, in gray slacks and an argyle sweater, she had a warm smile and a relaxed, welcoming handshake. "Let me show you something out in back, before we go inside," she said, smiling, and took me around the side of the house to show off a fifty-foot yacht that was sitting on wooden foundations in the backyard. "My husband made it," she said proudly. "He can't wait to get it into the water." He doesn't have far to go; the lapping water at the edge of the Lough isn't more than 500 yards from their lawn.

Both the Sandfords were widowed and have only been married to each other for eighteen months. As I walked through the front hall into the living room, we stepped under a painters' scaffolding and into a handsome living room with a coal fire burning in the grate. In the short interval of leaving the car and walking into the house, the sun had disappeared and rain began to spatter against the tall windows.

"I grew up in County Antrim, went to Queens University for a year before I quit to marry and have children. In nineteen sixty-eight, I went back to school for a degree in Social Administration and went to work with the juvenile courts system and delinquent children. I was appointed to a training school for both Protestant and Catholic boys, the only 'mixed' school of its kind in the country."

"Is there any tension because of that?" I asked.

"No. I'm always asked that question. The staff is about fifty–fifty also, more by coincidence than design, but I want to keep it that way. I'm told that the kind of youngsters we get don't have much religious background anyway, so it makes no difference to them.

"We have a day center in Belfast as well as a residential 'secure' unit, and a remand unit in County Down. The boys who are there on a training school order are eventually allowed to leave each day, and an attempt is made to rehabilitate them; the 'remand' boys are not permitted to leave until their case has been heard by a court. These would be the most serious juvenile offenders in Northern Ireland."

Mary's appraisal of the juvenile delinquency situation in Northern Ireland, based on her long experience dealing with such boys, refutes the common assumption in the United States and elsewhere that the political violence in the country has created a generation of emotionally disturbed children whose criminal activity is the result of that violence.

"Northern Ireland still has a very low rate of juvenile delinquency compared to the rest of Europe," she said. "And very few of the boys are political offenders. Most are in for car thefts and burglary. Studies have been done which show that the Troubles have had very little effect on the offending rate of children; in fact, very little effect on the children generally. The ones who suffer the most are the children of young men put into prison for long periods — lifers. Usually their wives don't wait for them, strange men come into the house, those children don't really know who their father is, and they are disturbed by that situation. You could say that was a direct result of the Troubles, and you can point to the areas where it is most likely to happen, such as West Belfast.

"The age of criminal responsibility is ten, and they can come before the court between ten and sixteen, but you wouldn't get a custodial residency much before the age of fourteen. But children who can't be contained in the children's home would appear in a training school because of really serious problems. And we are getting an increasing number of very disturbed children, mentally affected children, because there is nowhere else for them to go in Northern Ireland. We don't have a juvenile psychiatric unit."

I asked if there were many more of those children than before.

"No, no more, but we would have three or four at a time in a training school, and I think they are inappropriately placed there."

"Tell me more about your own background," I urged Mary. "Are you a deeply religious person?"

She smiled. "I think I'm pretty apathetic about the whole thing. I go to church, but perhaps not for the right reasons. And I question things a lot!"

"Are you a Unionist?"

"No. I was a member of the Alliance Party. Now I'm not really a member of anything, because it doesn't function well here. I would like to see everyone being Alliance, but unfortunately the extremes have rather pushed it out. My first husband, father-in-law, and uncles were officers in the Unionist Party in County Londonderry, but gradually when they went to meetings they were ousted from their various offices because they were too moderate. Then I thought Alliance was the best way forward. I've never been involved in local politics, though. In this country I'm afraid that men rather look down on women and think they should be kept in their place. They are very chauvinistic. I'm quite sure they are. The women who do make their way are looked upon as being a bit pushy."

"Do you consider yourself a feminist?"

"No," Mary laughed. "No, I don't think so. I very much like for people to get up and give me their seat on the bus and that sort of thing. But still . . . yes, I would like to see equal pay for equal work."

"Is your own husband a chauvinist?"

"Oh, dear, that's difficult! No, I don't think so. I think he is most understanding. Sometimes he resents the things I do because it takes me away from him, but we have only been married for eighteen months. It's rather a different situation than it was with my original husband with whom I had been married thirty-two years. But I think most men are slightly chauvinistic! Women are at a great disadvantage in that they want to bring up their family and be at home with them, and in doing that they lose a lot of rungs on the ladder. It's hard to come back at forty or fifty and find your place in the world again."

(At the very moment we were discussing Mary's husband, as if on cue, the door of the living room opened and he walked in, carrying a tea tray filled with cookies and scones. We both burst out laughing and decided on the spot that we would exonerate him of all taint of chauvinism!)

"Have the political troubles affected you personally in any way?" I asked as Sandy poured our tea.

"Not more than the slight irritation of having to be frisked going into shops and not being able to go into certain parts of Belfast, and so on. We've had bombs in our town, which made me very angry indeed, shops blown to bits for no reason whatsoever, and people losing relatives. My husband was for fourteen years in the Ulster Defense Regiment, and someone blew himself up at his gate, which could have been a bomb being designed for him. But personally I have been very little affected. It's very much a working-class war. Policemen, their wives and families are the worst hit. And the UDR."

"What are your own personal views of the political problems facing the North, and what do you think the churches could have done — now or in the past — to ease the path for reconciliation?"

Mary sighed. "Oh, that's a big question. I think that . . . as a child I never met anybody of the opposite religion. Never. Not until I went to university. I sat on the same bus going to school and saw other children — Roman Catholics. I went to a state school, and it happened that there were no Catholics there. In some state schools there would have been Catholics if there was no Catholic school in that area. I must admit that I do hold the Roman Catholic Church responsible for the segregation of schools, in that they insist on having their own. Catholic children who go to state schools are not regarded very well by their bishop. He has refused to confirm some of them, and that sort of thing. But I have spoken to Catholic people recently, and they say the same thing: they never had the chance to meet Protestant children across the divide, and that was forty or fifty years ago."

"Did you grow up thinking Catholics were peculiar?"

"I don't think I ever really knew they existed! It was never . . . certainly my father never belonged to the Orange Order or anything that would have been controversial. I just didn't know anything about them. I knew the girls went to the convent school, and we used to play hockey matches against them, but we never knew them as individual persons. I do think the churches could have smoothed out a lot of this a long time ago, by encouraging relationships across the divide, but then I think those who are in the church come from families to whom the same conditions would have applied. They didn't know any of the others, either, so they never really had any need to meet. I do think there is a very great cultural difference between the Roman Catholic and the Protestant religions."

"In what ways?"

"Well, you have lived in the South of Ireland. You know the sort of 'mañana' outlook there. They arrange to meet someone at nine o'clock, and they might get there at eleven! In the North of Ireland there is a more hardheaded business community, where if someone said they would be there at nine o'clock, they would. They look to England for their history and culture, whereas the Roman Catholic population here looks much more to the South of Ireland, the Irish culture, traditional music, Irish history, and so on. Irish history is not taught in the state schools here. Only once did I have Irish history, and it was taught by a very good teacher, who was also the headmistress, and it was taken along with American history and European history; in other words, foreign history.

"Oh, we have a terrible lack of identity here. That struck me very forcibly in the early nineteen seventies when we went to stay in a hotel in the South of Ireland. On the registration card it asked: Nationality? I would have written 'Irish' if I had been abroad, but I couldn't there, because I have a British passport. When we travel abroad, we prefer to be thought Irish rather than English, because there has been a time when England was not the favorite country in the world, with the unions causing trouble and so on, but I think of myself as British first. But I live in Ireland!"

"So you think of yourself as 'Northern Irish'?"

"Oh, yes. But nobody would know what you were if you said you were 'Northern Irish'! When I am asked, 'Where do you live?' I simply say, 'Ireland.' Then if they say, 'North or South?' I say, 'North,' because I know they understand a bit about our situation here. It isn't easy!"

"Do you think that the cultural differences you speak of are more class differences than cross-border differences? The working class here, the Protestant working class, have more of a work ethic than they do in the South."

"Well, I don't think you can generalize. Now those two," — Mary nodded her head in the direction of her front hall, where the painters were at work — "they are very hard workers, dependable and so on, and they are Catholic. You get a great cross section of dependability, but I understand what you mean, there is a cultural difference. There has been a great difficulty for the Catholic professional here because he has had to be very careful not to appear 'establishment.' Not to be a 'Castle Catholic.' [A "Castle Catholic" in Ireland can refer either to Dublin Castle or to Stormont Castle. It is a derogatory term suggesting that a Catholic living in either the South or the North is actually more "British" than Irish, more Protestant than Catholic in his cultural and social attitudes.] Therefore they have to walk a tightrope, trying to promote their professionalism and yet not lose their credibility in their own culture."

"Whom are they afraid of? I mean, to whom would they lose their credibility?"

"Politicians are afraid of voters, and I suppose professional lawyers are afraid for their practices. This is still the case, although there are certain barristers who get a good name and anyone would go to them, Protestant or Catholic."

"Would you?"

"It wouldn't matter in the least to me, as long as they were good at their job. I have a Catholic doctor here, who was recommended by my Protestant doctor where I lived before."

"When you were growing up, and went to Queens, did you have a sense of belonging to a majority in a country where the minority were treated unequally?"

"That was beginning to dawn on me at Queens, and I will still say they were not treated fairly."

"Did that make you more understanding toward their feelings of frustration?"

"Yes, I think it would have done, even to the extent of disagreeing with my family — my first husband's family. But there is such a history of what has become a ghetto situation now, which, sadly, was beginning to get sorted out in the early nineteen seventies. We had a lot of mixed housing developments then, which were being designed that way. In County Londonderry, where I used to live, they have mixed estates. But then, in the same town, we had a very extremist Unionist councillor who insisted on having a new estate called the King William III Crescent; that precludes any Catholic from ever living there! It is so provocative!"

"How would he get by with doing that?"

"Because at that time there was a majority of Unionists on the local council. Now of course it has gone the other way, and the SDLP and Sinn Fein have a majority on the council, and they are doing the opposite things. Although I must admit, I think they are being fairer."

"Do you admire John Hume and the SDLP?"

"I do. But I think they should give more support to the police. I think, until they do, this country cannot prosper."

"When you say 'support the police,' what exactly do you mean?"

"Encourage people to join it, for one thing."

"What about the intimidation that people, but particularly Catholics, face if they join the RUC?"

"Some very brave ones do."

"If you were a Catholic, would you encourage your son to join the RUC?"

"I think if there had been a lead from the Church and the Party, we would never have got to the state where we are now. I do think they are using this as a trump card. I think John Hume has disappeared into the background now. I don't know why. But Seamus Mallon [the deputy head of the SDLP] seems to be the one doing all the talking at the moment."

"What do you think of him?"

"I would prefer John Hume. He's an idealist. Mallon is more practical. He is always finding fault with the establishment."

"Are there any moderate Unionists anymore?"

"The Ulster Unionists really have lost their way. There is no leadership. That is exactly the problem. There is no real leader in Northern Ireland. I am so sorry that Brian Faulkner is not still with us. He was the only statesman we have had in the Unionist Party."

"What do you think about the Anglo-Irish Agreement?"

"Personally, I would say that we [Protestants] all feel very hurt that we were not consulted. But I can see the reason why we were not consulted. I must say — and perhaps my family and friends won't agree with me — that I can't see that there would be any problem in giving it a try. There are safeguards built into it, and after three years if it didn't work, we can throw it out and try again. The problem is that it hasn't been given a chance to work, so it can't possibly. My own family don't like the thought of Dublin having any interference in their daily life. I doubt very much whether they have thought very deeply about it."

"Where does all this deep-seated anger of the extremist Protestants come from?"

"I think it is ignorance. It is a great deal of ignorance of how the other half sees things. I had a Protestant woman in the house who helped me, and she could never bring herself to say 'Roman Catholic' aloud. She always whispered it! She would say, 'So and so is a very nice woman but she's [whisper] Roman Catholic.' Then I would say, 'Well, but you know Jack, he's a Roman Catholic.' And she would say, 'Aye, but he's different.' You see, she *knew* him.

"We come back to this notion of getting to know one another. The Roman Catholic Church thinks they have to educate their own, and that keeps us separated. I don't know whether they think we can't do it for them or that they can't do it with a mixed staff and have a good education, but they even insist on young offenders going to a Catholic establishment —"

"Except for yours."

"Except for that one. But then that is when they finally can't cope with them any longer. School integration wouldn't be the end of it, but it certainly would help."

"Do you have close Catholic friends?"

"I had more before I came here, I think. I'm still finding my way here. But yes, we both have one whom we have known forever. It's funny, but one never thinks of him as Catholic, if you know what I mean!"

Go back up the Sandfords' lane, make a few turns right and left, a mile this way, a mile that way, and you come to an area with the most improbable but charming name of Ballywillwill, with neat farmhouses, modest but prosperous, and fields filled with grazing livestock. Ethel Smyth lives in this part of the county. She's a Unionist councillor with a reputation of being a fiery pro-Paisley, anti–Anglo-Irish Agreement, anti-Catholic activist. She's also a determined feminist, a trait that would set her apart from most of her Unionist female colleagues.

The Smyths' farmhouse is handsome and well-kept. Protestant women are indefatigable housekeepers. Ethel's house shines. We sat down in the living room, an unused-looking formal room, with an upright piano, an artificial fire in the grate, and the ever-present Irish floral carpet. Ethel is a good-looking woman, with striking bright blue eyes, and she was all dressed up for the occasion in black lace stockings, red shoes, and makeup. Her very pregnant daughter brought in the tea tray when we were settled, and we eased into our conversation by talking about pregnancy and babies. Once we got into politics, though, Ethel was off and running and needed no prompting from me.

"I come from right around here," she said, "the third child of six in a Protestant working-class family. I passed my Eleven-Plus examination, which means I got a free secondary education. That changed my life."

Ironically, she was educated in a local convent school, because there was no public grammar school (high school) in the neighborhood.

"At first I felt like a fish out of water, but then I got on with them. I thought the nuns were wrong, of course, but they were sincere. And they certainly were good teachers."

She stayed in the school until she was eighteen, when she had to leave to return home and nurse her ill mother. "I opened a little grocery store while I was home," she said, "to save money to go to England. I worked in a boys' home in Staffordshire for a while, but had to come home again when my mother got worse. I took care of her until she died."

The Smyths have four children of their own, and the imminently expected grandchild will be their first.

"I was elected councillor in nineteen seventy-seven. There were nineteen men and me! I was the first women ever elected to that council, although there have been two since. They accepted me, all right, although in Northern Ireland it is generally accepted that even the most stupid man knows more than any woman. I got involved and I have strong views. I fought for my views. It was the Troubles that got me interested, although even in the convent I was interested in politics.

"One of the things that got me started in politics here was a school situation that affected my children. They went to a mixed primary school. It was a good school and everyone was happy there. Then a priest went round and told the Catholic children that they had to leave, and they did. I will tell you that I created a stink! I wrote a letter to the paper and went to the Minister of Education. I finally got a minibus to bring in more children. And a few of the Catholic children stayed, so we were able to keep the school open. You see, otherwise it would have had to close because there wouldn't have been enough local children.

"In nineteen seventy-three, education boards were set up. Catholics are involved and they can teach, but Protestants can't teach in Catholic schools. Catholic schools get state aid. I just don't think that's fair.

"So I began to go to Unionist Party meetings and the men were proposing me. I got to be vice-chairman, and then treasurer. The men were more supportive of me then than the women. But if you want to go higher and get a seat in Parliament, forget it.

"I'm involved in boycotting the council meetings now because of the Agreement. [Unionists all over Northern Ireland decided to boycott their local councils in protest against the signing of the Anglo-Irish Agreement.] We live in a nationalist area here, so it doesn't really help. But I think just having council protests isn't militant enough. We should have more fire in our bellies!"

I asked Mrs. Smyth if the Anglo-Irish Agreement had changed anything in her life.

"It hasn't. But I fear two things: The Flags and Emblems Act; they would have the right to fly the tricolor. And they would change the electoral laws where people in the South could come up here and vote. Lots of cheating goes on in elections in Northern Ireland.

"Now personally, I never felt there was an imbalance between the Catholics and the Protestants. Poor people have nothing, no matter what they are. There's a fallacy to think that there was a difference. Protestants think the Catholics are getting everything now. They have their own schools and they are sectarian. Northern Ireland people brought us up to believe that the most important thing was union with Great Britain. Because we felt insecure, we must band together. We saw the civil rights movement as a threat to Unionism.

"Twenty years ago, having a united Ireland would have been a lot easier than it is now. Now there have been too many bad things happen to too many people. In nineteen eighty-one, bombs were planted at my house in October. Two big bombs hung in the front yard. My husband phoned the police, and they came right out. I got the children up, and got a roast beef out of the fridge to take with me! Isn't it funny what you will do at a time like that? Thinking of my roast beef! Anyway, the army defused the bombs; they were set on a timer and there had been a mistake. You see, my public image is terrible. There were threatening phone calls in the middle of the night, crude, threatening calls. They didn't bother me as much as one educated, cultivated voice that said: 'Come a day, go a day, death to Ethel.' That sent a cold chill up my spine.

"Another time, the army had to guard us at night. They had had a tip off, so they sat at every window with a machine gun. The UDR stayed for three weeks. Honestly, we would stumble over them in the house.

"I said the IRA were cowards and lying rats, and I hoped they stayed on their hunger strikes. I couldn't ask God to forgive them. If the

Catholic Church weren't so powerful, we wouldn't mind unity. But the Catholic Church would be running the country. Also the IRA. Now there is so much bitterness. The Protestant paramilitaries have been much less effective. They do random murders on picked targets.

"I can tell you there is no democracy in Northern Ireland now. There is no free speech, we can't have protests. The DUP is more straightforward than the Official Unionists. I align myself with Paisley and Robinson [Peter Robinson, the deputy head of the DUP]. You just wouldn't know what Molyneaux [the head of the Official Unionist Party] wants."

I asked her what she thought about some of the vicious things that Paisley has said about the Catholic Church.

"Well, if you are a member of a reformed church, you have to preach about the errors of their way. Now I don't believe in name-calling myself. My attacks are all political. But I wouldn't want my children to marry a Catholic and see my grandchildren brought up as Catholics.

"The future of Northern Ireland will be terrible if the Anglo-Irish Agreement stays in. That Mrs. Thatcher, she sent men to the Falklands, but she never did anything here. I don't believe in power-sharing either. Brian Faulkner was a total traitor. Total! They didn't let the people vote. He stood as a Unionist, and he made people pledge to him, then he went over to Sunningdale and signed that agreement. I think he is a traitor to his own people. After that, he couldn't appear in any Orange Hall. He committed an act of treachery! *I* wouldn't have accepted any power-sharing! The party that wins the election should have the government. So what if the Unionists win? We are the majority. The SDLP had only twenty percent of the vote. Why should we share the power with them?

"You Americans don't want to hear the Unionist side. We have suffered murder and mutilation, and you don't want to hear about it. You Americans just listen to the nationalist side."

"But Paisley is your spokesman," I said, "and the kinds of things he says are unacceptable to most Americans who are interested in Northern Ireland."

"An awful lot of what Ian Paisley says is true. Journalists know he is speaking the truth. He's dead on center!"

I asked Ethel what she did during the March 3, 1986, strike, when militant Unionists protested the Anglo-Irish Agreement.

"We organized a strike here locally. Had a cavalcade of cars out to block the roads so people couldn't get to work."

"In the nineteen seventy-four strike [the countrywide strike that succeeded in bringing down the Sunningdale government], I was in charge of the strike for south Down. I gave out dockets for nurses and doctors and controlled the petrol stations and so on."

"What," I asked Ethel, "do you see in the future for women in the Unionist Party?"

"Women are our worst enemies, but we will gain experience and self-confidence. That's what we need. And finally women will see that we are all in this together. I think women have more fire in them than men. I want to see more angry protests against the Anglo-Irish Agreement, that's what I would like to see for the near future."

Although there is very little female participation in loyalist organizations, or in paramilitary activities, women who support the extreme side of Unionism seem to be angrier, more militant, more frustrated than the men. They speak often of betrayal, of the timidity of their leaders, of walking blindly down a road with no known destination.

They long for action, although on what front and toward what ultimate goal is unclear. They use the same buzz words ("flying the Irish flag over our land," "Papist supremacy," "Taig [slang for Catholic] murderers," "Mrs. Thatcher's treachery"), and they do truly fear for their future in a country that seems to have turned upside down on them. With no leadership, no tradition of independent action, no practice in thinking politically on their own, and no examples of earlier women leaders to follow, they seem pathetically pummeled by the chaos of their political lives and ill-prepared to do anything about it. They have only the personal and folk memory of generations of rabble-rousing preachers telling them how to be saved. They are fearful, too, of "their own," all the Protestant paramilitary organizations that prey upon their lives, extorting support, loyalty, and fidelity to actions and programs that are, to them, unfocused and meaningless. There is no outlet for their anger, no constitutional route they can take to defend their cause, no room in the men's clubs for their voices. There are no women in the Orange Order, the Ulster Volunteer Force, the Ulster Protestant Action Group, the Ulster Protestant Volunteers, or the Tartan Boys. With a few notable exceptions, they are Northern Ireland's biggest and most silent majority. (A brief, horrific foray into militant violence occurred in 1974. A group of loyalist women attacked a young woman named Ann Ogilby who was allegedly involved with an unmarried prisoner. To "teach her a lesson," the women beat her to death, while her six-year-old daughter stood outside the door listening to her mother's dying screams.)

Loyalist women seem to be more isolated, lonely, and without access to the kinds of community support available to nationalist women. By nature not so gregarious and by tradition not so open, they are more tightly bound within the confines of their neighborhoods, their culture, and their loyalties. The pressures that Protestant paramilitary organizations put on them are just as heavy a burden for them as the IRA is for Catholic working-class women in Twinbrook or Turf Lodge. The tattooed musclemen who pose as their protectors can turn in a flash and become vicious antagonists.

Andy Tyrie, until March 1988 the head of the Ulster Defense Association, the largest (and the only legal) paramilitary loyalist organization, says that he is trying to recruit women into the organization and to define a role that they can play within the group.

"I would really like to have more women," he assured me (pronouncing *women* as "weemen"). He sat in his office at the UDA headquarters in East Belfast, casually greeting people as they came and went. "But I would like to see them in the jobs that they can do better than the men, not just emulate the men. They have to win respect for themselves. Right, Hester?"

Hester agreed. She had obviously won respect for herself in the UDA. I had come to their headquarters on a beautifully warm, May day in search of Hester. People had said to me: "If you want to talk to a sensible loyalist activist woman, see Hester."

The offices were bright and clean. Emblems, pictures, flags, and posters lined the walls of the offices, and men wandered in and out with multiple tattoos on their arms, flags and emblems imbedded into their very skin. They all seemed to be blond and muscular, except for their leader, Andy, who looks like a jovial Italian barber with his big, black mustache, blue-tinted glasses, spacious midsection, and green sweatshirt. In the middle of all the masculine company sits Hester, tiny and blond, keeping middle age at bay with her short, curly hair, tight leather pants, spike-heeled black pumps, and sleeveless tee shirt. She has kept her trim dancer's figure.

Andy told us to use his spacious office for the interview. He sits in modest splendor at a big desk flanked by the Ulster flag and the UDA flag. He left us alone there, telling us to call him back in when we got to talking about sex. As he walked out the door, he stuck his head back in with a malicious grin. "The trouble with you weemen is that you are your own worst enemy. You don't have the self-confidence to stand up to men." He made a quick exit on that line.

Hester and I sat down across from each other at a long table in the middle of the room. The front windows of the second-floor office look out over a busy commercial street, and the rumble of passing cars and trucks came in through the open windows. She lit a cigarette, made the customary offer to share her pack with me, sat forward on her chair with her arms on the table, and began.

"I'm secretary, receptionist, P.R. person, and dogsbody. I used to volunteer, but now I work full-time, although it's for a pittance. I do it because I believe in it. I'm working-class Protestant, but I didn't grow up here in East Belfast. We were raised in the countryside and as a child I didn't know anything about East Belfast or what it stood for. I wasn't really aware of Protestants and Catholics until maybe the eleventh or twelfth of July, when I was scrubbed up and taken out to see the Orangemen march. Or maybe taken to Bangor [a seaside resort] for the day and that would be our summer holiday!

"My dad wasn't an Orangeman. He was born in England and moved here when he was seven. My mom was a strict Presbyterian and I was brought up that way. I was much closer to my dad, though. He has a brilliant imagination and he encouraged me in anything that was artistic. He was a shipyard worker and did loads of overtime to make more money, so his time for us was limited. My mother's strict religious sense finally came into conflict with me when I wanted to take dancing lessons. I just always wanted to dance! I would put on a pair of red "wellies" and imitate tap dancers. But my mother was very puritanical. She used to say: 'Dancing is using your feet as drumsticks for the devil.' Finally, just to shut me up, she said I could have lessons when I turned sixteen. I started off with ballroom and modern and so on, but of course by then I was way too far behind to catch up. I finally began to do cabaret work part-time on my own.

"I really didn't want to leave school. I liked it and wanted to stay on, but the money wasn't there. My dad apologized to me for not being able to afford to keep me on in school, no matter how hard he worked, or how much overtime he did. So I had to quit, and I went to work in a shop and began to do their window dressing. The boss saw that I had good ideas, so I ended up doing window dressing full-time and dancing on the side.

"I married my dancing partner. I married him on the rebound because I had been engaged to someone else, so he was more my friend than boyfriend, and I did him a big injustice by marrying him. He was a lot older than me, and I don't think I was aware that marriage is for life. The good thing out of that marriage are my two children; they aren't *just* my children, they are my friends, and they are brilliant. I separated from my husband when they were nine and eleven, and had to leave them with their dad, although I saw them as often as I could. One thing about him is he's brilliant with children, absolutely brilliant. He's not so good with women — although having said that, he's good with my daughter. Well, it's wrong to have regrets and feel bitter, but I do regret . . . if there could have been some other way of ending the relationship without the children being separated from me, I wish I could have done it.

"Their dad was a real pacifist. We lived in a mixed area called Lenadoon that was very troubled, just outside Belfast. I was becoming socially aware, and he would sit and read a book while bullets were flying around him. Maybe if he had taken more of an interest, I wouldn't have tried to right so many wrongs, but that did add a strain on the marriage. I thought he wasn't man enough. Now, looking back, maybe he had strength of a different kind.

"Our neighborhood was being taken over by the republican cause, and there was a lot of injustice in that particular area, but to bury your head in the sand when other people are talking about it . . . well, he just didn't want to know. I didn't want the children growing up with a chip on their shoulders, and I tried to be objective and fair anytime they questioned me, and it came up often because of the trouble area. Some of my peers thought I was off my head for being so involved, and by answering their questions the way I did. They saw shootings, bombs, the IRA at work in the area, but I always told them, 'Those are only the bad boys doing that.' I always tried to encourage them to mix, but it was hard because of the troubled times. Before the troubled times they were able to mix with Catholics, with the result that now they mix well. When things got real bad in Lenadoon, I could always take them across town to stay with relatives. Now some people in Lenadoon didn't have relatives like that, so maybe they were more bitter. Still, you can't hide everything from them. Once my daughter went to Sunday school and I asked her to buy the papers on her way home. A bunch of Catholic kids beat her up on the way. Small incidents like that made me angry. I have two more children now, by my second husband, and they aren't as privileged in that sense as the first two. Even though they would get the same answers from me as the others did, they wouldn't be able to live in a mixed area now. I just arranged for them to go to Holland for three weeks this summer in a mixed group. That will be the first time for them to mix with Catholics. It should be all right. I hope so. I want them to learn to mix.

"Anyway, I started being socially aware because there were a lot of amenities lacking in our neighborhood. A youngster got knocked down by a car because there was no pedestrian crossing and I got involved trying to protest about that, and we got a crossing. I met a few Unionists in the neighborhood and found out there was a Unionist headquarters there and I went there and gave them a bad time. 'Why are you just sitting here making coffee when there's things to be done?' I asked them. So they made me the secretary. It was all bread-and-butter issues.

"Meanwhile, there was lots of unrest, and I started to watch political programs that were topical; previously I hadn't bothered with things like that. Then I started to read quite a bit, and I was so ignorant. I didn't even know there was such a thing as the one-man, one-vote issue and so on. Prior to that, I wasn't even interested enough to vote. I suppose it sounds strange to say, but I really didn't even know there had been injustices, and I told my Unionist friends that I was very angry about this and that I was going to start to march in the civil rights parades. They nearly went mental! They told me, 'Oh, it's just a pack of republicans — the usual nonsense!' But I was angry. Some Unionist people shunned me because of those views; some republicans shunned me, too! And although I was becoming socially more aware, I was becoming discouraged with the republican side. They were better at making bigoted remarks than addressing themselves to the problems in both communities. It was a mixed community and a very pretty place to live. My family thought I was mad to move into a mixed estate, but I didn't care.

"I was naïve enough to go into Andersonstown [a nationalist neighborhood] and canvass for local elections for Unionist politicians. Some people were so surprised at the cheek of me that they would just take my brochure. But once I was in Lenadoon and stopped by this house where a man was bent over, tying gladiolas to bamboo sticks.

"'Hello,' says I. 'I'm here canvassing for the Unionist candidate.' He didn't hear me at first and I repeated it. He stood up then and looked at me and shouted, 'A fuckin' Unionist? Here? In *my* garden!' He grabbed a bamboo stick and started chasing me down the street. Think of the state of me!

"Well, the Troubles got worse in our area, ranging from stone-throwing to shootings and bombings, but I still tried to steer a middle-of-the-line course and argued with Unionists and loyalists in the area. Internment morning was bad. I woke up, and my door was being knocked in. It was neighbors saying, 'Hester, Hester, get up, something terrible is happening!' There were all sorts of noises. Then a lorry came by with fifteen or twenty youths on it, throwing bottles and shouting, 'Get out of here, you orange bastards!'

"More neighbors came running in. 'It's internment!' they was shouting, and I says, 'Right, get the army. Get the police.' But then I says, 'Hold on a wee minute.' I wanted to think what to do with the kids. It was getting worse by the minute. There was a fire. Lots of noise and smoke. I tried phoning my sister, but the phone was out of order. I got the kids washed and dressed, packed a bag, went round the corner to another phone, and got through to my sister. She didn't know what I was talking about because she lived on the other side of town. I got the kids out in a taxi and went back to the house. Lots of people were coming in now. See, they had started to think of me as some sort of agony aunt in the area. 'What are we going to do?' they all wanted to know.

"'Right,' says I. 'Let's ring up the army or an MP.' We rang one. Got his wife. Tried to get the police, but there wasn't any. For hours we were left without any security. They had pulled so many of the security forces out to lift people that we were left alone, and we were a small enclave of Protestants completely surrounded by republicans, so when they were being interned, they turned on us.

"So things got bad then. There were riots. People were moving out. I tried to encourage people to stay, not to give up their homes. 'I'll stay here with you,' I said. But in the mornings they couldn't get to work. Or someone would be held at gunpoint and told, 'Get out!' So there were various degrees of intimidation, shootings, stones through the windows, verbal. And others just made up stories."

"Where is Lenadoon?" I asked.

"It's adjacent to Andersonstown. The actual place is called Suffolk. But the people from Andersonstown said they would take it over, and they practically have. That one week maybe seventy people left. Then dribbles left. Six months later, they started some aggro. Every few months they would start up, and finally they all trickled out. When it was first built, that housing estate was awarded an architectural prize it was so nice. Now it's a slum. I cry whenever I see it. But I stayed on for a few years afterwards.

"My marriage was shaky now, and I started going out a bit socially, sometimes with other men, sometimes with women friends. Five of us women went out on Monday nights. Their marriages were shaky, too, and I encouraged them to go out with me because I wanted company. Well, there was a good gig on in Woodlands, and I knew the band, so on this particular evening my boss's wife — she was a bit neurotic, going through a bad patch after the breakup of her marriage — she went with us.

"I saw a foot patrol as I went out. I knew some of them. They saw me go out. So I went to the Woodlands and met my friends. They give you a ticket and you can have this cheap, horrible champagne. There was a group of fellows next to us, and they drank ours. They would have drunk anything. About ten P.M. there was a call for one of my friends from her babysitter, who was hysterical, saying that Lenadoon was burning. We tried to get a lift home. There were two soldiers sitting beside us in civilian clothes, but they said they couldn't take us. We eventually got there. There had been a lot of bother. Someone said the loyalists had gone on a rampage. No one had been hurt, but everyone was frightened. There was nothing I could do, so I went on home.

"The next morning, the police came to me and questioned me about my movements the night before. I told them. A week later they came back again and questioned me some more. I gave them names of people who had seen me in Woodlands, and they went to their houses to question them. A few weeks later — I remember it was quiet around the neighborhood, and I was washing venetian blinds — the police drew up and said, 'Hester, would you like to come down to Lisburn [police station]?' And I said, 'What for?' And they says, 'Oh, we just want a wee chat with you.' So I says, 'Well, I have to collect my children at two.'

"'Oh, no problem,' they says, so they took me down there, and on false pretense. They didn't take me to the police station at all, but to a special court, and they charged me with leading a hundred men on a rampage in Lenadoon!

"Well, I wasn't sure of my rights, so I says, 'Can I make one phone call?' The lawyer got me out on my own bail and I was out for eleven months before my trial. Now my marriage was shaky anyway, and then after this I got my name in all the papers about being charged with leading a rampage, and people nearly went mad. On top of that, my dad's heart was iffy and I was trying to keep the news away from him. And Norman — that's my former husband — he was going on at a great rate. And then I got loads of obscene letters. They threatened me and the family, and I thought that was so unfair because Norman and the kids hadn't done anything, so I thought it would be better if I left them and went to Scotland. When I told Norman that, he said, 'Well, Hester, you'll not be taking the children. You regard me as a pacifist, but if you attempt to take the children, well, I'm not a violent man' — nor was he, but he spoke so quietly you didn't doubt his word — 'I'll not be responsible for what I'll do to you. And if I can't do it myself,' — he pointed towards Lenadoon — 'I'll get some of your lovely friends over there to do it for me.'

"I says, 'Well, Norman, I wasn't going to take them now. I don't know what I'll do in the future.'

"And he says, 'I'm talking about the future, and you won't be having them.'

"So I went to Scotland. I came home to Belfast every three weeks, the most I could afford. I phoned three or four times a week, wrote to them once a week, and saw them every three weeks. Then I met John. Now I was lonely and vulnerable, and I should have taken a lot more time on that relationship. I know that now. Anyway, after eleven months I went back to Belfast for my trial. It was unbelievable. At lunchtime they adjourned and took me down into the dungeons and put me in a cell with four men who were charged with me. The four guys were neighbors. They brought me food on a tray, but I couldn't have eaten a bite. I guess this policewoman meant to be kind. She said, 'You must eat.' I said, 'Well, fuck it,' and bounced the tray off her and me. So they sent for my lawyer and he got me out of there.

"They sent for the four women plus my boss's wife to come and testify in my behalf. To say I had been in Woodlands that night with them. They were terrified and nearly crying. They had to be begged to come. I'll tell you one thing: republican women wouldn't have had to be begged to come, but they had to be.

"Then the court flew some soldier all the way from Germany to say that he knew I had led the rampage. They didn't believe the women's testimony. I thought I was going mad. I told my lawyer about the two soldiers we had asked for a ride home that night. I knew their first names and that they were stationed at Aldergrove. Their commanding officer wouldn't let them out, and yet they could fly a soldier all the way home from Germany to testify about something that wasn't true! I thought I was being sawn up!

"Finally they got the soldiers out of Aldergrove and they testified on my behalf. So finally I was proved innocent. What made me mad was that in the papers it said I was charged, but it never said I was proved innocent. So that all made me feel that justice just wasn't on. I had always believed in the courts up 'til then. This was November nineteen seventy-three. I used to hear a lot of republicans complain about being charged wrongly, and I always said, 'Ha! A lot of bloody nonsense.' Now I know it's true, because it happened to me. And see, it's an awful insecure thing you are handing to your kids. You should always be able to say to your kids, 'Trust the police.' Well, I still say that to them, despite it all.

"So I went back to Scotland after the trial. I had two children by John. He's Scottish and maybe because I had thought Norman appeared weak I went for the opposite, not realizing that aggression could come back at me. He also had a drink problem. So take that combination . . . but I was determined that the second time wasn't going to fail. The failure of my first marriage was largely my responsibility, so the second time round — no way. Well, then he started to drink and go out with other women, and after we all came back to Belfast he couldn't keep a job. See, I was a common-law wife and didn't have a lot of rights. I finally had to go to court, and it was a knife fight in front of the children that brought it to a head. He pulled a knife on me.

"Everyone said, 'Why stick it?' Especially on account of where I work. [At the UDA], I mean, they were dying to do it, no problem! But I couldn't say to John and Jamie, 'Look, I had your dad beaten up.' That wasn't the answer. So I took him to court, and now I've gone back to work."

I asked Hester how she first began to work for the UDA.

"Well, Andy had asked me at different times to work for him, but I had always refused. Then things started getting tough, my marriage was breaking up, and I started working part-time. It helped me keep my sanity, and gradually I became more aware, read more, got more into the problems. I was lifted with Andy and a group of them five years ago. Seemingly I was the first loyalist woman held under Section Twelve, which means they can keep you seven days before they release you. They had raided headquarters and found old ammunition and some papers around the office and books that could have been used in help with terrorism. Anyway, they lifted Andy on the Wednesday, and on the following Monday morning they came for me . . . two policemen at the door.

"They took me and threw me in a cell, took my handbag; they would take me out and interrogate me for two hours, back to the cell for two hours, back to interrogation:

"'Your boss is charged. The UDA is now nonexistent. Your wee ones are threatened.' Anything they could think of to intimidate me. It wasn't the army doing it, it was the RUC. They even took my shoes away. 'Why?' I asked. 'So's you won't beat yourself.'

"'Do *what!*'

"'In case you beat yourself.'

"Then they started in about my having been a dancer. 'Did you dance for the UDA?' they asked, trying to make it dirty, you know. I would get so bored in the cell I wished they would interrogate me, just to break the monotony. Andy and the rest were charged. He had to go on bail, and we had to move to these offices."

Andy had returned to his office by this time and joined our conversation, keeping up a free-flowing political commentary. He is very genial and relaxed, and there was a lot of easy bantering between him and Hester.

"We have four women working here now," Hester continued. "That's some improvement."

"Weemen create problems for themselves," Andy said. "They won't stand up to the men. They have no self-confidence."

"But that's not only in the UDA," Hester contended. "In the loyalist community you would get that attitude in any shop or factory. Our women still have to learn to stand up and be counted. And to win respect for themselves."

I asked Andy if there were many women in the UDA.

"I'd like to have more."

"Are there women making decisions here?"

"I'd like to have more doing that, too. I'm going to set up a course for weemen in the organization. The weemen we have are under their local commands. They are all volunteers. All the men volunteer too. No one here is salaried, including me. Some of them work and volunteer on their days off, others are on the dole. The basic core of the organization is ten thousand, but only about three hundred are active. Ordinary people here don't know what the UDA thinks. People expect too much. Promises are made and not kept. Change comes slowly. People want jobs, holidays, a car, and a house. But there are traditional patterns they think they must keep: they must go to church, they must parade on July Twelfth. I hate parades."

The afternoon light was fading. Andy stood up to switch on a desk lamp, and I got up to leave.

"Send me your book," he called after me.

I forgot to ask him why he calls women "weemen."

The drive to Iris and Peter Robinson's house takes you through East Belfast, over the Albert Bridge, right past UDA headquarters, and through a poor, scruffy neighborhood of tiny, red-brick row houses, many churches, shops, small business agencies, car-rental offices, filling stations. Gradually the neighborhood takes on a more prosperous air. The houses grow larger, the shops bigger, and finally suburbia meets the city. Handsome brick and stucco houses surrounded by large, pleasant lawns give the area the look of a prosperous English small town: neat, unimaginative, and conforming.

As I drove up the hill on their street, I saw a huge Union Jack flying from a tall flagpole in front of a large white stucco house. With its green tiled roof and wide drive, it looked more Southern Californian than Northern Irish. I wondered, as I parked in the driveway, where a working-class Northern Irish politician obtained the money for a house like that. (Mrs. Robinson told me later that the previous owner had gone bankrupt and they had gotten it "cheap.")

I rang the bell and it was answered immediately by Mrs. Robinson. (She could see me coming from a television monitor inside the front door.) A friend of mine in Belfast had said to me that morning, when I mentioned my date with Iris Robinson: "Be sure and tell me what she is wearing. She's the best-dressed woman in Belfast!" That didn't fit with my image of a respectable Protestant loyalist woman, but it turned out to be a fair assessment. She appeared at the door looking as pretty and as well-turned-out as any fashion model. Tall and slim, with long brown hair (stylishly curly) and an expert makeup job, she was wearing a mustard-yellow silk blouse with a sleeveless sweater, purple tweed pants, flat shoes, and gold hoop earrings. Gransha Road could have been Fifth Avenue.

Cordial but cool, she led me through a handsome, large foyer into a lovely, modern pine kitchen, which looked out over a long, green lawn. Everything was spotless. Protestant puritanism may have been thrown out the window when it came to clothes and makeup, but Mrs. R. was holding her own on the domestic front.

We took coffee and cookies on a tray into the library, lined on one side with books and on the other with pictures of Peter in various political guises; a large Union Jack also hung there. We sat on a comfortable leather sofa and chair. Iris Robinson is not one of your floral-rug Unionists. A chess set and a guitar propped up against the wall were the only signs of habitation in the room.

Peter Robinson is a longtime supporter, colleague, heir apparent, and — some say now — aggressive rival of Ian Paisley. He has the reputation of being an immovable bigot, trained in Paisley's vindictive rhetorical style. He has been a vocal opponent of the Anglo-Irish Agreement, and, as a protest gesture, he led a loyalist mob on a provocative march across the border into the Republic of Ireland, where they attacked a police station and beat up on the local Guarda (police). He was duly photographed, interviewed, arrested, tried, and heavily fined. As a publicity stunt, it added notoriety to his already simmering reputation.

Robinson has brought new organizational and political skills to the DUP. He won his seat in Westminster in 1979, defeating William Craig in a well-organized campaign. Intelligent, articulate, and shrewd, he calculates his moves to be in a position to take over Paisley's reins whenever that old war-horse is put out to pasture.

Iris Robinson is representative of a new breed of Protestant loyalist women. She doesn't mince words. She feels hostile and defensive; she's angry about the Anglo-Irish Agreement and eager to initiate confrontation about it. She, like Ethel Smyth in County Down, is disgusted with what she calls a "lack of fire" on the part of more cautious male politicians.

She comes from a working-class background and grew up in a housing development in East Belfast. Her father, who was English, died when she was seven, and much of the responsibility of bringing up her sister and four brothers fell on her shoulders. "I didn't resent it," she said. "I always loved working in the house."

Obviously a perfectionist, she says she would far rather do her housework herself than have help from a man who would "do it badly."

She met Peter at a technical college. "He was very popular. All the girls were chasing him, so I decided my best technique would be to play hard to get. It worked."

Robinson was interested in politics right from the start of their marriage. He heard one of Ian Paisley's speeches and thought: "That's the man for me."

The pervasive fear in Northern Ireland, which Mrs. Robinson shares with other militant loyalists, is that the nationalists will force a united Ireland on the Protestant community. "That's their goal," she said. "And the Anglo-Irish Agreement is just the forerunner to eradicating the border. Article I of the Agreement says Britain won't let the Protestants be pushed into an agreement they don't want, but in Eire they say they already have their foot inside the door.

"You see, they're just playing with numbers. They say they will follow the majority wishes, but the minority can become the majority very soon. The British government lets citizens of Eire vote in Northern Ireland after they establish a short-term residency. Well, they could just come across the border, move in with a friend or relative, establish residency, and then vote. That would change the numbers game."

She was warming up to her subject, speaking rapidly, pointing her finger and tapping the arm of her chair for emphasis.

"I'll tell you something else. I'm annoyed, very annoyed, that a foreign government would have a say in the running of my country. Britain, Eire, and the United States. Now if *you*" — pointing her finger at me — "were perfect, if everything ran perfectly in your country, maybe you could tell us what to do.

"There is a big Irish-American vote in the United States. They have a fantasy of freeing Ireland from foreign involvement. Bigots here are only too happy to promote that in the United States. The Anglo-Irish Agreement is an agreement by the United States and Britain. The United States will promise Britain money and aid provided that Mrs. Thatcher supports the Agreement.

"Catholics here are better off than Catholics in Eire. Protestants in the South have dwindled in number; it's a Catholic country and wants Rome's dominance, but when the Protestants here want to be united with England, then it's called bigotry. The Catholic Church in Ireland tries to tell its people what to do. Like the divorce referendum. Now I personally don't believe in divorce. Scripturally it isn't allowed, except in cases of adultery. But they forced the divorce referendum down their throats.

"The border is a frontier. Eire is a foreign country. It could be a friendly foreign country, but now it is an enemy foreign country because it can extradite wanted murderers, and because it is a Catholic Ireland. Why, they even sent an envoy to Rome to report on the Anglo-Irish Agreement!

"Our school system here is segregated. The DUP believes in integrated education. You can't talk about reconciliation until children go to school together. Ecumenism? The Church of Rome sees itself as the only true church; how can you have ecumenism if they believe that? Protestants just wouldn't take it from their churches. We don't make an issue about contraception, either. It's all a personal choice. All churches are against abortion, but some people should be entitled to it, in certain circumstances."

I asked Iris if she and her husband agreed politically on all major issues.

"I'm one hundred percent behind Peter on everything, and I give him his freedom to be out as much as he wants to or needs to. We don't socialize at all. I have two close girlfriends, and I might go to one of their houses for an evening. The DUP has a lot of social functions, especially around Christmastime, so we have to go to those. Neither of us smokes or drinks.

"I was so incensed at the betrayal I felt by the Agreement. For the first time ever, I participated in demonstrations, protests, and of course I signed our petition to the Queen. [Anti-Agreement Protestants in the North signed a petition to Queen Elizabeth stating that Mrs. Thatcher had gone over the heads of the majority of Northern Irish citizens in signing the Agreement.] If our petition is rejected, no one is to blame if there is a bloodbath. Terrorism is still rampant here, don't forget. And Eire won't send our terrorists back. They will get their pound of flesh, such as a three-judge court, before they agree to sign the extradition treaty. A friendly neighbor would concede extradition to help its neighbor, but Eire isn't a friendly neighbor.

"Now it's in my interest to have peace in Northern Ireland. I have children — they are fourteen, eight, and four — and I want a peaceful world for them. And I don't want to be called a bigot. The media has projected a dreadful image of Northern Ireland. The Protestant schools have a priest on their boards; they have a voice in the running of the school. But Catholic schools don't have a Protestant on their boards. The Catholics have the SDLP running down to Dublin to represent their interests. It's farcical to think that we have any input in our government here. The Agreement is John Hume's baby. It left Unionists out in the cold. But our two leaders will up the ante; the rates [tax] protest was effective. The DUP is also supportive of resignation from council seats in protest. The Official Unionists are not united with us on this. Of course, our enemies would love to see us scattered. If we had only the DUP to lead the fight against the Agreement, we would have shown more spunk. We would have brought the country to a standstill. The power-station workers told us they wanted to 'pull the plugs.' We could have done it. We could have pulled off another nationwide strike. Of course, it's nonsense to think that we accept everything that Paisley says. We are close, but we can deal with differences in the DUP. You have so many facets in the whole Unionist crowd, for instance, men like John Taylor [Unionist member of the European Parliament and member of the British Parliament]. But we must preserve our unity now.

"Until the Agreement was signed, you didn't see Britain churning out any propaganda against Irish nationalists. Now their propaganda machine went into full swing against the Unionists for being against the Agreement. They condemn us for everything we do to protest the Agreement, but you don't hear anyone complaining about intimidation."

Her anger and frustration against Britain for what she saw as its betrayal in signing the Agreement led me to ask her why she even wanted to stay "British."

"My allegiance is to the Queen, not to Parliament!" she said emotionally, banging her hand down on the arm of the chair. "This Agreement is not a bill, not an act. It can be scrapped anytime. I will remain British as long as I breathe, and I'll take to the streets if necessary. I won't have my birthright taken away without a fight. Oh, I despise what Thatcher has done! A lot of MPs now know they have done wrong. They admit it. Why doesn't Thatcher admit that she has done wrong? I'll tell you why. American dollars, that's why. It's a vicious circle: America, Eire, Britain. Britain gets Star Wars if she can produce a united Ireland, she knows that will please the Americans, and they [the Americans] will get a NATO base out of it. If we went behind backs and spoke to the Russians, they would just love to get in here; of course, we'd think twice about that, but it's an alternative. We'll try anything. But I'm British and I'll remain British. I have no intention of living under a tricolor or Vatican Rule."

"What real difference," I asked, "would it make in your life — your own life and your family — if there were a united Ireland?"

She didn't answer.

I asked her what she felt about women participating in politics.

"We only have about a half a dozen women DUP councillors; there should be more. Letters are always coming in, asking: 'When will you give the women a chance?' I think we are a resource that hasn't been tapped. Men think women are too emotional. They write them off. That always annoys me. Women can get things into shape and get loose ends tied up. One problem is, they don't know how to get involved. I personally would love to be more involved and I am more so now than I used to be. I thought I would wait until my children are older, but the Agreement has gotten me involved. Also, my fourteen-year-old helps me at home with the younger children. He's gotten interested in politics lately and he is angry with the British establishment.

"At first, I was proud of Maggie Thatcher because she is a woman.

'Good on you, Maggie,' I thought. But now I dislike her intensely. She had to be polished and groomed. She is a woman who will never say she is wrong. She is egotistical, power-hungry. She can't recognize in her heart that she is wrong. She's arrogant and overbearing. She could have done so much. She could have brought in a woman's angle. I myself would dearly love to be involved. I'm a housewife, but I love my country. All this security that we have to have — locked doors, cameras — who needs it? We've had so many threats: wreaths sent to the house, the door kicked in, obscene phone calls ["we fancy your wife"]. Peter is very cool and calm about it all, but I long for the day when I can go out in the garden and cut my roses in peace.

"Peter is all for women in politics. So is Ian [Paisley]. His wife, Eileen, was in politics in the early days, but then everything was anti-Ian, so she retired. Now Rhonda [Ian Paisley's daughter] is aspiring. She'll stand on her own two feet; she's popular as the mayoress. [She acted as Sammy Wilson's hostess when he was Lord Mayor, since he is divorced.] I've told Ian that we should get more women involved, but you know, if I got more involved, women would be my worst enemy. It's just always been a man's world and most women think that, too.

"I used to be such a homebody, staying at home taking care of my brothers and sister, then marrying Peter and having my own family. I never really had many friends. And until the Agreement was signed, I was happy doing my own thing, and happy that Peter did his thing. Now, I'll work as hard as I can to fight the Agreement. Now I'll be outspoken! I'll not be browbeaten! I'm hurt, and I'll talk to anyone about it!" Her wide-set brown eyes flashed as she talked. "I'm a Virgo and a perfectionist. I'll not stop easily!"

Besides her family and politics, her hobby is flower arranging. But she has a secret form of relaxation which I found endearing. And totally unexpected.

"I like to put a rock tape on my car tape deck, turn it up to blare force, and drive very fast down the M1," she confessed, smiling for the first time in our interview. "I find that so relaxing. I like Bruce Springsteen. I would have loved to have heard him last summer. [He gave a concert in a small town in the Republic of Ireland.] I couldn't go, of course, because I don't cross the border on principle. I haven't been there since nineteen sixty-eight, except for Peter's trial this year."

I told Iris that with her strongly held political beliefs and her articulate manner, she should consider seriously going into politics. "You are a natural politician," I told her, although I'm not sure she is one whom Northern Ireland needs at the moment.

She smiled again and seemed to like the idea, but then she made another startling confession. "My real ambition is *not* to be a politician," she said. "I really want to be an articulated-lorry driver." [Articulated lorries are huge trailer trucks.] "I plan to take my advanced driver's test soon. I really like good, fast driving."

The world is full of surprises.

One thing that strikes me about most of the Protestant women I talk to in Northern Ireland is that they deny with varying degrees of intensity that they are "feminists," and yet, by any standard, many are. It is as if they believe that if they avow feminist values, they are admitting failure as good, Ulster Protestant women. As in so many other aspects of their lives, the reality of the present has caught up with them and surrounds them, but they either can't see it or don't like to admit it.

Lady Kinahan is, by my standards, a feminist. She is outspoken in her views. She is a talented artist and has published one novel and finished another. And yet she denies being a feminist. "I'm not even sure what a feminist is!" she laughed.

Sir Robin and Lady Kinahan have retired to a cottage on the grounds of their family home, Castle Upton, the oldest castle in Northern Ireland. They bought the castle twenty-five years ago when it was derelict and spent two decades trying to restore it to its original beauty.

"It is the most historic house in Northern Ireland," Lady Kinahan said. "We just couldn't bear to see it falling apart, so we bought it and thought we would take a rattle at it. We tried to get it back to the bones of what it was meant to be, but we couldn't afford to do it up the way it had been."

Their son lives in the castle now, and they live in comfort in their smaller house, with a big, modern kitchen and a bright floral-and-chintz living room. Lady Kinahan's art gallery is on the second floor. She is also a skillful needlewoman and has made fourteen petit point covers for dining room chairs and was just finishing the fifteenth while we sat and talked.

"I'm fed up with it now," she laughed. "This is the last! I also make all my own clothes and every curtain, pelmet, and chair cover in the house. There just isn't time to do everything. I like doing buttonholes sitting in front of the fire if the light is good. You can do small things like that in company."

A pretty woman with graying hair and sparkling brown eyes, Lady Kinahan was rather stiff and formal when we met, but warmed up as we talked. A giant schnauzer named Fred took one uninterested sniff of my boots, then curled up in front of the fire to sleep through the interview. A tiny miniature schnauzer puppy named Albert, who was about the size of Fred's head, nibbled steadily on my pencil, notebook, sweater, and anything else that came his way. "They are named after exiled Austrians of royal birth," Lady Kinahan explained. "The standard is the common sheepdog in Austria. The giants make good guard dogs because they don't actually eat people, they just sit on them. Over here, they think Fred is a Kerry blue, and they *do* bite, so people are terrified of him.

"I'm a naval daughter," Lady Kinahan continued. "My father comes from the South of Ireland. His family were sent over in eleven ten to subdue Ireland, intermarried with the Desmond family, and owned so much land that the English came over and took it all away from them again. However, they went on living there, near Limerick. We are very proud of our ancestor Hussey de Burgh, who was in Grattan's Parliament and tried very hard to make the English allow the Catholics to be members of Parliament. And the English wouldn't.

"I came to Northern Ireland after the war [World War II], and I realized that it was where I belonged, and I never wanted to go away again. I had always felt a stranger in England. When I came here, I discovered what it meant to be on the same wavelength with other people. I laughed at the things they laughed at, and shared the same attitudes. People were friendly and sincere and meant what they said. When they said, 'Do come and see us,' they were delighted when you came, whereas in England when they say, 'Do come and see us,' they are appalled if you show up!

"So I am very pro-Ulster. My mother comes from Ulster. I met my husband two or three years after I first came; we were married in Belfast Cathedral, and we've got along very well ever since. Eventually my parents moved over here, too.

"Robin asked me when we were married if I wanted to live in the country or the city, and I couldn't think why *anyone* would want to live in a town. I couldn't live in a town! He was an alderman and businessman and eventually became Lord Mayor of Belfast, and I had never been exposed to civil life at all. It was a total and complete mystery to me."

I asked if she enjoyed her duties as the wife of a civic leader.

"No! Not at all. But I did it dutifully. Bits I enjoyed. I enjoyed making speeches; I liked writing my own speeches and saying what I thought. You have to say something to make them listen. Once I was asked to speak at the opening of a Cruelty to Animals project, and I began by saying, 'There are far too many loose bitches in Belfast!' That got them listening!

"I'm very glad you are writing this book about Northern Ireland," she said. "The misconception of Northern Ireland in America is appalling. Also in England. *And* in the Republic. They never come north. My relatives in the Republic came up to my wedding and that is the only time they have ever come here. It's just extraordinary. They felt that the hunting was poor, the racing was poor, and they didn't play golf, so there was nothing to come up here for!

"Do you go to the South often?" I asked.

"We used to go down a great deal, and everyone I know used to go down for the hunting and for the Dublin Horse Show, and I liked to go to Connemara or Donegal to paint. I've had three exhibitions in the South. Alas, with each exhibition I had, I had problems getting my money. They were very dishonest. I won't mention any names, but they are well-known galleries.

"I have always painted. For four years in London I did book illustrations, then portrait painting. Had my first picture in the Royal Academy before I was twenty-one. Then I got married and came over here, and they don't understand much about painting here. I didn't paint when I was having my children. All my creative energies went into my five children. They are grown now; the three girls are married and live in England, and one of the boys is in London. We hope our other boy will stay here. It's very much touch and go. It's hard to make enough money to keep up a house that size."

"Do you have women friends who are creative like you?" I asked.

"I find I am a bit out on a limb. My sister paints. And we are both looked upon as odd, indeed. No, there aren't very many who do these things. But our family has a strong creative thing. My husband is supportive, but of course they would all much rather you sat and listened to them, if you know what I mean. He hates it when I spend the evening typing. He is very proud that I can write a book, but he wishes that it would happen when he wasn't there. They are all the same. They want your full attention when they are there."

"Are you interested in politics?"

"Technically, we are nonpolitical, but it would be hard to be more political! Our politics are Unionist, but I wouldn't guarantee that I would vote Unionist this time. My husband had a terrific win over Paisley's right-hand man to get a seat in our local house of Parliament. That was thirty years ago. We had five recounts and he won by forty-five votes. He won almost entirely on the Roman Catholic vote. They put it out from the pulpits that he was Father Murphy's choice! He is the Lord Lieutenant now, which is a nonpolitical role, representing the Queen. So he can't take part in politics, but we certainly all think about it."

"Have you ever thought of going into politics yourself?"

"Not in the slightest! But I do a jolly good backroom job, entertaining, talking to people, and getting through to as many people as I can, unofficially. But no woman will get on in politics over here. I'm not a feminist, but . . . women are just out. They are expected to stay at home and darn the socks and that's that."

"You may say you are not a feminist, but you sound like one to me," I said.

"I do all right because my husband doesn't try to stop me doing these things. I have a good friend who is a marvelously capable girl and would have been an extraordinarily good councillor, but she couldn't get a vote at all. We are fed up with our members not going to speak in Parliament. We don't see how the English, who are totally ignorant about Ulster, are ever going to become less ignorant until they learn something from us, and learn that we aren't all Paisley or IRA. We wish the Unionists would go back and take their seats. [Unionist politicians in Northern Ireland boycotted Parliament in protest of the Anglo-Irish Agreement.] Everyone in England says how awful your Ulster MPs are, but take a look at some of the English ones!"

"What would you do then, just abstain from voting?"

"I can't make up my mind whether to abstain and risk letting in someone like Gerry Adams [the head of Sinn Fein in Northern Ireland]. I don't want to encourage them. Equally, the other ones are pretty poor. I will just have to wait and see. Our local one has a very nice voice in the choir, but he is very ineffective. He came to see us to ask us what we thought he should do, and we said, 'Go back to Parliament,' and that was three months ago and he hasn't gone back.

"You see, in England they say we should bow to the majority vote, and the majority of English people say that we should be put on to the South, but the majority of the English people don't know the first thing about Ireland. It is very well known that when Ireland is being discussed in the House of Parliament, there are never more than six English MPs in the House. Therefore, how can they possibly know what is best for us? And if our own MPs don't try to tell them? And you can't get a better type of MP here because every time you get a good one he gets murdered. So we have no platform now; not having a local Parliament, we have no young candidates coming up. So we are up against a faceless bureaucracy. They do exactly as they like and don't have to answer to anyone. Everyone I know writes endlessly to MPs, but they never get an answer."

"Have you or your husband ever felt personally under stress from the Troubles?"

"I'll tell you a funny story about that. A few years ago, an IRA 'hit list' of businessmen was found. They were listed in the order that they were to be shot. There was a lot of publicity about it at the time. So Robin pricked up his ears and said, 'I wonder who's on that list?' And he went off to his office. When he came home that evening, he said, 'Guess who was at the top of the list?'

"But there is no point in thinking about it. You are certainly not going to change your way of life. That is the first step towards giving in. I can't understand anyone going around surrounded by guards. Then you are the prisoner. Now Robin is very much loved by everyone except the IRA. Ordinary Catholics are very fond of him, and they know he is true. He has always been famous for hiring equal numbers, but the IRA doesn't take notice of things like that. They just want to bring the whole thing to a grinding halt. The people who live in the ghettos are intimidated by the IRA and they can't get away. They are having a far worse time than we are. Far worse. I would like to think that I wouldn't be subjected to their intimidation, but I know perfectly well that if they said, 'Right, we've got your son and we're going to deal with him,' you would have to be jolly brave to stand up to that.

"I feel very strongly that magnanimity is what we need, and the British government ought to be magnanimous enough to stop the Anglo-Irish Agreement, which is causing all the trouble, because the situation was just about cured before they started that, and it has put us right back. Now the English should be magnanimous enough to say, 'Right, we'll halt it while we talk,' and I think they would be staggered at the results, because it has given everyone cause to think, pause to think what values they think are worth sticking up for and what values are not worth sticking up for. And I think they would be amazed. Now the English government says 'No!' as often as Paisley does. They don't say it as loudly, but they say it just as rudely. England never sticks up for the right thing; they have more scandals in big business, more dishonesty, and more violence. I don't say it is Mrs. Thatcher's fault, but it is happening. I always say to an English MP, 'Take the beam out of your own eye before you take a whack at the mote in ours, because look at your own community and your racial violence.' We don't have that here. We have our crime, but it is entirely political. It's much less than the crime in Merseyside [the Liverpool area], and yet they treat us as if we were appalling. We get very annoyed about it. What really infuriates me is when they talk about 'out here.' I say, 'Do you mean over here?'

"Anyway, you poor thing. You've heard enough from me." She put down her needlepoint and picked up Albert. "Let me go make you a cup of tea."

Priests and Preachers

"I'm an agnostic," she told the census-taker at her door.
"Right," he said, pen poised, and then he stopped, scratched his head, and asked: "Would that be a Catholic agnostic or a Protestant agnostic?"
— PORTADOWN HOUSEWIFE

RELIGION PERMEATES NORTHERN Ireland — at least it seems that way to a visitor. Coming into Belfast from Derry, you see a maze of tiny red-brick houses made symmetrical by a straight row of chimney pots lining their roofs. Above them hangs an enormous sign saying "Belfast Still Needs Jesus." The *still* is enigmatic, but the message is clear.

Later, walking along the Shankill Road, a Protestant thoroughfare in Belfast, I stopped in a butcher shop to buy some bacon for dinner. The plastic shopping bag I was handed carried a scriptural message; one side said: "1 Peter Ch 3 V 18: For Christ also hath once suffered for sins, the just for the unjust." The other side read: "1 Timothy Ch 2 V 5: For there is one God, and one mediator, between God and men, the man Jesus Christ."

One's name, one's school, one's neighborhood, one's favorite sport identifies one's religion. Religious graffiti decorate walls and buildings. (My favorite, scrawled on a wall in a scruffy Protestant neighborhood, said: "No Pope Here!!!"; underneath someone had added a sweet riposte: "Lucky old Pope!")

Part of the ongoing debate about Northern Ireland is whether the political violence there derives from "religious differences." One often hears, "Religion has nothing to do with it." But religion has almost everything to do with it, both symbolically and realistically. Ireland has, for centuries, been a country in which religious denominations — both as powerful organizations and as channels for fervor — have played exaggerated roles. Religion has been used as a political tool to divide the population in Ulster since the beginning of the Scots Presbyterian implantation. In the seventeenth and eighteenth centuries, the snobbish theological and social attitudes of the established Church of Ireland gave the newly planted puritanical Presbyterians a deep and resentful sense of inferiority.

The Presbyterians suffered much of the same humiliating deprivations of their civil rights under the Penal Code as the Catholics. That degrading treatment lives on today in their almost paranoiac fear of being somehow "done in" or "overrun" by an "enemy." The Catholic population, having suffered similar treatment, has responded with their own hard-nosed, don't-give-an-inch republicanism. Is there a surer prescription for lasting emotional damage — either to an individual or a nation — than to inflict a harsh blow to self-esteem? In Northern Ireland, the results are predictable, obvious, and lasting.

To keep this religious cauldron bubbling, it is necessary to maintain fear and loathing at a certain temperature. That requires a skill that over the centuries dozens of heavy-handed, zealous fundamental evangelical preachers in Northern Ireland have developed. (Evangelical zealotry, however, is not unique to Northern Ireland; don't forget our very own Pat and Oral, Jim and Tammy, the Reverend Swaggart and Madman Jones. The only difference is that our American fundamentalist movement is so cheerfully greedy it has forsworn bigotry for dollars.)

Cultural and religious belligerence, combined with a heritage of primitive theological teaching that has passed for "Christian doctrine" in the North for generations, has distorted the thinking of too many Protestants. Over the decades, Belfast has spawned weird religious sects to appeal to almost any social or cultural bias. When the mainstream of Ulster Presbyterianism couldn't accept the Paisley brand of religion, he broke off and formed his own Free Presbyterians. The same thing occurred with the Plymouth Brethren, another fundamentalist Protestant sect; some of its members decided they were even more sin-free than their brothers, so they broke off and became the Exclusive Brethren.

* * *

I found that most of the Protestants I spoke with really do fear and/or dislike Catholicism, and not all are willing to put on a public face of tolerance. (And a public face is all a population needs to live side by side peacefully in a pluralist society; everyone is a fireside bigot about something or other.)

Protestants make a distinction between Catholics ("Some of them are my best friends . . .") and the Catholic Church. When pressed, they'll tell you that what they dislike is (1) the Pope; (2) the control over its people that the Church exercises; (3) the pomp and ceremony of Catholic rituals and the liturgy (although they enjoy the royal pomp and pageantry of England); (4) the "goings-on" (sex) between priests and nuns, priests and parishioners, priests and priests, and priests and possibly the devil.

Protestants honestly fear that if the North were to become united with the Republic of Ireland, the Catholic Church would try to impose its practices and beliefs on them, particularly in family and sexual matters. Given the track record of the Church in the Republic, they have good reason for their apprehension. They say: "We have nothing against Catholics. It's just that we don't want their religion inflicted on us."

This point was given enormous validity during the debate in the Republic of Ireland on the divorce referendum in 1986. There is no question that the hierarchy in Ireland influenced the outcome of that election in which the constitutional amendment was defeated; it was welcome ammunition in every anti-Catholic pulpit in the North. That vote alone damaged the work of a decade of well-meaning ecumenical gatherings in the North of Ireland.

It seems to me that the Catholic Church in the North is more fair-minded, more willing to give a little, more self-confident about its position in the country than the Protestant church. Having been the underdogs for so long, Catholics have little to lose, much to gain. They have a much more laissez-faire attitude and don't seem to search so assiduously for sinners as their Protestant neighbors. There is no Catholic parallel to Ian Paisley among the Catholic hierarchy, and one doesn't hear the virulent religion-bashing among Catholics that seems to stimulate a certain kind of Protestant mind. Roman Catholicism gives Catholics in the North an ancient, European cultural tradition that Protestants don't have. While Catholics can relax in the well-practiced liturgy of their church, the Protestants sort of have to make up their liturgy as they go along. New sects spring up with regularity in the North.

Nevertheless, it would go a long way toward lessening tensions between the two communities if the Catholic Church clarified and hardened its position toward paramilitary organizations. Its official anti-IRA stance is clear and public. It decries both the violence and the radical Marxist philosophy of the organization. But too many priests and some nuns, while publicly denouncing specific acts of violence, feel that members of the IRA have gone astray but are still "our lads." They give the IRA moral support, covertly or openly. Although the Catholic hierarchy can't discipline every nun or priest who is sympathetic to the gunmen, I think that the Catholic Church in Ireland, beginning with the Papal Nuncio in Dublin and on down the line, should take a stronger, less ambivalent lead in combatting paramilitarism.

Because both Catholic and Protestant churches are male-dominated, their influence on Northern Irish life has profoundly undermined the self-confidence and the self-esteem of women. Where religion is deeply woven into the national psyche, where major life decisions are controlled by a religious hierarchy, whether it is that of orthodox Judaism in Israel, or of Moslem fanaticism in Iran, there is a denial of women's basic rights and freedoms.

Many of the women I spoke to in the North felt more angry and frustrated with their own church in terms of their feminism than they did toward other denominations because of sectarian bigotry. Young women particularly felt that their church made no concession to feminism, and that they were treated in a condescending manner.

"Once I actually sat through a Sunday service and copied down the number of times that *he* and *him* were used, and I can assure you that if an invader from Mars had been attending that service, he would have been quite unaware that there was anyone but men in that church," a disaffected Catholic woman told me. But not all women are alienated from their religion. Many of those I talked to, particularly nuns and ex-nuns, are trying to work within the framework of their church to find a comfortable niche for themselves.

A good friend took me to meet an old and dear Protestant friend of his in County Down. After the introductions were made, he left. Over the next two hours she talked frankly and thoughtfully to me about a lot of subjects, including her views on the Catholic Church.

She is a hardworking farmer's wife who, having raised her family, works in a women's dress shop in a nearby village, a change of lifestyle that she enjoys very much. She laughingly says her husband is learning, in his own middle age, to become a good househusband. She has never traveled far afield, not even to visit Dublin. Buying trips to Belfast for the shop provide her windows to the world. Her pretty, cozy farm home bespeaks the hand of a talented homemaker. She has a modern kitchen, which was added on to the house a dozen years ago. A glorious view of the rolling Down hills stretches outside her front windows. Each of her two sons and their wives and families lives in a cottage on either side of her. She and her husband, a thin, cheerful man who looks more like an accountant than a farmer, lead a life of tranquillity. Her brother-in-law lives with them, and the three of them dote on the two neighboring grandsons. It is impossible to imagine hate or violence or bigotry entering the doors of their home or minds. They are totally without bitterness as a response to the violence they have seen going on around them for the past eighteen years. A faithful Presbyterian, she has "no time for Paisley and his crowd," although she says she does not like the Catholic Church, either.

"I have individual Catholic friends," she said, "and I like them and respect them very much, but I don't like the Pope. I don't think he should call himself an anti-Christ." I pointed out that he didn't call himself that, that it was a name long used by Catholic detractors. She seemed surprised and said she had always thought it was one of his titles!

The ideas of feminism are firmly entrenched in her character and in her life, although she might call them by a different name.

"Working women?" She smiled. "I've worked all my life, side by side with my husband, and now in my sister's shop."

"Domestic equality?"

"My husband has dinner ready to cook when I come home from work now. He's getting very good at it!"

The attitude of religion toward women?

"Well, I wouldn't mind a woman preacher."

When I recounted these views to my friend later in the car on the way home, he was surprised that she was so open with me, had actually thought of these subjects, and had views on them! I said to him, "Well, maybe you never asked her." He replied, "Oh, no, I would be afraid to. I would think that we wouldn't agree on things and then talking about them would make us uncomfortable and ill at ease with each other."

The young woman in an office in Belfast offered to make me a cup of coffee while I waited to meet her boss. While we talked, I asked her about her religious background.

"I don't mind telling you about the religion I was brought up in," she said, "but I can tell you that I left it behind me a long time ago, thank God.

"It's called Exclusive Brethren. It's a very strict sect, a real clique. It's a group that broke away from the Plymouth Brethren. When I was a child in school, we weren't allowed to mix with the other children. We couldn't even take lunch with the others; we had to bring our own lunch and sit in a separate room to eat. We were that closed in. At home we weren't allowed to play with other children on the block.

"As I got older, it seemed to me that everyone should be entitled to believe in what they want to believe in. It doesn't matter to me what you believe, as long as you believe in something. But the Exclusive Brethren are bigoted and fearful of others. When I left school and started to work, I felt as if I were two different people: the religious girl I had been brought up to be, and the real me. I knew I had to make a decision between the two, and I chose to be independent. My family totally rejected me for that. If I met one of them on the street now, they might say hello but that would be all.

"I guess I was looking for freedom. I live by myself now; I've just bought a house, and if I were to get married it wouldn't matter what he was, Catholic or Protestant; it just would not make any difference as long as he left me alone to be what I wanted to be. I like my independence. I hate this bigotry."

Ian Paisley wins hands down as the best-known religious figure to come out of Northern Ireland in this generation. Preacher and politician, founder of the Free Presbyterian Church and the Democratic Unionist Party, Paisley has done as much as anyone in Ulster to keep alive the flame of religious fear among the Protestant people. He has been unflagging, creative, and charismatic in his role of theological provocateur, playing on the obsessive suspicion that many Protestants in Northern Ireland have about Catholics.

When moderate Protestants in Northern Ireland tried to meet nationalist demands halfway in the early 1970s, the extremists felt they had their backs to the wall and wanted no part of the conciliatory measures. They found just the man to reflect their implacable bigotry, and to do it behind the "respectability" of the pulpit: the Reverend Ian Paisley. Recipient of a diploma from the Theological College of the Reformed Presbyterian Church in Belfast, Paisley with his vicious diatribes against Catholicism and his traveling vaudeville satire of "The Mass" collected large audiences. He didn't preach, he bellowed; eyes bulging, fist shaking, voice quaking, he moved his audiences to shout back "Amen!" and "Halleluja!" He even won admirers in the United States. Bob Jones III, of Bob Jones University in Greenville, South Carolina, conferred an honorary doctorate on Mr. Paisley in 1966, to commemorate the occasion of his release from prison. Straight Presbyterians couldn't quite stomach vintage Paisley, so he parted with them and began his own brand of religion, called the Free Presbyterian Church. Although there are only 10,000 followers of Free Presbyterianism, the sect has fifty-nine congregations in Ireland, England, the United States, and Australia; it runs Whitfield College, a radio station, and a publishing company. It is a highly successful enterprise, organized along the lines of the various fundamentalist American television religions.

One of the key elements in his success is Paisley's ability to play off the paranoiac fears of Roman Catholicism that seem to be almost a genetic defect of so many Ulster Protestants. He uses that fear with consummate skill, creating an emotional state of siege among people who, in reality, are leading perfectly safe, quiet, reasonable lives. Any act of republican terrorism that takes place in Northern Ireland can be put at the foot of the Catholic altar by Paisley.

The eldest of his five children, Rhonda, who lives with her parents in Belfast, is following in her father's political footsteps. She was elected a city councillor in 1985, and also serves as an unofficial hostess to the city's unmarried Lord Mayor. People in Belfast say she serves at her father's whim; others say she is strong-minded with a will of her own and writes her own script. Protestant women in Northern Ireland are even less emancipated than Catholics; the Protestant ethic for women insists on a docile, male-dominated homemaker. Those who break out of that mold are the exception. Rhonda seems to be one of those exceptions. Small-boned and thin almost to the edge of anorexia, everything about her is physically fragile, and she looks more like an American teenager than a twenty-six-year-old Belfast City Councillor. Although she studied art at Bob Jones University, she is now running a youth program for the homeless in Belfast called "Reach." Both Catholic and Protestant youths are welcome in "Reach," but Ms. Paisley, like her father, is not an advocate of Christian ecumenism. She is convinced that the Catholic Church in Northern Ireland backs the IRA, and therefore there can be no meaningful relationship between Catholicism and Protestantism in the North.

Sweet-voiced and charming with strangers, this pretty, large-eyed young woman is the same Paisley daughter who accompanied her father to St. Anne's Protestant Cathedral in Belfast when Cardinal Suenens, the former Primate of Belgium, came to preach an ecumenical service, and joined 200 other Free Presbyterians in shouting down the Cardinal as he tried to hold his service. Paisley had objected to Suenens's visit to Belfast in a letter to the Dean of St. Anne's. Quoting from a Belgian press agency, Paisley accused Suenens of presiding over a congress in Brussels in 1970, where ". . . the young delegates were dragged towards the altar. There something was beginning to rise and take on an unbelievable shape. It was at first greeted with gasps, then giggles and finally pandemonium broke loose as the transparent plastic forming the shape was seen to represent a gigantic penis. The delegates screamed themselves hoarse, feeling it was a challenge to . . . their virility. . . . Suenens, like the Pope, was not a Christian at all. Both were masters of a heathen temple where 'atavistic rites, all with sexual undertones, take the place of religion.' . . . 'When the adolescent girls shrieked with delighted embarrassment as the large plastic penis rose up before them, Cardinal Suenens knew perfectly well that they were . . . commemorating the heathen god Baal whose name . . . has several meanings. Among them are lord, master, possessor or husband, while others refer to a controlling male's penis with its forceful boring and thrusting. So what the Cardinal arranged for the young, mostly girls, of Brussels was a show of phallic worship, which symbolises the generative power contained in the semen . . . which streamed down upon all life and nature from the mighty penis of Baal.'" (Moloney and Pollak, *Paisley*, pp. 2 and 3.)

It was a beautiful, warm Easter morning and the congregation was streaming into the big, modern stone church as Maria, my American friend, and I arrived at Martyr's Memorial. All the ladies were in their Easter bonnets. It appeared to be a middle-class parish; the men in their conservative blue or gray suits looked as though they felt at home in them. There were few small children, almost no teenagers, very few young adults. The congregation was overwhelmingly middle-aged or older. Contrary to our expectations, the church remained half empty. We were met in the vestibule by an energetically friendly man who seemed to be posted there to wait for us.

"Good morning, good morning," he beamed. "You must be our visitors." He took me by the hand and led me to a guest book, which I signed, and then we slid unobtrusively into a back pew to await the arrival of the famous preacher.

The service started promptly. The Reverend Paisley walked out with great presence. His height, broad shoulders, prominent eyes, and regular features make him an impressive figure. His pulpit, more like a stage setting than a lectern, was enormous. He could stride from side to side and still remain behind it. His voice was deep, resonant, and controlled. One might be angered, frightened, or possibly repentant during his sermon, but I doubt if anyone would fall asleep. He began the service by welcoming all the visitors to the church that day, "especially our two visitors from America." Happily we were not called upon to stand up and take a bow. As the service progressed, there was much energetic singing of hymns.

One of the announcements that preceded the sermon contradicted the publicized reports that Paisley would be marching in Portadown the following day in a provocative Orange Order parade through Catholic neighborhoods in the town. He said that he would be giving a sermon as was his custom in another part of the province. He then went on to remind the women in the congregation that the church would be serving tea to hundreds of visitors that evening and he needed their help. They should remember to bring knives to spread butter on the bread. Then he made a little joke. The newspapers would carry headlines saying: "Reverend Paisley urges women to carry knives on a march down the Ravenshill Road." It got a few chuckles.

The sermon that followed more hymns and announcements was a standard Easter Sunday sermon; there were no political overtones, no Pope-bashing. Instead there was hellfire and damnation rhetoric; Paisley strode from one side of his wide pulpit to the other, lifting his arms high in the air, pointing his finger fiercely at the sparse congregation, lowering his voice to a whisper, raising it to a shout. (It is said that as a young man, Paisley used to go out by himself into the mountains and practice projecting his voice to the empty hills. One can hear the results of that practice even now.)

The sermon lasted fifty-six minutes. What with prayers, hymns, announcements, and the collection, we had been in Martyr's Memorial for over an hour and a half when the service ended. People were invited to stay on for more prayer and meditation, but we declined and left along with most everyone else. The congregation at Martyr's Memorial was mixed in gender, but the collection baskets were passed by men; the "greeters" at the door, the preacher, and the ushers were all male. The only indication women were involved in the congregation was that they were reminded to bring their knives to spread butter.

On subsequent trips to Belfast, I visited several other churches, including an Elim service, a fundamentalist Protestant sect, in a working-class neighborhood of the city, and a posh Plymouth Brethren church in central Belfast. (Ian Paisley's brother, Norman, is a Plymouth Brethren minister.) An actress friend joined me in my "church crawls," and we got ourselves dressed appropriately for Sunday services, which means a demure suit, blouse, high heels, hose, and gloves. Very 1950-ish. We didn't have hats, which more or less gave us away as "strangers," since hats are very big in Belfast Protestant churches; the bigger the church, the bigger the hat.

When we arrived, late, at the Elim congregation, everyone was in place on folding chairs, and the minister, a small, thin, young man with a rather downcast air, was already giving an earnest, soft-spoken homily. While he was speaking, a man in the front row spoke aloud softly "in tongues," which, to the uninitiated, simply sounds like unintelligible sounds. The theory is that it is the spirit of the Holy Ghost speaking through you.

A woman sitting next to me seemed to be holding her own private service; she kept her head bent, held her forehead tightly with her hand, and murmured: "Oh, you darling Jesus! Oh, you beautiful man! Oh, help me, darling, baby Jesus!" She more or less kept up this refrain throughout the service, but no one seemed to notice or mind either the man's or the woman's interjections during the main service. It was their private spiritual domain. When the minister finished, he asked for testimonials from the congregation.

Two people got up to speak, and they were straightforward and touching. A woman had had a broken love affair. She spoke of her sadness and loneliness, and said how Jesus had been a comfort to her. A man spoke about the necessity of reaching out to others who needed help, and how he took off Saturday afternoons to try to do this by preaching on street corners. Then we sang hymns from words printed on a screen in front of the pulpit while a young man played a guitar and the preacher played the organ, and finally a layman from the audience got up and gave a sermon on biblical interpretation.

To my surprise, a communion basket was passed around. Expecting it to be the collection basket, I dropped in a pound note. My friend nudged me, and I realized to my horror that the basket was full of crackers! (I had assumed that the practice of communion was too "high" for the Elims.) I retrieved the note, took a cracker, and hoped I had not disgraced myself. (Everyone else, it seems, broke off a tiny portion of a cracker as a symbolic communion wafer; I was left holding an entire Carr's Water Biscuit and had to crunch loudly for an eternity before I finished it.) Then they passed around individual thimbles of "wine," which tasted like cranberry juice. More hymns, more prayers. A pleasant, low-keyed Sunday service, with not the slightest overtone of Pope-bashing or anti-Catholic ranting. The congregation was mostly middle-aged, both men and women, few children, no teenagers. All the women were in hats, plain, small, and sensible.

We had to leave the service before it was finished to get to the big, fancy Plymouth Brethren Church across town. The street in front of the church was clogged with Mercedes, BMWs, and other new and shiny manifestations of business prosperity. The church was packed; we had to go to a seat in the upper loft. Rows and rows of hats with feathers, bows, and veils made a little jungle of color to look down upon. The men and boys were in coats and ties, women in rather frumpy, 1950s-style flowery dresses, taking advantage of what must be one of Belfast's only warm spring days.

A handsome, sleek minister, white hair coiffed and (could it be?) blow-dried, was in the middle of his sermon as we arrived. (A young woman sitting in the loft with us was repeating the sermon in sign language to a group of deaf parishioners.) The minister was urging "civil obedience" in his sermon, in an oblique manner. His voice was clear and low-keyed, his message simple and spoken with clarity and elegance. Was he actually telling his flock that they should accept the Anglo-Irish Agreement? The substance of the sermon surprised me, because I had read that the Brethren remove themselves from all forms of political activity, even to the point of not voting in elections.

A beautiful, rousing hymn ended the service. After the last verse of the hymn was finished, people poured outside into the warm sunshine, flowered and feathered hats bobbing in the breeze, a happy and smiling crowd. Several people made a point of saying hello to us on the way out. There were more men than women in the congregation. A friend in Belfast tells me that the Brethren are very good businessmen and maintain a tight and impenetrable skein of economic assistance among themselves.

As we walked through the crowd of churchgoers back to our car, I said to my friend, "Nothing we have seen or heard today fits the stereotype of Northern Irish evangelical Protestantism, although the two congregations we visited are supposed to be in that mold."

"Of course not," was her reply. "This is the way I remember churchgoing when I was growing up here." She looked at me out of the corner of her eye and grinned. "We're not all crazy here. At least, not all of the time."

Annie's Story

The belief in a supernatural force of evil is not necessary. Men alone are quite capable of every wickedness.
— JOSEPH CONRAD

THE YOUNG WOMAN'S NAME is made up, as is the name of the village. Otherwise, all the events in the story are told exactly as they happened. The woman, who I call "Annie," is tall and slim with striking good looks. Her long, straight Grecian nose and pale skin are set off by masses of auburn hair. She speaks with rapid intensity, but her spontaneous humor and breezy, informal manner lightened the shadows of the gothic tale she told me. The village, which is the setting for the story, is also lovely, a small, seaside town with a picturesque harbor full of well-kept, brightly painted fishing boats. Only the story itself is ugly, a modern-day Salem witch-hunt.

Annie had a middle-class Belfast childhood. University-educated and adventuresome, she lived abroad for five years and returned to Northern Ireland when a long love affair came to a sad end.

"I came home to start a new life for myself," Annie said, sitting beside me on the sofa in a friend's living room. "I wasn't sure what that would be, but I knew one thing for sure: it wouldn't include a man again!"

She wanted to live out of Belfast, to find a pretty little village and settle in it. She didn't want to be part of village life, she is far too sophisticated for that, but she sought the peace and quiet of the countryside and she also loves the seashore. Her best friends, a couple she had known from university days, suggested that she come out one weekend and look over their village. Annie loved "Ballylittle" the minute she saw it. It wasn't too far from Belfast; her city friends could easily come for weekends. It had all the ingredients she was looking for, and it also had an intriguing house for sale right in the center of the village — a beautiful eighteenth-century Georgian house, derelict but with great possibilities, perhaps as a bed-and-breakfast business or an antique shop. She could swing the cost if she did most of the restoration work herself. She wasn't a do-it-yourselfer, but that was no deterrent. She would learn. Within a month, the house was hers, and she loved it. She had no money left over for furniture, just enough in her checking account for her one essential: a stereo system.

And, as luck would have it, the man who owned the stereo shop in Belfast was free that weekend to come to Ballylittle and deliver it. One thing led to another, and happily — and predictably — Annie did not stick to her resolution to give up men. But that isn't part of this story.

She moved into the house. Everything needed to be redone, repaired, restored. The garden and the outbuildings were as derelict as the house, so there were months and months of hard, ten-hour-a-day work. The men in the hardware shop in Ballylittle were enthusiastic purveyors of advice, amused and impressed that a lone woman had moved into their village and was taking on the renovation of the big house. They dispensed tips on painting, plastering, plumbing, plowing. Her newfound Belfast friend began coming down regularly on weekends. He, too, proved to be a talented handyman, particularly in the garden. By summertime, there were homegrown vegetables. Annie would usually go into the city one or two nights during the week for a movie or the theater and an evening with her boyfriend. Things were progressing very nicely. The unhappiness of the failed love affair was fading.

Annie's parents had originally been aghast at the purchase of the house. They thought it needed too much work, and that she was just pouring money down the drain. So after a year's work, she had an enormous family party: parents, brothers and sisters, an uncle . . . fifteen in all came and stayed in the house. Everyone was impressed by the beautiful home that Annie was creating.

As this idyllic restoration progressed, things were not totally tranquil in Ballylittle. I should mention at this point that Annie had been brought up as a Catholic, although she no longer practices her religion. Ballylittle is a Protestant town, through and through. Maybe 100 percent. Now how the good citizens of Ballylittle knew that Annie had been baptized a Catholic — and knew it on the day she moved into her house — is a mystery understood only by born-and-bred citizens of Northern Ireland. During the first night she spent in the house, some local worthies crept through the sleeping village and daubed slogans on the front of her house. Nothing very clever or threatening, just old hackneyed phrases like "Taigs Out." They also broke a few windows for good measure. (Annie was sleeping on a mattress in the front room and the glass fell all around her.)

"My loving neighbors," she remembered thinking, getting up to sweep away the shards of glass. But Annie is not a woman of frail resolve. She simply ignored her nighttime visitors and made no attempt to wash off the paint. That was annoying. No one likes to be ignored. So they came back the next night and painted on "UDA" and "UVF." That stayed put, too.

"I figured if I left on the slogans, most of the people in the town would be embarrassed and would make whoever was doing it stop," Annie said. The following summer Annie painted the exterior of the house, covering up all of the slogans. Then they began kicking in the door.

"I guess the front door got kicked in a dozen times. I finally had to buy a new one. They wouldn't come in, or try to steal or anything. They would just smash in the door. I'll tell you, it's bloody frightening to be in a big house alone at night and have someone kick in your door. I would be terrified and phone the police, and they would come round, but of course no one would be there. I finally barricaded the front door and went in and out of the back. And then the first July Twelfth that I was there, they smashed the bottom windows and daubed more slogans. Then they stood outside and banged their lambeg drum until half-four in the morning!"

"Did your neighbors say anything to you the next morning?" I asked.

"No. You see, I knew this was a Protestant village when I moved here. My friends who live here, the couple who told me about the house in the first place, may be the only Catholics here. But no one bothers them!"

"Why?" I asked. "Why you and not them?"

"A mystery," Annie smiled. "Known only to the citizens of Ballylittle!

"So I thought, well, I'm a woman living alone here, in the 'big house' of the village, and maybe they just have to get used to me. And I thought: I am *not* going to have my choice of a place to live dictated by bloody fucking sectarian politics in Northern Ireland! I was determined to stick it out.

"I guess I was out of touch. Remember, I had been living out of the country for five years before I came here, and before that I had lived in Belfast and had gone to Queens University. Most of my friends just don't have those entrenched, narrow views. And also, the people in the village were friendly to me at first. I'd act like the village idiot in the hardware store and they would tell me how to install my kitchen sink. I wasn't looking to make bosom friends here. I import my own friends, but I wanted to live here, buy my food, be a good citizen, and all I wanted in return was for people to speak to me in the streets and be nice and friendly in the shops. I knew they wouldn't take me into their homes, because in villages people don't do that. You have to be born there. Since I wanted to lead my own life and not have everyone know my business, that suited me fine. A lot of people told me they were delighted I was fixing up the old house. It had been an eyesore for so long.

"My parents knew that the harassment was going on, but what could they say? They hadn't wanted me to go there in the first place. My mother said, when she first saw the town: 'It's very Protestant.' Well, I was brought up with Protestants. There were six of us in the family, and my father wanted a big house, and all the big houses in Belfast are in Protestant neighborhoods. But my mother said: 'Well, *our* neighbors don't paint their curbstones red, white, and blue!" (A loyalist tradition in Northern Ireland, particularly on special holidays, like July 12.)

"'Oh,' I said to my mother, 'you're just being a snob. You think it's all right to live with middle-class Protestants but not with working-class ones!' As it turned out, she was quite right!"

Sometimes Annie's neighbors would call the police if her door was smashed in and she wasn't home. (It happened with numbing regularity.) And one neighbor explained to her many times that it wasn't sectarian in origin, it was just hooligan vandalism. Annie wanted to believe that. She wanted to think that she was singled out for persecution because she was a new face in town and that eventually they would get used to her and she would just fade into the scenery.

"I think that might have happened," Annie said, "except that the Anglo-Irish Agreement was signed, and then everyone started looking for a scapegoat. Halloween and July Twelfth rolled around again, and both were bad times. I really felt like I was just sitting there under siege. I think — looking back on it now — that I didn't realize how terrified I was at the time. You tend to adapt, you know. The bizarre seems to be the norm.

"Well, finally one night, someone threw a petrol bomb in my window. I was around the corner, visiting my mates, the Catholic couple, but it looked as if I was there because I had left the lights on. One room was totally destroyed, the room where I lived. And one of my chickens was killed!

"There was a fellow in town who had put in a new ceiling for me; he had the Red Hand of Ulster tattooed on his arm, and yet he was the one who called the fire brigade that night, ran to my friends to tell me about the fire, and then physically restrained me from dashing into the burning house — now, maybe that was because he knew there were still guys in there and he didn't want me to see them! But nevertheless, he stood underneath the burning floorboards with a hose, trying to put the fire out. Then later he was 'lifted' by the police for being a suspect. Well, I don't think he was. I think he had a heart of gold and was truly trying to help me. There are, after all, good people in the village!

"Anyway, I started putting the place back in order. I got bulletproof windows; as far as I was concerned, I was going to keep living there. The bastards weren't going to get me out with one petrol bomb! But I also decided that I had better find out who had done it and whether or not I was in any serious danger. So a friend of a friend contacted someone in the UVF to find out if they had a hand in it.

"One night, late, I heard a knock on the door, and a voice from the other side said: 'Can we come in and talk to you? We're from East Belfast.' Oh, my heart sank. 'This is it!' I thought. 'They've come for me.' I ran upstairs to try to look at them out of a window, and one of them yelled: 'Are you still there?' and I said: 'Yes, I went upstairs to try and look at you out the window,' and he said: 'Oh, we thought you had gone to phone the police.' It was a crazy conversation!

"'Listen!' he said. 'We'll back out into the middle of the street so you can see us under the streetlight,' so I ran back upstairs and looked out and there they stood, waving up at me. I mean, if they had had a gun, they could have put it in their pocket! It was getting to be more like a Tom and Jerry cartoon than an encounter with a terrorist organization! So I waved down at them, and then ran downstairs and opened the door. I thought at the time it might be a foolish thing to do. You are always reading about prison officers or policemen who open their doors to a stranger and get a stomach full of bullets, and you think what fools they were, and here was I ready to do the same thing.

"Anyway, I let them in. One was a hood type, but the other was very respectable and charming. Charismatic, really. He was the Big Cheese from Belfast. They came into my kitchen and introduced themselves. 'We're from the UVF in Belfast,' they said, and I thought: 'Oh, no, this isn't happening to me. I'm not standing here in my kitchen shaking hands with these two individuals who tell me with a straight face that they are members of the UVF!' Well, they stayed about a half hour. The Big Cheese was totally charming. He thought it was terrible what was happening to me. He said they wouldn't condone it, and as far as they were concerned they couldn't care less whether or not I was Catholic or Protestant or Hindu. I had just as much right to live here as anyone else. And they would see that it didn't happen again. They would put the word around; they would tell people. This house would be protected from now on, and if I ever had the *slightest* bit of trouble, I was just to call them, and they would sort it out. He gave me his telephone number."

"Did you believe him?" I asked.

"Oh, yes! He told me to tell people that he had been around to see me, to let them know. Well, I thought it was just great. Slept like a log that night. Even caught myself thinking: 'See, this is what these organizations do; they protect innocent people! My house is now under UVF protection!' You see, it doesn't take long to come around to that way of thinking.

"The next day it seemed to me that people in the village gave me strange looks, and I thought: 'They know! Good!' Well, I was okay for about five days. And then my contact reported back that *his* contact had found out that Ballylittle was a *UDA* village! And so the UVF couldn't promise anything. 'Does it fucking matter?' I asked. So my contact then went to the UDA and asked if my protection could be arranged, but they said they couldn't promise anything because it was known that I had 'republican' visitors. Well, I have friends from the South who visit, naturally. But I am not involved in politics and never have been. So I felt totally persecuted then. I could hardly tell my friends not to come and visit because they were 'suspect' in Ballylittle.

"Then the final blow fell: I got a letter saying that the next time they burned the house they would be sure that I was in it, because they didn't want any Fenian [Catholic] bitches in Ballylittle. So that was it. I sold the house and left."

"Could you sell it to anyone, after all the things that had happened to you there?" I asked her.

"If the police say a place is too dangerous to live in, the government will buy it. But they only gave me a pittance. And now it's worse than it was, empty and derelict, just sitting there like the old eyesore it was. It's totally obscene. I went back in July to get my stuff out of the place, and I thought I wasn't going to get out alive. The yobs were sitting on a wall across from the house and screamed obscenities at us; a friend had come with me. He's six foot eight, and he offered to go speak physically to the guys on the wall, but I said no, leave it. I just wanted to get out of there."

Annie moved out of her house in 1986. She still visits Ballylittle occasionally to visit her old friends who live there. They are trying to sell their house, also, but haven't yet. I asked Annie if anyone in the village ever told her they were sorry for all the turmoil she was put through.

"No, no one did. Right after the firebombing, they were sympathetic, but then one by one they stopped speaking to me. It was a survival instinct; they didn't want to alienate the local boys."

We talked about the reasons why Annie might have been chosen as a target for such unrelenting persecution; the other Catholic family in the village had not been forced to endure such blatant sectarian harassment.

"Do you think it was because you were a woman living alone, with a boyfriend who came down to spend weekends with you?" I asked.

"No! Absolutely not. Anyway, most of the people in the village thought he was my brother."

"What about the fact of you — a Catholic — buying the 'big house' of the village?"

"I don't think so. I really think most people were glad to see it getting fixed up. It had been empty a long time and was an eyesore. No, I think I was just in the wrong place at the wrong time. Or — the only other thing I could think of — I have a long-dead relative who was a famous Irish politician. Maybe someone knew that — but how could they know? — and spread the word and I was a target for 'revenge.' You know how the Irish are about ancient grudges! But honestly, I really don't know. I never will."

When Annie made the trip back to Ballylittle with a borrowed van to get the last of her things from the house, she found that most of them had burned in the firebombing, but her treasured mug collection was still intact, plus some clothes, books, and her family christening shawl. She packed up her few possessions, put them in the van, and drove back to Belfast. En route she stopped to do an errand in another village, and during the short time that she was away from the van, it was broken into and all her things were stolen! The fitting epilogue to a long, sad saga.

"I really don't think about it," Annie said. "This is the first time I have sat down and told anyone the whole story. It's just too painful. I try to put it out of my mind. Like Scarlett O'Hara in *Gone With the Wind*, I'll just think about that later! I'm living with my boyfriend now, and I have a job. But it takes a long, long time for those experiences to be erased from your mind."

Somehow, Annie's story bothered me more than almost any of the other gothic tales I have heard from women in Northern Ireland. It wasn't a life-shattering tragedy; Annie is young, well-educated, and strong-willed. She will make a new life for herself. I think it was the unrelenting meanness, the cheap and tawdry bigotry — carried out with such blatant acceptance by the entire village — that makes the story so malign. The more I thought about Ballylittle, the more eager I became to see it for myself, to look at Annie's empty house, and walk the streets of the village, to see and hear what the people there are like. It wasn't many days after I talked to Annie that I found myself driving in the general direction of Ballylittle. A fifty-mile detour would put me right in the town! Anyway, it was a beautiful day for a drive. The sea was in sight for much of the way, and mountains rose darkly in the distance. The fickle sunshine gave way to a heavy, quick spring shower, then made a majestic reappearance, lighting up the sides of the mountains. A yellow, gorse-covered fence running along the side of the road lined the steeply banked field on my right, and hundreds of black-faced, horned sheep grazed peacefully in the lush, green grass. New spring lambs clung close to their mothers' legs.

Suddenly, I saw the sign, "Ballylittle." I swung off the highway and drove slowly toward the center of the village. I had a strange feeling of déjà vu as I drove; everything seemed so familiar, from Annie's vivid descriptions, and yet I knew I had never been there before. But I knew where everything was going to be: the hardware shop where the men had been so helpful; the corner butcher; the chemist's shop . . . and then I saw her house, unmistakable. Burnt-out and trashed, just the way she had left it, with the windows smashed in and the whitewashed front wall covered with graffiti. The front door was boarded up, but I peered in through one of the broken windows. The room was in shambles from fire, smoke, and water damage.

I felt odd and slightly furtive poking around the empty house, as if unseen eyes were watching me from curtained windows up and down the street (which they well may have been!). I walked away from the house and through the small main business street of the village, noting, as Annie had described it, how pretty and well-kept it was, with much more charm than most Northern Irish towns. A friendly, talkative man was working on a car in an outside garage and chatted with me about the weather and the fishing in the area. I entered a small tea shop for a bite of lunch, an immaculate, bright room decorated with blooming plants. I ordered tea and a scone, and as I ate, the woman behind the counter chatted with me. Soon a middle-aged man came in and ordered fish and chips. He had a very red face and a very large midsection, and he talked with great animation about trivial, local matters. He and the owner of the shop indulged in good-natured banter, with me as an appreciative audience. They were both clearly curious about the reason for my being there, and asked many circuitous questions before I relented and told them I was a writer and might write a piece about their town. And I added that I thought it was very pretty, with its brightly painted house fronts and window boxes.

"Aye," the man said, pleased. "It's a nice wee place."

"Everything here is so neat and clean," I said, "so I wondered about that big, burnt-out house with the smashed-in windows. Kind of an eyesore, isn't it?"

Instantly the woman behind the counter disappeared without a word into the kitchen, and the man, so gregarious and friendly, found that his fish and chips took all of his concentration. I tried once more.

"Whose house is it?"

"There was a woman who lived there alone," the man answered curtly. "She was trying to repair the house herself and had an electrical fire. It burned her out. She gave up on it and went back to Dublin. She never came back."

He got up, paid his bill, and left. He didn't say anything else to me, and the woman behind the counter never reappeared. I finished my tea, paid the young girl who was minding the cash register, and followed the fat man out. As I passed Annie's house again, on the way to my car, I stopped to take some pictures of it, and while I was standing on the other side of the street, camera poised, I saw a young man running down the empty street toward me. For one second I froze. Oh, my God! I thought. They know why I'm here! The young man was swinging something in his hand — a club, I thought, to knock me over the head! Could I get to my car in time? What kind of a crazy place is this? Within a second, the boy was alongside of me, smiling, and holding out my umbrella, which I had left in the tea shop!

"I thought I wouldn't catch ye," he said, out of breath. "The sun is shining now, but you'll need this before the day is out." He turned and walked back up the street. I sighed and fumbled for my keys, turned the car around in the narrow street, and headed back out to the highway.

Ballylittle. Such a pretty town.

Beyond Politics

Does the road wind up hill all the way?
Yes, to the very end.
Will the day's journey take the whole long day?
From morn to night, my friend.
— CHRISTINA ROSSETTI, *"Up Hill"*

RADICAL PERSPECTIVES

A WEEK IN LATE MAY brought summer to Belfast. During the warm days, parks and lawns were filled with people baking their pale, Northern skins into a sore and unfamiliar pink. The night before, the members of Charabanc, a women's theater company in Northern Ireland, invited four guests to dinner. We sprawled out in summer dresses and cotton pants on blankets and rugs in the tall grass of the back garden, where we lined up bottles of cold white wine and settled down for a long talk about politics and feminism.

Two of the guests were Eileen Evason, small, dark, and intense, and Marie Mulholland, the epitome of the "Big, Strong Woman" (a song that she belts out with startling energy and volume). Eileen is a senior lecturer in social administration at the University of Coleraine and a popular commentator for the BBC in Northern Ireland. Marie is a dedicated community worker in West Belfast, one of the prime movers behind the effort to destroy and replace the infamous Divis Flats. Both women are committed feminists and articulate critics of the political, social, and economic structures of Northern Ireland, although they disagree radically on the potential fusion of feminism, republicanism, and socialism. They both are also bright, feisty, and funny, qualities that leaven their anger and frustration.

"Look," Eileen said, when I asked her why so few women were active politically in the North, "the political parties here are allied with the different components of a civil war, which consigns women to a particular role. This is not a proper political struggle. We would expect feminism and socialism to be raised in a normal conflict, and this isn't any of those things. People fail to recognize that in the conflict in Northern Ireland all the combatants are fascists. This has a number of implications. Radical women are quiet because they can't get into the debate. How do you get into a debate between the IRA and the UVF!

"The first problem is the peculiar and distorted nature of the conflict. It is *not* about are we going to have a thirty-two-county socialist republic. It is essentially about which group of fascist men we are to be ruled by — fascist men from London, Dublin, or Belfast. I'm not terribly fussed about that. Our women are excluded from that debate because feminism encompasses socialism and it also encompasses other important issues, which are nuclear disarmament and ecology. The border is pretty small beer by comparison; so are the kinds of things which preoccupy feminists here.

"That's a primary problem. The other aspect is that in Northern Ireland radical women go. They leave! Large numbers of women have left, everyone with radical perspectives. So we have this situation with a province with one and a half million people, and within that context we have to run the whole apparatus of a state. That has implications for the rest of us. For instance, if you are in women's aid, you don't just work locally, you have to work nationally, getting housing policy legislated and so on. So radical perspectives don't get a hearing here.

"And thirdly, the few of us who are left are doing an incredible amount. It's just a threadbare place here now, so many have left. If you have firm ideas about how a society should look, it would be hard to stay in Northern Ireland!"

I asked Eileen, who is English-born, why she came to Northern Ireland.

"I came here for work. Most people leave here for work! I come from Birmingham and was twenty-two years old and was offered a lectureship at Queens. I went up later to Coleraine.

"I think women are keeping the place going here. They are having the most creative ideas, the most creative political thinking. They are involving themselves in a whole range of things. Now we don't go around telling the world about it, but the world doesn't come to us and ask us, either. People just don't ask the right questions! The right question is 'Tell us what is really going on here,' not 'Give us material that fits into our narrow political perspectives elsewhere.'

"This is the typical colonial struggle. How many ex–British territories are there that have ended up as socialist? The typical struggle is against the imperial British power, but essentially the struggle is conducted by reactionary elements. They try to cobble together a modernist view of society, but they keep in enough reactionary elements in relation to women, because all so-called modernist nationalist movements have to address the question of women; then those reactionary elements reassert themselves after independence. We see that everywhere. Ireland is no different.

"The important thing to remember is that revolutions are *for* things. I have been here eighteen years, and what I want to hear is What is it for? I'm not interested in what it's against. We all know that. I want to know that it is for something that is better. A litmus test of a good society is the position of women. If this revolution doesn't have a commitment to women and doesn't have a commitment to socialism, what are we talking about? Okay, if we're talking about ending the oppression of the Catholic population, then I'm totally for that. But you couldn't say there was anything very revolutionary or radical about that struggle. For years I have wanted someone to explain to me the difference or the connection between republicanism and feminism and I have not yet found that person!"

Marie, who had sat silently until then, joined in the conversation.

"I've spent years trying not to make republicanism and feminism a polarized thing in my life, and I found that almost impossible."

"Look," Eileen said, "I came here and was in the civil rights movement. I started out here as a republican socialist feminist. Now I've ended up as a feminist socialist. Query: republican? As far as I am concerned, as far as republicanism goes, it depends on what is on the table. I can't get worked up about man-made boundaries. Now you *could* have a drastic political change in England and end up with a government there which had a far more radical perspective. As a woman, if I had to choose between that government and a government in Dublin which is the same old bloody rubbish, I would choose London. So that's the difficulty. I came to a simple conclusion: I would stay with whichever ruling group gave women the best deal."

"But what," Marie interrupted, "if the 'ruling group' gave someone the best deal at the expense of someone else?"

"We are the majority," Eileen answered.

"Do you mean radical change coming through by way of the British Labour Party?" Marie asked.

"Any kind of British government which would make it worthwhile for women to remain in the United Kingdom is not going to be the kind of government that sanctions what we have seen in Northern Ireland over many years. Hypothetically, if you could envisage a British presence here which was not oppressive and at the same time was radical in terms of women's and labor issues, then you could stay with London. If you had that on the one side, and the thirty-two-county Republic on the other, with its Fine Gael–Fianna Fail government [the two major political parties of the Republic], which would you choose?"

"I don't see it as a choice," Marie answered, holding firm to her Irish nationalism.

"If you could *logically* set up a different situation and *logically* envisage yourself staying with London, then it becomes a non-nationalist situation. Nationalism is an infantile kind of situation. An infantile disorder!" Eileen said with exasperation.

Marie retorted: "If that was my only choice, I would stand on my own and say no! I've got my rights as an individual to determine my life as an Irish woman and not by a British government or a thirty-two-county government."

"But that's where we've been misled! I see it in terms of class and in terms of women, and if my class and women were better served by staying with London, then I would stay with London. Okay, so you have a sense of being Irish, like a sense of being Welsh or Scots or whatever. But what matters are jobs, housing, and liberation for women. Therefore, if we could get those things through London instead of Dublin, then there is no connection between republicanism and feminism!"

Marie held fast. "I still believe it is our right to make our own mistakes."

"Who is the 'our'?" Eileen asked her. "You have this idea of nationalism, which I think is a red herring. There is no 'our.' The 'our' between men and women is different, between the working class and the ruling class is different. Look, what I am arguing about is the assumption that there is a necessary connection between the departure of the British and feminism, and there isn't. Feminism and socialism matter to me, and I'm pragmatic. So if the government of Iceland came along just now and said: 'Right! Link up with us and you will be part of a socialist society, and women will be liberated,' I would stand up and shout: 'Brilliant! Let's join Iceland!'"

Eleanor, one of the Charabanc Theater Company and also a hostess for our evening's dinner forum, spoke up for the first time.

"I want a socialist republic that implies feminism, too. But I also want my own people; it's nationalism in the most benign sense, but it is something that I feel and recognize."

"Well," Eileen retorted, "have your different identities recognized, like they do in different parts of the Soviet Union. What I am arguing about with Marie is this peculiar idea of owning a piece of land. Here we are, and those of us who have a sense of being Irish own this piece of land and we ought to be able to determine what happens on this piece of land."

"Everyone else has had that chance, so why can't we?" Marie asked.

Eileen sat up straight at that remark.

"No, no! Not everyone else has had it. Most people have never had it."

I ventured in at this point. "When you have it, what do you have?"

"A forum to make mistakes," Eileen answered, laughing.

Another Charabanc voice entered into the fray, Maureen's: "It's not just a piece of land; it's history, culture, environment."

"Yes," Eileen conceded, "but you can have it in the framework I described. Also, from the ecology point of view, this idea of owning a piece of land is bad."

"It's not really the *land,*" Eleanor said. "It's the people. I don't wax lyrical about the Sperrins or the Mournes [mountain ranges], but I do wax lyrical about the people here. I think they are fucking magical."

Eileen was the patient professor, trying to teach her recalcitrant class. "We are talking about political options and political struggle," she said slowly, emphasizing each word. "I am not prepared to struggle for nationalism and territoriality."

I wanted to steer the conversation back to the participation — or lack thereof — of women in politics.

I asked Eileen, "Why don't you encourage women to become more powerful in the political structure, because that is a framework in which you will make these changes that you all want."

"Because there isn't a political party that we would stand for," she answered shortly and succinctly. "Now the point about feminism is the same point about human liberation. Feminism encompasses socialism; it's not possible to envisage the liberation of women except in a socialist society. Feminism is about the liberation of women and about the idea that there is a vast range of capacities that people may have that they would be able to pursue without stereotyping, without assumptions being made, and their abilities should be realized. It is socialism in a far, far broader sense. The concepts of socialism began as a concern about human waste and human potential.

"If you say you are a feminist, you are saying 'Right. Let's break down the ideas that we have had about what people do, let's break down stereotypes, break down compartments we have about sexuality, let's rethink our economic structures.' The ideology of feminism is far more advanced than the idea of socialism. Admittedly, in practice, things are pretty terrible, but my concern is with the ideas. The ideas I find in socialism, although good, are limited. With feminism, you move on. Socialism is concerned with economics and is limited; it has no concern with the world, with disarmament."

I tried again.

"Why don't you translate these feminist goals into politics?"

"I think we do. In our everyday lives that is what we are trying to do. But the political system is corrupt."

"Well," I replied, "make your own political system. Make it into power that every woman in Ireland can make use of. Make that possible in a political system. Don't just try to change laws. Be the people that make the laws in the first place."

"Women fought very hard in the nineteen twenties and 'thirties to get a reasonable structure for women in society, and they lost," Marie said. "The Constitution of nineteen thirty-seven was a terrible defeat for Irish women, and the same thing happened last year in the referendum on divorce. The Catholic Church there was the great obstacle. But listen! Ireland isn't the great ogre against women! In America they bomb abortion clinics! We close down well-women clinics, but we don't bomb them! Ireland is too often used as the example of what not to do."

"You're right," I agreed. "Nevertheless, in the United States, abortion is legal. The Supreme Court made it legal. That's a great difference."

"I don't have much faith in laws," Marie said.

"The law gives you moral advantage," Eileen countered. "'Not only do *I* say this, it is the law of the land.' We knew the Fair Employment Act wouldn't change much, but nevertheless, there is a statement, and you can say: 'This is the *law.*' What do you want to do, live in South Africa where there is no law? The law gives us guidelines."

Marie turned to me, but by this time it was so dark I couldn't even see her face. The cool dampness of the grass was beginning to seep through our blankets, dampening the fervor of our conversation, and hunger was drying out our stream of thoughts.

"You put a lot of emphasis on political activity," she said. "But there are two ways to break an egg, hammer it from the outside or be the chick inside pecking your way out. The women's movement here hasn't adopted the political system as the end all and be all. It's not a political party. Within a political system it becomes constrained."

"If the system were broad enough so that it was something resembling a labor party, I would be there," Eileen conceded. "Our problem here is that not only is the system corrupt, it is so narrow that no one with any honesty could be in it!"

"Join it and change it," I said, uncurling my stiff legs and trying to stand up.

"Join the Unionists? Join the SDLP?" The obvious absurdity of this option sent all the women laughing into the house, where we sat down to a lovely, candle-lit table and a chicken casserole. When I complimented our hostesses on their efforts, Eleanor gave me a nudge and laughed: "Bread *and* Roses, luv, don't forget!"

Lesbianism

The gay community in Northern Ireland, both male and female, is still far from the mainstream. Although some gays have "come out," many others fear being ostracized by family, friends, and church. They either leave the country or stay in the closet. For men and women, lay and religious, this can be a life of acute and intense frustration and unhappiness. Only in the past decade, and only in Belfast and Derry, would one find gay bars, clubs, support groups, newsletters, and so on. The Catholic and Protestant churches in the North make no room for sexual "deviation." When it occurs within a church hierarchy, it is a matter for embarrassed coverup.

In the winter of 1987, I spent an evening in Belfast with a group of women, some lesbian, some straight, talking about Northern Irish society and how one feels being part of a small sexual minority in a harshly conservative country, and how paramilitary organizations, with their "macho" image to uphold, deal with homosexuality.

One of them, a funny, vivacious young woman from Belfast, began: "I was eighteen, and I was having this great heterosexual relationship. We used to lie in bed and tell each other our sexual fantasies, and mine was always about making love with a woman. Finally my partner said: 'Look, this keeps cropping up. If this is something you really want to do, don't let me stand in your way!'

"I said, 'Well, I'm not just going to walk out on you. If it happens, it happens.' And it happened. And it was wonderful. The morning after the first night I slept with a woman, I walked to my classes and thought, Why didn't I do that sooner? There was no trauma, no doubt. It just felt so fucking good. I didn't feel any less for the man I was seeing, but sexually I felt this was better."

"Why?" Three of us — all straight — asked the question in unison.

"There was no competition involved. Nobody had to 'perform.' There wasn't any pressure. Also, the feel of a woman's body was so much more satisfying. That's how I know I am a lesbian. I felt that I was in bed with somebody who was like me. I'm not saying that's right for every woman, but that's right for me. I wasn't trying to be more feminist than everybody else, although I do think I'm too fucking much for most men to handle."

The woman who was speaking, whom I shall call Kate, has a vibrant, strong personality and a keen mind. Although she also has a generous nature, I can see how many men would find her a formidable companion.

Another woman, an attractive divorced businesswoman, spoke up. "You know, I enjoy the company of women so much. I mean, I would much rather spend an evening with a group of fun women than with a man. It's more relaxed, there are more laughs. Everyone is more truthful. But I don't know. I just couldn't stand the thought of kissing a woman!"

Kate laughed loudly. "Then you're no lesbian, honey," she said. "Simple as that.

"All my men friends had to accept that as part of me," Kate went on. "I've never had any bad relationships with men. That's why I am not prepared to be a separatist."

Kate stopped to roll a joint and passed it to the woman sitting next to her after she lit it.

"What did your family think about it?" I asked. "Did they know? Did they care?"

"There was a heavy lesbian scene in the place I was studying in England at the time. Some of the women wanted to come over here and support International Women's Day at Armagh Prison, so I rang up me mum here in Belfast and said, 'A couple of me mates are coming over, would you put them up?' So me mum did, and one night while they were there, two of them were out to a party and came back to the house at three A.M., then realized they were locked out. They rang the bell, and when me mum came stumbling out of bed to let them in, there they were, hugging and kissing on the stoop! Me mum was furious. Furious! When I came down for breakfast the next morning she was waiting for me: 'I want those women out of this house! Now!' I've never seen her so angry.

"'Why?' I asked her. As if I didn't know!

"'Because,' she says, 'I don't know why you know them, but I think I know what they are. Are they . . . ?' She couldn't say the word. There was a long silence while neither of us could look at each other. Finally she looked at me.

"'You're one of them, too, aren't you?' she said. 'I know you are. For the last six months, all you've done is talk about your women friends. You're one of them. God help you.'

"'Say the word,' I said to me mum.

"'Come here,' she said. 'Come here and stand in front of that picture of the Sacred Heart and put up your hand and swear that you aren't one of them!' She had tears streaming down her face by this time.

"'Say the word,' I said again. But she wouldn't. So I said: 'No, I won't swear that. It's not because I don't have respect for that Sacred Heart picture, but I'm not going to tell you a lie.'

"So that was it. It was out in the open, and she went berserk. I remember her getting up from the fire, and the teapot was on the cooker, and she got up to take the kettle off the cooker. She was shaking so much she spilled scalding water over her feet.

"'You've gone against God and you've gone against nature, and I don't want you in my house. I'm leaving now, to go to the ten o'clock Mass, and I am going to light a candle that you will change your ways, because you are unnatural and dirty. And when I get back, I want you and those women out of the house.' So I got them up and we left.

"That day we went to a conference and there were Sinn Fein women there, friends of mine. They knew something was wrong, and I told them, and they said they had known all along that I was lesbian. They were my only real support at the time. They told me to go back to the house and confront my mother and talk to her. 'Tell her how you feel and why you are the way you are,' one said. 'And if she won't accept you back in the house, come and spend the night with us.' So they gave me a few pints of beer and sent me home to confront my mum.

"We talked and talked. Finally she said: 'Okay, this is what you are. But I don't ever want you bringing this into the house. I don't want you ever mentioning it to your younger sisters.' I agreed to go along with that.

"'You and I will never be as close as we were,' she said. She took the burden of guilt on herself. She thought I was queer because she was a single parent, because there hadn't been a father figure in my life. 'If your father and I hadn't separated, you wouldn't be like this!' Also, as a Catholic, she had the added guilt of being separated from her husband. She felt that she had sinned and this was the manifestation of why she should feel bad for being separated — her daughter was a lesbian! The jewel of her eye was a queer! And all this would never have happened if she had obeyed the laws of the Church and stuck with her bad marriage!"

One of the other women spoke up, in a soft, gentle voice. She is a lesbian who had entered the convent but had left before her final vows because of her growing awareness of her sexuality.

"My mother never knew I am a lesbian; she died three years ago. But she suspected it, and she didn't like it! She hated to think about the physical side of it; emotional attachment, love, companionship, those were all right, just as long as you left out the physical side! It's like saying to a musician: 'You are a wonderful musician, just don't play any music'! And the irony was that she was so fond of my lover; she became like a member of our family."

"How about your father?" I asked.

"I told him, and he said: 'Well, I love every hair on your head, and I was brought up to obey the Ten Commandments above all else. I can't see that you are breaking a commandment, so how can I condemn you?' But he knows the Church is against it and that worries him. He is such a traditional Catholic that he is used to letting the Church make his moral judgments for him: what they condone, he condones, what they condemn, he also feels he should condemn."

"Now, I love my mother dearly," Kate said, "and I want to please her and make her proud of me. But no matter what I do, what I achieve, it isn't enough, because I'm queer. Everything I do, I am trying to say: 'Please, Mummy, please like me. Please respect me. I'm good. I try.' Well, she turned to me the other day and said: 'I know I haven't given you all the attention or the support that I should have, but it's not because I'm not proud of you. It's because I'm exhausted.' "

"What about your granny? Would she have known about you?"

"Granny? She wouldn't have known the word, that's for sure. But I'll tell you a wonderful story about her. She was always eccentric; you never knew where her political affiliations were going to lie. Whatever happened to be the going issue of the day, and whoever got the most points for that issue, that's who she was for that day. Anyone from the SDLP to fucking Paisley. If he had the right attitude on the right day, he was on!

"Anyway, she was dying of cancer, and we couldn't contemplate sending her away to die, so my mum took the year off to nurse her, and I took two nights a week and so did my sisters. Now her best time was nine P.M. when she got her morphine injection. One night I was on duty sitting with her by the bed and T., my lover, had come over to keep me company. Now T.'s mother had died the year before, and according to Granny it doesn't matter if you have a father, brothers and sisters, grandparents, stepmothers, half sisters — if your *mother* dies, you are an orphan, because your mother is the most important person in your life! Right? You are an orphan even if you are thirty years old, and you have to be looked after. So here is T., thirty, and me, twenty-four, and Granny always calling her 'that wee orphan you live with.'

"So here we are sitting by the bed and Granny having her morphine hallucinations, and she says: 'Is the wee orphan there?'

"'Aye, she's sitting at the foot of the bed.'

"Granny says: 'Ah, God love ya. Ya poor girl, no one else loves ya 'cause your mother's dead.'

"'Right, Granny.'

"'See that girl, Kate, sitting there?'

"'Aye, Granny.'

"'Then the two of you come up close.' We both went and sat on either side of her, by her pillow. Now remember, this is a woman seventy-six years old, a traditional Irish Catholic woman who has cooked for the priests for twenty-five years. They are the holy anointed to her; whatever they say, goes.

"So she says to us, 'Yous aren't like other girls, are you?'

"'No, Granny.'

"'I don't see any husbands around. So you two will have to look after each other.'

"'Aye, Granny.'

"She looked at me: 'That's your friend, the wee orphan, right? Well, you two are different, and you've only got each other, so take good care of each other.'

"We promised her we would.

"I remember once I was living in England in a gay commune, and there were two gay men and the rest of us were lesbians. One Sunday morning Granny rang me up there, and a man answered. When I picked up the phone, she was hysterical: 'I didn't know you were living with a man,' she said. 'Your mother will have a nervous breakdown if she knows that. Your mother is not a well woman. How can you do this to your mother?'

"Now if Granny had known that I was living in a house with all women, she would have thought that would have been great. No man to corrupt me! No man to get me pregnant! But lesbian? Never heard of the word. There was no point. But in the end, she knew.

"We are a very matriarchal family because all the men are either divorced, not living with the women, or dead. And among the siblings there are more women. So they came here, twenty-five women in the bedroom when Granny died. She was the matriarch. She had worked from the time she was eleven years old until she was seventy-five, when she got cancer, scrubbing doorsteps, cleaning factories, cooking. Her husband was killed in the Battle of El Alamein when she was in her twenties, and there was never another man in her life. There were no men in the house. They just weren't a part of her life. She died among women. It was women who walked behind her coffin and women who buried her."

Moving Left

Throughout the decades of the 1970s and 1980s, paramilitary organizations in Northern Ireland have split, regrouped, fought among themselves, disbanded, reorganized. The "Official" IRA, the remnant of the old army that fought for Ireland's independence in 1920, split in the mid-1970s, and the splinter group became known as the "Provisional" IRA (the Provos).

The Officials ceased their military operation and began to function as a political party, formulating radical political and economic goals. They became the Workers' Party and have a small, intensely devoted following in Northern Ireland. One of the most respected community workers in Belfast, a young, articulate woman named Mary McMahon, is also a prominent member of the Workers' Party. A big, broad-shouldered, thoughtful woman with short brown hair, bright blue eyes, and a warm, slow smile, she exudes strength and capability. One's first impression of her is, here is a woman I would like to have on my side.

The daughter of a schoolteacher, Mary grew up in Armagh, attended Queens University in the late 1960s, and joined the republican club there for the simple and only reason that it was banned by William Craig (a controversial Unionist politician who was serving as Minister of Home Affairs at the time). Her family are not political.

We met in the Crown Pub in downtown Belfast, not knowing one another and depending on descriptions given on the telephone. When I got to the pub, it turned out that *all* the young women sitting on the bar stools had on blue jeans, a sweater, brown hair, and blue eyes. But she recognized me immediately, and I drove her back to where I was staying for lunch and a long afternoon's talk.

As we ate smoked salmon and brown bread, Mary explained the Officials' break with the Provisional IRA.

"We didn't see ourselves in any sense as in competition with them [the Provos]. The media seemed to say it was two factions fighting for control of the nationalist population, but there was no question about us being involved in an armed struggle in the way they were. No question of us looking for physical control for safety for our members. We were then a developing, radical, left-wing organization. That might have put us in political competition with the Provos, but we didn't see it as a physical threat.

"For the IRSP [Irish Republican Socialist Party] there were no goals, no objectives. A lot of their activity was based on personal vendettas. All of them I knew in the IRSP based their politics on personal scores which began when they had been Provos. [The IRSP is linked to a tiny, violent paramilitary organization, the Irish National Liberation Army, or INLA.] They had chips on their shoulders because they hadn't been promoted quickly enough. There was also, among some of them, a terrible fascination with death and all that goes with it. I don't think there were any of them, honestly, that could have put their hand on their heart and said there was a political objective about what they were doing.

"Because they had no objectives and nowhere to go, I think they have effectively dissolved themselves now. I mean, if you just go out and kill people, you become psychopathic. Look at their behavior inside jail: one got his ear bitten off, another got his nose bitten off! Animal behavior. And look what happens when they get out. They themselves are admitting now that they had descended into futile, sterile violence and personal gain.

"Once the Workers' Party made its goals and objectives clear, our political existence was a lot easier, because we know what we are about and we can describe to the public what we are about. It also takes us out of the isolation of Irish politics and brings us into European politics, where socialists and workers are recognized as part of political life."

I asked Mary if the Workers' Party exploited the ties it should have with other socialist parties around the world.

"We don't have enough of them. It's a loose tie. We're not part of the Socialist International in Europe; they wouldn't allow us to be a part of it, because they normally only allow one party from every country to be a member. The SDLP got there first because of John Hume's influence and his ability to manipulate the international setup to his advantage. I'm not a fan of John Hume's; he's got more friends abroad than here at home. But I will say this, he has been very clever."

"Millions of Irish Americans are looking for someone from the North who will say the 'right thing,'" I said, "and John Hume fits that bill."

"Well, our political existence in the North is established now, it's accepted, it won't go away in the face of Unionist or nationalist opinion. In recent years the most significant point is not how badly we have done electorally in percentage terms, but that we have recruited members from across the whole range of the social and sectarian divide."

(Although the Workers' Party carries only a tiny percentage of the tally in local elections, Mary's assertion that they have crossed those social and religious barriers seems to be true. I have met many Protestant, middle-class men and women who have, surprisingly, told me that they "support" the Workers' Party. Whether they translate that support into votes seems improbable in the face of its poor showings at the polls.)

"You have a public leadership position in your political party," I said to Mary, "but you are one of the few. Why aren't there more?"

"There are lots of reasons. One, tradition. Women haven't traditionally been involved in Irish political life in any serious or leadership position. Second, if you accept the analysis that women in Irish society have been, as Connolly [James Connolly, Irish labor leader and 1916 martyr] described them, 'slaves of slaves,' then you have to accept that for every improvement and progress, you have to double that for women to get them anywhere near equality, even at the grass-roots level.

"Also, so many women in Northern Ireland are so pissed off at what passes for politics. They detest Unionism and nationalism because it is about flag-waving and symbolism and not about things that are important in their lives; it's not about food, it's not about jobs, it's not about housing. And therefore they think politics is irrelevant. Because politics in our society has been dominated by men, women don't have the confidence to overcome all the inhibitions and obstacles put in their path to get involved in the first place. Then you have to have staying power. Politics in Northern Ireland is wearying!"

"What about you?" I asked. "Did you have to fight your way as a woman to achieve your role in your party?"

"Well, I don't have family commitments the way a lot of women do. I'm single, and that's a choice on my part. It would be exceptionally difficult, especially in Northern Ireland where a woman might be caring for an aged relative as well as children, to be active in politics as well. The fight for equality was fought in the nineteen seventies and the formal barriers went down, but I was at a meeting in Belfast a few years ago, and the chairman kept talking about 'the boys,' and finally I said, 'Are women supposed to be part of this or not?' and he said, 'Must I watch every word?' I said, 'Yes, you must, because not to watch every word is to carry on with the same pattern.'

"But we have done some interesting things for women here lately. We had a seminar for women on health. Most of the women who came weren't members of our party. Then another one on women in politics. On the Friday night before it, I was asked why this was a women-only thing. 'You are barring Party members from attending!' I was told. This was from men who weren't good on women's issues. Anyway, fifty-two women came to that; some were Party members, some weren't. Now the men can't wait to get their hands on the report, to see what the women were saying. It will be out next week, and it has to do with day care and things like that, not what women think about men! That will disappoint them. One thing that will arise from wives and girlfriends of members is that the men who claim to be socialists are going to have to take a much bigger role in family affairs in order to allow the women to get involved politically. It will be interesting to see how that falls out. It will mean that for some of the men, they can't go out gallivanting four or five nights a week. They'll have to stay home and babysit while their wives go out! There are so many things that would draw women together across sectarian lines. The strength of women working as a group here has never been utilized.

"A feminist movement that cannot allow in its working-class women who are taking on effectively the political establishment of Northern Ireland — which is sectarian, corrupt, inward-looking — is about elitism and irrelevancy. Now I don't like the political system in Northern Ireland, but there is no point in running away from it. It would be a very comfortable, happy position to go to feminist meetings once a week and have all the consciousness-raising that you want!"

"What about women in Sinn Fein? Is there room for them there?"

"Well, they say there is. They have two women councillors in West Belfast. But I don't see how they can argue for women's rights when they take women down the street, put a gun in back of their head, and blow their brains out. There are three deaths in particular that stand out — they stand out because so few women have been killed. There was a woman from Derry who was shot dead collecting the census in the nineteen eighty–nineteen eighty-one period. The Provos admitted they did it and said she was a British agent. It was pathetic; I mean, the girl was standing at a doorway and they just walked up and shot her dead. At that time the Provos weren't fighting an election but people who were collecting the census returns [for the British government] were deemed legitimate targets. I mean, the Provos don't have anything that isn't a legitimate target! No matter who they shoot, they will find a reason!

"The second was a judge's daughter down there on the Malone Road. I thought that was particularly sad and morbid because the wee girl who was left with the guns coming away from the scene was nineteen years old, two years younger than the girl who had been shot.

"There is a girl from Ballymurphy. She is twenty-nine years old, married to her childhood sweetheart, the boy next door. They had no kids, which was a source of personal sadness. He worked as a taxi driver and did odd jobs. All we'll ever know is what the Provos say. They executed him for being an alleged informer, although he was not a member of theirs. They took them both to Turf Lodge, held them for two days. He was taken out by one group, she was taken out by another. She was made to stand at one end of an entry hall and made to watch while they shot him, and as she tried to go up to him as he fell, they shot her as well. What I'll never forget is Buckley, that ijit of a priest from Larne, standing outside the Crumlin Road Jail with placards complaining about strip-searching in Armagh, when the Provos are shooting a woman in Turf Lodge. I find it inconsistent. It's not to say that as a feminist one would endorse a campaign of terrorism if they only murdered men! Now some American feminists think that equality is getting women into the armed forces and getting them the same rank. That's not equality! It's bringing yourself down to the level of the oppressors instead of being about elevating people's lives and their philosophy of life to a greater public good.

"Now the Provos certainly don't have a woman in power inside the IRA, but their idea of equality is that they have some women who are well-known terrorists and they say, oh well, women are as good terrorists as men!

"I'd like to see an end to all that St. Paddy–whackery that you have in the United States, and see Ireland as an independent country in Europe that has a much more vibrant political existence from both East and West, and see Ireland as a significant country in that block that can contribute to international neutrality and better understanding in world peace terms.

"In the short term, it's hard to see what will happen. There won't be any changes in Westminster in the next elections. Charlie Haughey [the Irish Prime Minister] has been whipped into line by the United States, and it seems that the whole process has been determined by forces far removed from Ireland. In terms of achievable politics, I would like to see council [local] politics operating in Ireland and the Workers' Party have a very strong influence there. Ireland, North or South, is small enough for strong local government. That's where the strength of the left is in Ireland, if it has any strength at all. The experience of the Labour Party in the government in Dublin has been disastrous; it never used its strength in councils to assert a positive left-wing influence to change the system in terms of local services. Here, that's what we have to look at: what is achievable and what is attainable."

As Mary got up to leave, I asked her what she thought about American money and interest coming into Northern Ireland, as a result of the Anglo-Irish Agreement.

"Not much. The Irish influence in American politics has not been very positive or progressive. And the Irish-American influence in Ireland is even worse! It's the worst end of everything that Irish and American politics is about!"

The Peace People

On December 10, 1976, two young women from Belfast, Mairead Corrigan and Betty Williams, won the Nobel Peace Prize for their work in mobilizing a nationwide peace movement in Northern Ireland. Their male colleague, Ciaran McKeown, who had worked with the two women in the creation of that extraordinary grass-roots movement, was not one of the Prize recipients.

The movement began in the summer of 1976; Mairead's sister, Anne Corrigan Maguire, was out walking her young family along Finaghy Road North on Belfast's west side. An IRA gunman was being chased by a British Army patrol, which opened fire on the racing car and shot the driver in the head. His car careened into the young family on the sidewalk; Anne's six-week-old baby and Joanne, who was eight, were killed instantly. Two-year-old John died a few hours later. Anne's broken legs and pelvis eventually healed. All of Belfast was shocked by the accident. People were used to violent death in the city by then, but they found the death of the children too much to bear silently. Over the next few weeks, spontaneous peace vigils took place all over the city.

Betty Williams, a Protestant, contacted Mairead, whom she had never met, and offered to help. As the mass meetings grew, the two women enlisted the help of a young Belfast journalist, Ciaran McKeown, to formulate a peace platform and an organizational structure for the growing movement. They eventually became known as the Peace People, and for several years, they carried the torch for antiviolence in Northern Ireland. Men and women on both sides of the border met, marched, demonstrated, protested, and signaled their desire for a peaceful settlement of the Troubles in their country.

The movement spread to Europe and the United States. The two young women gained an international reputation. The Peace Prize was the culmination of their hard work and charismatic appeal to the thousands of Irish people committed to their goal of nonviolence. Unfortunately, the political parties in the North offered no structural foundation for the movement. After the demonstrations and the emotional marches, there was really nowhere to go, nothing concrete to do. Those who marched were already committed to peace; enemies of the movement, the gunmen and the terrorists, were never going to be won over. Gradually, the organization lost its momentum.

Betty Williams kept the money she had won from the Peace Prize. (The cash prize that went with the award was £80,000.) Mairead at first said she would not keep hers, and then was persuaded to. It was a bad decision on the part of both women, and it hastened the dissolution of the movement. Betty and Mairead quarreled. Betty moved to America and eventually married an American businessman. She lives now in Florida.

The saddest victim of all was Anne Corrigan Maguire. She never recovered from the tragedy; she and her husband tried to make a new life for themselves in New Zealand, but they missed their families and returned to Belfast. They had two more children, but in January 1980, the pain became too much for Anne to bear. She took her own life. Mairead tried to help Jackie Maguire keep his young family together, and in 1981, they married and have started a new life for themselves. They have added two more children to the family.

The offices of the Peace People are still open on the Lisburn Road in Belfast. Irish and American volunteers, committed to the goals of the movement, staff the office, arranging for relatives to visit prisoners, publishing a newsletter, and answering queries about the movement. But the glorious, hopeful days of 1976 are over.

Women in the Arts

There is an extraordinary volume of art and literature coming out of Northern Ireland today. I leave the theories of a connection between civil violence and an arts renaissance to literary critics and only note that the early development of Northern Ireland's most gifted poets began when they were students in the mid-1960s, a time of hope for Ulster's future and before the outbreak of violence in 1969. Were those young poets "picking up psychic history not yet enacted or resolved"? (Edna Longley, *Poetry in the Wars,* p. 10.) Or did they develop in spite of the growing unrest in their country?

The responsibility of poets and artists to use their talents to explain, analyze, and interpret the politics of the country, as against their right to abdicate that responsibility, is fiercely debated in literary circles in Ireland. Should Seamus Heaney, one of Ireland's most gifted poets, be asked to become "the most potent Orpheus who would lead us through that psychic hinterland which we shall have to chart before we can emerge from the Northern crisis"? (Mark Patrick Hederman, *The Crane Bag,* p. 102.)

Paul Muldoon, another gifted Irish poet, says that instead of reading political and sociological writings about the North, one should read Northern poets. While poets and critics and their public debate a writer's role in a violent society, the question of women within this renaissance is beginning to surface more quietly. There were no women poets of stature in the "the Group" at Queens in the mid-1960s where Heaney, Derek Mahon, Michael Longley, Jimmy Simmons, and others began their literary careers. And there were no women of note making their mark in the theater in those days. But, as in all things in Ulster, that too is changing. Medbh (pronounced "Mave") McGuckian is now poet-in-residence at Queens and can be a mentor to a generation of young female poets, as Phillip Hobspan was for the 1960s generation of young men at Queens. In 1985, Ruth Hooley edited *The Female Line*, the first anthology of well-known and theretofore unpublished women poets and writers, to celebrate the tenth anniversary of the Northern Ireland women's rights movement. Jennifer Fitzgerald is developing the first Women in Literature course at Queens. Jennifer Johnston has already established her reputation as one of Ireland's leading novelists and playwrights.

The theater is as much a part of Northern Ireland's cultural tradition as are literature and poetry. Here again women are beginning to play a more prominent role, not only as actresses, but as playwrights, producers, and directors. The Charabanc Theater Company, a small group of women in Belfast, write, produce, and act in their own productions. Marie Jones is a founder-member of Charabanc, and the coauthor, with Martin Lynch, of the company's first hit, *Lay Up Your Ends*, a musical tribute to the women in the linen industry in Belfast.

"It was a celebration of all those women who spent their lives in the mills," Marie told me, while she and I were having coffee one afternoon in Belfast. She is a small, dynamic woman, with bright blue eyes that gleam with fun and humor. The big wing chair she was sitting in almost dwarfed her. She bounced around from side to side in it, nervous energy propelling her.

"We interviewed the old women who are left; they have wonderful stories to tell about their days in the mills. While they worked, they would make up stories and songs to amuse themselves and pass the time. These were passed down from generation to generation and formed the base of a cultural tradition here in Belfast. Those women — and children, too — worked under terrible conditions, but they managed to have fun and find a laugh even in the worst of times.

They produced a heritage that all women in Northern Ireland can be proud of."

I asked her about the history of the Charabanc Company. (A charabanc is a long wagon that was used to take mill women to the seaside for an occasional Sunday outing.)

"Look," Marie began, "I'm an actress. And I was pissed off because there were so few good roles for women. I thought about it, and talked about it to lots of people in the theater. Finally Martin Lynch said to me one day: 'For God's sake, Marie, stop complaining. Write your own material.'

"'Right!' I said. 'On your bike!' [Pronounced "bake" in Marie's Belfast accent, it means "get going."] Well, how to do that? I thought about my mother, who had worked in the linen mills. Those women had a culture all their own; I had heard snippets of their jokes and songs all my life, and I knew what wonderful material it would be for the theater, so I started getting it all down on tape. I would talk to one woman, and she would tell me her stories, and then she would say: 'Now, luv, go down the street to that wee Mrs. Greer, because she was a weaver, and she will have different stories.' Pretty soon, I had all the material I needed!

"The man I live with helped me form a company, and we put on our first production in the Arts Theater here in Belfast in nineteen eighty-three. People loved it, and we had good reviews. We were a success."

Since 1983, Charabanc has toured in Russia, the United States, and the Republic of Ireland and performed in theater festivals in Munich, Toronto, and Baltimore. They received a standing ovation when they performed *Gold in the Streets* in Boston in 1987 at the Northern Irish Theater Festival. Besides evoking a warm and nostalgic sentiment for the Belfast working women, the troupe satirizes the political situation in the North, poking fun at religious and cultural traditions that the Northern Irish cling to, and with gusty good humor they are able, in their songs and skits, to demolish in minutes some of the paranoiac myths that separate the two cultures of the North.

"Do you describe yourselves as a 'feminist' theater company?" I asked Marie.

"No. If a man starts a theater company, is he labeled? Of course not. If you see *Observe the Sons of Ulster Marching to the Somme* [a powerful play by Frank McGuinness], you don't say, 'That's a "masculine" play — although the cast is entirely male. You just think that it is good theater. The same with us. It's important for women to write plays and important for us to have our own company. It gives us an outlet for our talents that we wouldn't necessarily have working with another company.

"The hardest thing about getting Charabanc going was not getting the material, or writing and producing our plays; it was the dialogue with men — the lawyers, producers, and so on — getting the company formed. That's where we really had no experience. I was brought up as a working-class girl, not to have an opinion of my own in the company of educated men! Now we have one middle-class woman in our company; she has an opinion on everything. It's amazing! But there I would be, poised on the edge of my chair, so nervous. There those men were, just sitting around, so relaxed, legs crossed, discussing this and that about the business aspects of the company. Jesus! But we learned."

The Charabanc Company has Protestant and Catholic members; as with the theater world everywhere, religious and cultural labels cease to exist. The theater in Northern Ireland is free of religious bias. Two of the women in the company live in a house just off the Ravenhill Road, and we went there to a party on Easter Saturday night to celebrate the closing of *Gold in the Streets.* The party began after a midnight supper in an Italian restaurant in central Belfast, where a loud and boisterous contretemps took place over the quality of the food in relationship to the size of the bill. Finally the chef was produced to defend his skill. He proved to be too drunk to rally a credible defense, so in the end the plaintiffs were the victors.

We then all transported ourselves to the Charabanc homestead where many hours were spent in the kitchen singing "sectarian" songs for the benefit of the American guest, telling stories, drinking wine, and planning new theater productions and grand world tours. I became acquainted with all the Charabanc members: Maureen Jordan, the public relations person; Eleanor Methven, the "middle-class woman who has an opinion on everything"; Rosena Brown, who looks twenty and has nine children to raise alone and got a new chance for a career when she nabbed a role in a television production about Belfast; and Carol Scanlon, who trained as a teacher of drama and English before she joined the Charabanc Company. In the wee hours, I met Christina Reed, the Belfast playwright who won the 1980 Ulster

Television Drama Award for her play *Did You Hear the One About the Irishman?* We made a date to meet later for an interview. People drifted in and out of the house. Some sat quietly in the living room, but the action was in the kitchen where spoons and the bottoms of pans provided an accompaniment to the songs. Pounding on a wooden tabletop with the flat of the hand isn't a bad imitation of a lambeg drum. Mysteriously, it was suddenly 5 A.M. Light was beginning to filter through the leafless trees outside. Maria, my American friend, and I made our way, cautiously and slowly, through empty Easter Sunday–morning streets. We passed Martyr's Memorial Church en route, and it was a sobering thought to realize that we would be attending the service there in less than six hours! I asked Maria, as we stopped for a red light (law-abiding even in the empty dawn streets), "Are you going to be fit to pray at eleven A.M.?" She was already asleep.

It was a year later before I had a chance to sit down and have a long talk with Christina Reed. We met in her handsome, modern mews house in Belfast, where she lives with her three daughters. Sitting in the kitchen, we talked while she made leek soup. She's a small, intense woman, vivacious and friendly, with a mod "crew cut" hairdo. Her teenage daughters and some of their friends wandered in and out as we talked.

She had just won the Giles Cooper Award for a fifty-minute radio play. I congratulated her.

"News travels fast in Belfast!" she laughed. "I just heard about the award myself."

"What about women in the arts here?" I asked. "Are they part of this great renaissance of creativity in Northern Ireland?"

"Well, the nineteen sixties and nineteen seventies saw this renaissance begin. Queens University had these poets, Heaney, Muldoon, Gormsby, and so on, but there were no women. I do think women have more trouble getting published here. Field Day [a theater company in Northern Ireland] has no women on its board, nor does the Lyric Theater, or the Arts Council. There is one woman director of radio plays in Ulster BBC. When Ruth Hooley produced *The Female Line,* she had a lot of trouble financing that book. There are few good theater roles for women.

"I'm working class, and working-class women spend all our time with other women and children. Most women here are satisfied with that lot. When I separated from my husband, the women sympathized with *him*, not with me!

"You see, girls, particularly working-class girls, are taught from early on to limit their expectations. That's just how the educational system here works. The lack of ambition among the girls is just fantastic. Ask one, 'What do you want to be, if you had your choice,' and she'll say, 'Oooh, I want to work in a record shop!' One of the reasons that sixteen- and eighteen-year-olds are deliberately getting pregnant now is just to get out of their parents' house, to change their lives. And that's the only way to get out that they know."

"What are the things in your own life," I asked Christina, "that gave you the self-confidence to write plays?"

"I can't remember. I've always written. When I was nine or ten years old I was given a little diary with a lock and key, and I always wrote in it very carefully, but everything I wrote was so boring I began to make things up. I come from a background where it was never considered that anyone would do something so fanciful as writing plays! We were practical, geared to going to school, leaving at fifteen, working, getting married . . .

"No one in my family went to university; my mother was keen on education, though, and she got us library tickets, so my early reading comes from that. Also, she and my grandmother were great storytellers, and I think that is where my writing comes from, because I am simply writing down what I heard from them, sitting around a kitchen table like this! My grandmother took great delight in frightening the daylights out of us, telling us ghost stories. I got so much material from the things that happened in my life and stories my mother and grandmother told. For instance, my mother's wake was like the old Belfast 'street wakes,' which went on for three days. They were a city version of the old country wake. The shades would be drawn, and it was a big celebration. Even though the body was laid out at home, it wasn't morbid at all. The writer in me kept sneaking around the house making notes. Lots of women who are writing in Ireland now will recount this: the telling of tales by other women forms the well of their creativity.

"So I used to write down the stories they told, but I never told anyone about it, never showed it to anyone. And then a number of things happened. My children were growing up, my mother died, my marriage was breaking up. I had a traumatic time, and I am hopelessly disorganized and dreamy about most things, but I made one decision: This is what I want to do. I want to write. There was a drama competition on at the time and I dramatized one of the stories I had written and I was very lucky very fast: I won. I was thirty-five then.

"Now, beginning last year, I earned enough from my writing to live on. My ex-husband supports the children. He was always supportive of my writing in practical ways, but, you see, an awful lot of what I started to write was my dissatisfaction with everything, and I think that it was inevitable that once I publicly . . . well, I didn't write him into plays, but things come out. Anyway, it was awful at the time but there is no antagonism now. He's a good father and he maintains the children very responsibly — not that I owe him gratitude for that: he should! But a hell of a lot of men don't."

"What kind of husbands do Northern Irishmen make?" I asked.

"Well, I think we are — pardon the pun — all screwed up about the sexual thing here. We are taught, both Catholic and Protestant, very early on that sex is sinful, that it is something for marriage and that women just have to put up with it."

"Protestants are taught that, too?"

"Oh, yes. Even more. Because you've got that big Scottish Calvinist thing that sex in itself is a sin.

"I was fifteen years old before I knew how a baby was born. I went to work, and the girls in the office were going to see some French movie showing a live birth. I mean, it was a documentary about natural childbirth, but here it was considered a 'dirty movie,' so these girls took me with them and I sat there dumbfounded! Now I knew how babies got in there in the first place — when I was ten years old a boy on our street told me — but I had this vague idea in the back of my head that they came out the navel! I was absolutely shocked by the violence of it, the hugeness of it. And I was fifteen!"

"Do you think that the combination of this puritanical attitude toward sex . . . I mean, if a woman only endures it instead of making her husband feel good about it, he certainly can't feel very macho in his role as a husband. Then if he doesn't have a job, and his wife is going out and earning the living, *plus* running the household, well, then, does going around with a gun make a man out of him?"

"I don't know," Christina said. "I really don't know about that. Certainly not among Protestants, because Protestant men have always had their secret societies — the Orange Order, the Masonic Order and so on — which have tremendous power here. And there is the tradition of men not being at home much anyway."

"Where does that tradition come from?"

"Too many babies at home, too crowded. The men created a pub life of their own."

"Do Protestant men go to pubs, too?" I asked. "I thought that was a Catholic tradition!"

Christina laughed loudly. "Of course they do! It's a myth that they don't. You are thinking of these very religious, fundamentalist Protestants, but they are a small group. If you go into a Protestant neighborhood, there are pubs and clubs all over the place. The first thing a paramilitary organization does here, whether it's Catholic or Protestant, is to open a social club."

"People are very social here," I said, "in the real meaning of the word. And they are kind to strangers. Where does all the cruelty come from?"

"You're right about the kindness. Hospitality has always been a big tradition here, and Irish people are very polite. We are sociable people. A friend of mine, a man in the theater, started coming here a few years ago to do a play, and now he loves it and keeps coming back. 'Belfast is the best-kept social secret in the British Isles,' he says. 'I love it here.' About the cruelty, I don't know. I think it comes from frustration and depression. I think when people are forced to live within a very narrow boundary, with a limitation put on the expression of their own individuality, I think that causes violence. I think the extremists have come to a point where that becomes a fanaticism; they can't think of anything else. And then violence comes from people not being allowed to express themselves. You see, so few people here ever get to vote *for* something. You have to vote against something. That results in a negative way of life. You are told that if you don't live like a Unionist or a republican, you are going to let the other side take over. It is this business of putting labels on everything.

"When I first started going to London, I had a set-to with feminists there because I found what they wanted from me was that I would be some sort of left-wing something or other, preferably lesbian if I could manage it, and I said to them: 'Look. It has taken me forty years to get rid of one set of labels, and now I'm told I've got to take on these new ones, or I'm not acceptable.' It's the same as saying that if you don't behave in a certain Christian way or a certain social way you are not acceptable.

"I have an Ulster Protestant Unionist background, but now I am much more left wing and don't support the Unionists at all. What they have done here is indefensible. Of course, I don't talk politics with my family. I love them, but it is a dilemma. I have dozens of cousins, and they are all opposed to violence, but they don't agree with the Anglo-Irish Agreement. They even find it a terrible shock now to know that a Protestant could get arrested! Nevertheless, it is true that the Protestant work force was also badly paid, and many of them lived in poverty. I personally think the nationalists have a very valid gripe, but most of my family doesn't. They would think, 'How dare they complain?'

"I never marched in the demonstrations; my children were young then, and I was busy with them. Also, I detest anything religious, and the Peace Movement was too religious for me. I belong to no church. My girls went to Sunday school because they wanted to, and now they go to an integrated school."

"Do you find any sectarian or political bias in the theater?" I asked Christina.

"Creative writers here are not under any threat. The theater is middle class here and there is no sectarianism in it. The paramilitaries aren't interested in the theater, thank goodness!"

I left Christina's house in the growing dusk, a beautiful, cold winter's evening when lights were just beginning to come on and smoke drifted out of small chimneys, disappearing in jagged lines into the darkening gray sky. Students with long mufflers wound around their necks and men with briefcases hurried along the sidewalks. I walked fast, to get to the Botanic Garden before it was locked for the night; it was my shortcut home, and I made it just before the watchman came to close the heavy wrought-iron gates. The park was empty as I hurried across its winding walks, and I thought again, as I had so many times there, of the irony of being so "safe" in a situation where, in the United States, it would be foolish to be a woman alone. The Garden at dusk holds no threats. Northern Ireland is a law-abiding place.

Where does the cruelty come from?

Relationships

Religion, politics, and violence affect the kinds of relationships that men and women have in Northern Ireland in a way unique to their country. Prison widows, real widows, family pressures on a "mixed marriage," men "on the run," the stress of massive unemployment — all contribute to strained and distorted commitments.

For the hundreds of young and middle-aged wives whose husbands have been in prison for five, ten, and twenty years, the stress of everyday living is shattering. Some, obviously those with good marriages to begin with, find the courage and self-confidence to carry on, to make their weekly prison visits, to give hope and encouragement to their imprisoned husbands, to work for their release, and to keep the home fires burning. For others, the spectre of a life alone for a decade or two is too much to bear.

I often talked with women in the North about "relationships." Widows, wives, and lovers each had their own experiences to relate, and it seemed to me that the strain of the past twenty years has taken its toll in this arena more than any other. Also, living in such a chauvinistic, emotionally repressed, and tradition-bound society, many of the women have suffered bad relationships alone and silently, often with only the company and support of valium to help them through. Not many priests or preachers are sympathetic to a woman's emotional or sexual needs. Women may rule supreme in the home in Northern Ireland, but when they need to reach out, the helping hand is often not there.

One good-looking woman of twenty-seven, the mother of four small children, talked to me about being left alone while her young husband did a twelve-year prison sentence.

"I was scared shitless," she said. "I just couldn't imagine being — what do ye call it? celibate? — for a dozen years. I mean, I know he's in there for what he believes is right, and I know he thinks he did the right thing. But here's me, right? He never asked me what did I think. And them kids. Look at them. They'll be grown before they know him again. So what are we supposed to do? Sit around and make a martyr out of him? That's what his so-called friends do. It makes me sick. This is my house now. I make the decisions. I'm raising the kids. If I do something wrong, I take the blame. I never thought I could do it on my own. The first month, I cried day and night until my wee daughter told me she thought I was going to die! Popping valium like candy.

"But I've done it. I can manage now, and I'll tell you something: He's not going to be welcome back in this house when he gets out. If he comes back, he comes back on my terms, and if he can't handle that, well, I say that's tough."

I asked her what her family thought about her independence and her attitude toward her marriage.

"My mother says she wishes she'd had the chance to do the same thing! My dad doesn't say nothing, but he doesn't like it, I know. My sister — her boyfriend is in now, and she's running around. I tell her, 'Don't wait for him, you'll grow old.' So she's having some fun now, like she should. I wouldn't have thought that ten years, or five years ago, but you get older, you know, and you think differently about a lot of things. I got married too young, had too many kids. But there you are. I love them, and I'm trying to make some kind of a life for myself. I see a man now. I like him and he's good to me and the kids, but I don't know what we'll do. There's not much of a future here. We just kind of live day to day, you know?"

Another prisoner's wife, loyal to her husband and faithful about her weekly prison visits, feels that it's her duty and responsibility to support him while he's in prison.

"I know he wanted his wee son to grow up without the risk of being interned or beaten up or being arrested unfairly. So if he had to sacrifice his freedom, that's it. It's not much of a sacrifice for me to keep things going while he's in. He was a good husband."

"But his son will grow up without him," I pointed out. "He was sacrificing his fatherhood as well."

"Better than growing up without his freedom" was her rejoinder.

"Do you go out, see friends, date?" I asked.

"I don't go out with other men," she replied angrily. "I'm married. I don't think much of the sluts who go running around with their husbands in prison. Sometimes I go out with a few women friends or with my mother. That's all. My job is to raise this here wee one and to make a home for him when he comes out."

Sinn Fein people tell me that most of the prison widows remain loyal to their husbands and await their release. Social workers and prison officials say the opposite, that breakdowns in prison marriages are almost universal and are accepted now by the community. Some years ago, a prison widow seen dating another man would have been ostracized by her community and probably her family. Now, there are special funds raised by supporters of paramilitary organizations for both Catholic and Protestant widows and prison widows, the "Green Cross" and the "Orange Cross." Nevertheless, it is often hard for these women to make ends meet, and their children's futures are sometimes tainted by the political connections of their fathers.

Other women develop a new confidence and become politically active on behalf of their husband's release. Women who never in their lives had stood up in a meeting or made an independent political statement suddenly find themselves protectors and defenders of their men. They become adept at using the media and community resources to get their cause publicized. Although some of these women have been tremendously effective in this role, they usually melt back into the nonactive wife/mother role as soon as their husbands are released and home again. Many women are involved at a less public level, organizing marches and pickets, speaking at local community meetings. As well as working for the release of their men, these women try hard to keep alive the myths and legends that make prison life less sordid and more heroic. I noticed that the legends always seem to revolve around republican prisoners and seldom if ever around loyalists.

The most potent of the legends, of course, deals with the hunger strikers, those ten republican prisoners who starved themselves to death in 1981. Enormous pressures were put on the wives, mothers, and sweethearts of these prisoners from every side — IRA supporters, the Catholic Church, the government — either to support them or to take them off the strike. These women were either held up as brave heroines, partners in a patriotic performance, or they were castigated as unfeeling perpetrators of their loved ones' unnecessary deaths. They — parents and wives — had the excruciating decision to make when the starving prisoners went into a coma whether to continue their strike, which would result in certain death, or to be guided by their own feelings and take them off. Either decision cost them pain, anguish, and harsh judgment by family and friends. The wives or girlfriends who had left the prisoners before the strike were considered villainous traitors. One of them, Mickey Devine's widow, Maggie, who had left him for another man when he went to prison, still has nightmares and hallucinations about him, and requires psychiatric treatment. (David Beresford, *Ten Dead Men*, p. 424.) If the strikers had lived, all but one of them would be out of prison by now; their mothers, wives, and children are the living victims of their act of self-destruction.

Bill Rolston, a teacher and journalist in Belfast, has written sensitively and sympathetically about the lives of the prison widows, and I asked him why the mythology and legend seems only to include republican prisoners.

"Well, why is there such a dearth of mythology on the loyalist side overall? You can accuse republicans of being romantics, casting back to the golden age of Celtic society, but at least they have something to be reminded about. Loyalists aren't sure what to cast back on. It's interesting to see how some of the young DUP types are trying to rewrite sections of Irish history, trying to say that St. Patrick was "one of ours," and that Cuchulain was a UDA man but he didn't know it!

"The problem with loyalist women is that in the literal sense of the word their ideology is reactionary. It is reactionary in that they are not working towards a goal, and they are trying to prevent other people from achieving their goals. They aren't standing *for* something, they are standing *against* something. Both sides have idealists, it's just a question of Who is the enemy? For the republicans, that's clear. For the loyalists, it is more of a problem. Their enemy could be anybody, not just the IRA. It could be any Catholic, a government figure who doesn't pursue Catholics enough. Rome. The Kremlin. Television. They have lots of enemies."

There are certain rules of prison-wife protocol: The wife must remain sexually abstinent while her husband is "inside." If she dates at all, she must date someone "higher up" in the organization. She must never miss a weekly visit to the prison and, while there, must regulate the conversation so that she does not "unload" on the prisoner with her own personal or family problems, such as finances or a child's misbehavior. If called upon to do so, she must relay messages from prisoners to outsiders. Some women are made into quasi-madonna heroines in their community because of their husband's position; those unfaithful may eventually have to leave their neighborhoods or even the country and resettle where they are not known. Whatever the choice, whichever direction they take, the relationship suffers a nearly fatal blow. "I was taking valium all day and all night," one prison widow told me. "I'd say to myself, 'None tonight, May,' but by ten o'clock I'd be all sweating and shaking and I felt like I couldn't breathe right, so I'd go next door and beg one off a neighbor. One thing here is that you always know you can get a valium off your neighbor!"

Most of the women prisoners in Northern Ireland (and there are only a few left inside) are, by choice, single. The role of an active paramilitary does not include domesticity. Some of the women form lesbian relationships; others have boyfriends outside who usually don't wait for them. Some, like the Gillespie sisters, urge their boyfriends to seek out new relationships.

Catholic girls who dated British soldiers in the early days of the army's occupation of Northern Ireland were severely punished by their own communities. "Oh, the IRA would catch her sooner or later," a woman remembered, who had seen a neighbor girl punished for being seen in a pub with a British soldier. "They came and got her out of the house one night. She was screaming something terrible, but no one would do a thing for her. They tied her to a streetlamp, cut her hair off, shaved it right down to her scalp, painted her body, and stuck feathers to her. Then they put a sign on her saying 'I am a disgrace!' They left her there all night, tied to the streetlamp. No one would dare untie her until dawn."

Maybe the girls don't date British soldiers anymore, or maybe the IRA gave up on that form of punishment, but nowadays you don't hear of a "tar-and-feather job."

Women in Northern Ireland, as everywhere, are experimenting with new forms of relationships, ones that would be shocking to their parents' generation, but hardly new nowadays in London, Paris, or New York. But Northern Ireland is both a small and a conservative country, and independent lifestyles are harder to maintain. Nevertheless, because of, or in spite of, the Troubles, women are fashioning new domestic policies for themselves that give them more independence than they had in the past.

Two attractive, university-educated single women sat in the living room of a Belfast flat one evening in May 1987, drinking white wine and talking about their relationships with men. They seemed cool and self-assured about their attitudes, less intense, less introspective than American single women who endlessly analyze their current relationships.

"I like having a man in my life, but I will never marry," one said firmly. "I think marriage spoils a relationship. And I wouldn't mind if my current lover had a 'fling' on the side, as long as he was honest and told me about it. I would like to know the kind of woman who was also attracted to him! I guess I would expect mutual trust and commitment, but not marriage. The only reason I can see for marriage is to have children, and I don't want children."

"I won't even tell my mate I love him!" the other one said. "I was so badly hurt in a love affair. I lived with a man for five years; we were both waiting for our divorces to become final and then we were to get married. Out of the blue, totally unexpectedly, while I was visiting home here in Belfast, he wrote me to say that he was getting married to someone else. He had seen me off at the airport the month before, tears streaming — *streaming!* — down his face, swearing that we would never be parted again. It will be a long, long time, maybe never, before I trust a man again. Of course I know you can't legislate for a man to stay in love with you, but at least you can expect to be treated like a human being. Now, looking back, I don't know if anything he ever told me was true! I have a new relationship now, and it's fine, but I will never say 'I love you.' I think that makes things bad between us.

"When I began this new affair, I think I was getting too doormatty. So once, just out of the blue, I flew off to London for two weeks and stayed with a friend. When I came back, he was an awful lot nicer. I would like to think that I am above playing those games, but it always works, doesn't it? He said, 'I missed you while you were away, far more than I thought I would.' And three or four months later he told me he loved me. And I probably won't hear it again for another year! But I hold out on him, too. I just don't want to risk it. You ruin a good relationship that way. He knows I love him. I just won't keep telling him. Something makes me hold that back."

Two Queens students and I sat in a noisy little restaurant near the university. Both were pretty, quick-witted undergraduates, committed feminists. Both had boyfriends; one lived with hers, the other didn't but wished she could.

"My parents would kill me," she said, eating a tasteless lasagna that we all had ordered. "They would find out soon enough, and they just wouldn't let me stay here."

"My parents wouldn't like it, either," the other one agreed. "But they don't know. John has to pay for his room, because his parents think he lives there. He had his phone removed because he was never there to take calls, but he stops by and picks up mail. It's silly, expensive, and hypocritical, but it's the only way we can work it."

"Will you get married when you finish school?"

They both laughed as if that were a good joke instead of a serious question.

"Maybe. I'm not sure I want to," one said. "I don't know. You lose a lot of independence. I don't particularly want to have children, so I don't see why I should be married. And I want a good job. I would always want to work. I just can't imagine sitting around a house all day, polishing furniture and washing nappies. But I guess a lot of that would depend on what my boyfriend wanted."

"We both want children," the other one said, "so I suppose we will get married someday. But I would always work. I wouldn't want to be stuck at home, either."

"What about your friends?" I asked. "Do they think that marriage fits into their future plans?"

"Everyone does his own thing here," she replied. "Most of the students who have a serious commitment wish they could live with one another before they get married. But I guess most of the parents wouldn't like it."

"Do you ever talk about your relationships with your mother or dad?" I asked.

They roared with laughter. Nothing had struck them so funny in ages. Finally one said, "My mother would lock me up if she knew what I do up here in Belfast!"

In Northern Ireland young Protestants and Catholics meet, fall in love, and get married: a "mixed marriage." Both families cringe with the disgrace of it all, bellow with rage, forbid them ever to enter the house again, predict a dire ending for them both, don't attend the wedding, refuse to speak to either one, go into mourning. Time passes. They miss one another. A baby is born. Everyone wants to see the baby. The wound heals. They begin to live in peace with one another.

That's a typical scenario with a mixed marriage. Sometimes — rarely — both families are accepting from the beginning. Sometimes the wound never heals and the offending couple ceases to exist for the rest of the family forever. In Portadown, Christine told me of a friend, a Protestant who had just married a Catholic girl. "It caused such a great to-do," she said. "The parents were so upset. But it often happens. Protestant families especially hate it when their sons marry a Catholic and he becomes a Catholic, too. That means their name will become Catholic. But it's happening here more and more often. It used to be that girls and boys met in clubs, and the clubs were either Protestant or Catholic. But now they go to discos, which are mixed, and they meet each other there."

In May 1987, three months after this conversation, a Belfast couple, Margaret and Gerald Caulfield, were shot in their beds while sleeping. Margaret was killed, Gerald seriously wounded. Married only three weeks, the Caulfields were neither practicing Christians nor political. Their crime was that she had been raised as a Protestant, he as a Catholic, and they had fallen in love and married. Police believe that loyalist gunmen committed the murder.

I asked one of the most sensible, open-minded women I met in Northern Ireland what she would think about one of her children marrying a Catholic. (She had previously told me that she was a "lukewarm Protestant" and went to church more for social reasons than because of deeply religious feelings.)

"I have to say that I wouldn't be very pleased. No one in the family would."

"What would be your objections?"

"I'm quite certain that it is just an in-built prejudice. I have lots of friends whose children have married Catholics, and I don't think they liked it much at the time, but they have grown to accept it and to see that no one has suffered from it. You know, it's really a fear of the unknown."

What's Normal, Anyway?

So many gods, so many creeds
So many paths that wind and wind
While just the art of being kind
Is all the sad world needs.
— *ELLA WHEELER WILCOX*

DESPITE IT ALL — the fear and suspicion, the paranoiac hatreds — life in Northern Ireland, for the majority of its citizens, marches on like it does anywhere else in the developed world. The tension, the stress, the extortion mainly afflict the poor and the working classes. They are the innocent victims of their own people.

But even the "normality" of the middle class is the conscious achievement of a population trying to carry on with their lives while just under the surface the potential of violence seethes and swirls, ready to break out at the beat of a lambeg drum or the *ping*! of a plastic bullet bouncing off the pavement.

After three uneventful trips to Northern Ireland, I was lulled by the illusion of a country going about its business. Then, suddenly, something would happen to bring me up short and make me realize how fragile and tenuous is the achievement of normalcy, how easily the façade collapses. What is more shocking is the lack of response to violence, a numbness that makes life bearable in the midst of horror.

I was walking along Grosvenor Road one spring day in the five o'clock Friday afternoon rush hour, watching the cheerful faces of people greeting the weekend, when suddenly there was a loud thud, like the first peal of distant thunder in an approaching storm. My only reaction was to hope that the rain held off until I got home, being without umbrella or coat. Stepping up my pace, I passed two elderly women walking slowly arm in arm and hurried toward the bus stop. Within seconds the thud was followed by another, this one much louder, and I could feel it underfoot.

I looked around me. No one seemed to take any notice whatsoever. I looked back at the two old ladies. They were still arm in arm, strolling slowly, heads bent toward each other, talking and smiling. As they approached me, I stopped them and asked, "Excuse me, but was that a bomb that just went off?"

"Yes, dear," one said, and they went on their way.

(Later I learned that the bomb had been exploded in a small Belfast hotel; the Chinese owner of the building didn't seem to know why he had been targeted.)

Another evening I was coming back to Belfast from a visit in the country with a friend. The County Down roads were empty, dark, and quiet, and just as I was commenting to my friend about the intense stillness of the countryside, brilliant lights flashed into our windshield, blinding us with their glare. Four police cars formed a barricade at a small crossroads, and a dozen policemen waved us down. We stopped and they approached our windows on both sides of the car.

"I.D., please," one said with quiet courtesy. John produced his; I showed them my passport.

"Car registration, please."

"Open the boot and the bonnet, please." They were so polite. You would have thought the conversation was about the chances of rain or the price of hay.

"Where are you going? Where have you been?" And so on. Nice as could be, they closed up the "boot" and "bonnet," handed us back our papers, and sent us on our way.

"What was *that* all about?" I asked John. I had seen military roadblocks from time to time along the major roads, but had never been stopped at midnight on a back country road. Neither of us knew what was going on until we read the papers the next morning and learned about a major army ambush of an IRA bombing squad in the little town of Loughall, in County Armagh, the night before. Eight Provisional IRA men were killed as well as an innocent bystander.

The next day I drove to the Falls, parked, and walked up and down the road. News of the "massacre," as the killings were being called on the Falls, had reached the city, and the Catholic population in the area was mourning the deaths of the young men. "There'll be mayhem on this road tonight," a shopkeeper told me as I bought a newspaper. "They'll tear the place up." I returned on the following morning, early, and the street looked like a war zone. Still-burning cars were upturned along the curbstones, acrid black smoke pouring out of their flames. Streetlamps and utility poles were downed, lying like giant pick-up-sticks across the roadway. Broken shards of glass were everywhere, and storefronts that hadn't been boarded up were smashed with rocks and bricks. The rioting had gone on all night; like the black population in Washington that erupted so violently upon the news of Martin Luther King Jr.'s assassination, the nationalist population along the Falls destroyed and defaced their own territory. Their protest turned inward upon themselves.

As I walked slowly up the now-quiet and nearly empty street, I saw a tiny ice cream shop that was open, the only sign of life on the road that morning. A handwritten sign above the shop said: "Hand-Made Italian Ices!!" A line of small boys was in the shop, buying cones, intently licking the ice cream as they came out. At the edge of the curb in front of the shop a car lay on its side, flames licking its rusted hood. Not one little boy stopped to look at it, to marvel, to exclaim. They simply licked their cones and walked by it as if it didn't exist. A burning car to them was "normal."

Still, babies are born, toddlers go to play groups, and their mothers carpool; old folks chat on park benches when the sun shines. A prodigious amount of stout and lager gets consumed in smoke-filled pubs; women take selfless care of their young and their old; men play tennis and golf, sail and fish and garden, go to work and come home, pray on Sundays, eat a huge midday dinner, and take their families on outings to the beach. The poor worry about their unpaid bills, their out-of-work sons, their pregnant daughters; the well-off worry about their children making high enough marks to get into university, or the lack of well-paying jobs when they get their degrees; farmers worry about too much rain and the price of beef; professors worry about the quality of their students; students worry about the quality of their professors. Out in the countryside beautifully groomed horses jump over stone walls, chasing a fox, and the lakes and coastal bays are clogged on summer holidays with sailboats racing in the wind.

People drink more tea and coffee, smoke more cigarettes, and swallow more valium than Americans. They also talk more, laugh more, eat more chocolate, and have a far lower crime rate and suicide rate.

They are not a stylish people: the well-off are too formal and old-fashioned, and the poor are too flashy. The Belfast telephone directory doesn't list a psychoanalyst or a periodontist, although tattoo shops are big. Weddings and funerals are very big. Family ties, particularly mother-daughter relationships, are strong, tenacious, and binding.

Because of a two-decade saturation of television coverage of Northern Ireland showing scenes of violence and rioting, it is hard for a stranger coming to the North to relax at first in the humdrum, daily, normal routine of the country. One listens for a bomb, looks for a sniper, sees a truckload of soldiers and thinks the war has started; but these days the terrorist activities of the various Catholic and Protestant paramilitary groups are aimed at a small circle of marked enemies. The random "tit-for-tat" murders of the 1970s are rare now, as are the bombings that once maimed and killed so many innocent people. Also, the technical skills of the terrorists have improved enormously with eighteen years' experience. In the beginning of the Troubles they were often blowing up themselves or the wrong person while trying to devise a homemade bomb. (There is an often-quoted but untraceable statistic that more young men in Northern Ireland have died from accidentally self-inflicted wounds than from being planned targets.) Now their bombs are more sophisticated, their bullets better aimed, their logistics better planned.

In central Belfast, where I often stayed with a friend, there was a convivial, informal social life that swirled around the house all the time. Guests — invited or unexpected — seemed to climb up the steep staircase to the second-floor living room with cheerful, dependable regularity. Students coming for a cup of tea at the end of the afternoon would often still be there when I returned at midnight. Tennis partners stopped by for a drink and stayed for dinner. When a quiet evening seemed to be winding down at 10 P.M., the doorbell would ring and someone from a suburb or neighboring town would arrive after a dinner party or theater, eager for coffee or a nightcap and a chat. In the ordinary course of conversation, politics was seldom discussed unless it was for my sake. Then I sometimes had the feeling that barriers were lowered and surprising disclosures made. Because it was a disparate crowd that came to the house, backgrounds and traditions varied and sensitive subjects were often skirted for the sake of civil discourse. I think people were often surprised to hear a sudden explosion of past anger or buried hurt on the part of a guest in an unexpected turn of the conversation. (One very attractive, vivacious woman spent an hour telling me how free from bigotry or sectarianism her childhood had been, then, an hour later, was weeping over a forgotten memory of her beloved father — a poor Catholic farmer who loved horses — being told by a Protestant neighbor that he had "no business" raising horses.)

The technical things that make a society pleasant and easy work well in Northern Ireland. The telephone system is faultless, and operators are endlessly helpful and patient. The highways and roads, country and urban, are wonderfully maintained and marked. Mail comes twice a day. Shopkeepers are friendly and human. All these services function well in this "war-torn" country.

People on the street are unfailingly, almost aggressively, kind, helpful, and patient with strangers. I was once coming into Belfast by train from Dublin and wanted to get a taxi from the station into the center of town. As I stood looking (and feeling) forlorn in a mean, raw wind with rain blowing in my face and no taxi in sight, a city bus pulled up to the curb where I stood with a heavy suitcase. The bus driver rolled down the window and stuck his head out in the rain.

"You look lost, luv," he shouted. "Where you headed?"

"Anywhere near Great Victoria Street," I answered.

"Hop in" was his cheerful reply as he rolled his window back up. I lugged my suitcase to the far side of the bus and pulled it in behind me. The other passengers didn't seem either perturbed or particularly interested in the recruitment of a passenger at an unscheduled stop. I took a seat right behind the driver and listened to his steady stream of jaunty observations as the big double-decker bus swerved around the tight corners of a dozen narrow streets.

As we neared my destination, he made a sudden stop in the middle of a block and said: "This is as near as I can bring you. It's a one-way street, but you just head up that there street and you can't miss it." He got up, picked up my suitcase, and put it down on the sidewalk for me.

"Wait a minute!" I shouted after him as he started to get back on the bus. "I forgot to pay."

"Ach, let it go," he said.

"You've been very kind," I yelled up to him as he got back into his seat. "I'll return the kindness to someone today."

He grinned. "Forget it, luv. We like to do nice things for strangers here. It's only ourselves we hate."

There is a certain frowning, puritanical, tight-lipped side to life in Northern Ireland that has absolutely nothing to do with sectarian feuds, employment statistics, or republican ideals. It's just the way some people are, part of what is normal. Because of their overdeveloped sense of tribal loyalty, people in the North have to defend "us" against "them" in every possible situation. It makes sticking together more important than facing the truth, and if you won't join in the ceremony of denial, you are easily labeled a troublemaker.

I have a friend in Belfast I'll call Evelyn. Her story, grotesque though it is, illustrates the dark, fearful nature of the puritanical Ulsterman.

Evelyn is sensitive, independent, intelligent. By the time she was thirty she had a good job and enough money in the bank to buy the little house in a nice Belfast neighborhood, on a quiet, tree-lined street. Although she had her own social life, she was friendly with the neighbors and said her hello, how are you's dutifully and cheerfully. She especially enjoyed chatting with two little boys across the street, who whizzed up and down the sidewalk on their bikes, watching for her to come home, waiting for the sweets that she brought them.

People on the block felt sorry for the family who lived directly across the street from Evelyn. They were quiet and kept very much to themselves, although they had lived there for years. The man was old and getting senile. The only son, a man in his thirties, was "not quite right." The mother, dour and overworked, hardly put her head out the door and had no time for any of her neighbors.

Evelyn began to notice that the son took a more than passing interest in her comings and goings. She would drive home from work in the late afternoon and he would be sitting on his stoop, waiting for her. She would leave for an evening's engagement, and he would stand in his yard to watch her go. She would arrive home late from a date, and he would be standing in his bedroom window on the second floor of his house, looking at her through parted curtains.

She began to feel spooked. On the other hand, as a friend blithely pointed out, perhaps she was ultra-safe. He was always watching her, so if someone did try to harm her, her not-quite-right protector might sound an alarm. Evelyn didn't feel comforted by this theory, but nothing more ominous than his constant vigilance occurred, and she began to get used to it.

Then he became more brazen. His face appeared at her window sometimes in the early evening as she sat in her living room. He would disappear quickly if she went to the door. On Saturday nights, at exactly midnight, her phone would ring, and it would be he, asking for himself by name. Finally one night she asked a boyfriend who was there to pick up the phone and bellow: "Who the hell are you and what do you want?" The phone calls ceased.

Then came a beautiful day in May.

"The kind of day," Evelyn said, "that just makes you know everything is going to be wonderful all day. You wake up singing and you know great things will happen!"

She ran some errands, worked in her garden, did a small laundry (it was a rare sunny day to hang it out on the line), then left for an afternoon's outing with a friend.

"We had a marvelous time," she remembered. "I came home in the early evening to dress for dinner, and I just felt that the world was smiling. I ran out into the back yard to bring in my line of laundry, and to my amazement it was gone! Not a stitch there! I was totally bemused and the only possible explanation I could think of was that my next-door neighbor had thought it was going to rain and had taken it in for me.

"I knocked on her back door and her husband answered; they were an older couple and had been friendly neighbors. I asked him about the laundry and he was strange and evasive. 'I wouldn't worry about it, dear,' he said, 'I'm sure it will show up.'

"Show up! I mean, does laundry take a walk and then come home again? It was so weird I just left him standing there in the doorway and went home. Nothing inside the house was touched; it clearly hadn't been a robbery. Who would want four towels, two sheets, and a pile of underwear?"

The euphoria of the afternoon was gone. Evelyn dressed for her dinner date and worried. That night she returned home late, maybe two or three A.M. Just as she turned into her drive, the second-floor light in the bedroom across the street flicked on and he stood in the window, watching her. As she made the rounds in her house, turning off lights and locking up, she glanced out her kitchen window into the back yard. The laundry was hanging neatly on the line. She went straight to the phone and called a friend.

"I am losing my mind," she stated flatly when he answered the phone.

"Go to bed" was his sleepy advice.

She went back out to the kitchen, unlocked her back door, peered around the small, dark yard, and ran out to gather in the laundry. Her panties and bra were stiff and soiled. It didn't take a thorough inspection or a lot of imagination to figure out what they had been used for.

"I knew then that he was sicker than I had thought," she said. "And I didn't really think it would stop there. It's one thing to stare at me all the time; it's another thing to borrow my underwear and masturbate on them. What would he do next?"

Her friends now urged her to call the police, although she was loath to do it. "This was the middle nineteen seventies," she said. "They were being called out dozens of times a night for bomb threats, kneecappings, riots, murders, God knows what. And here I phone up and say, 'Excuse me, but my neighbor steals my bra and panties and, er, uses them for his own, ah, carnal pleasure, er, if you get my point.' I mean, they would think I was totally mad! They would lock *me* up!

"But my friends insisted. One of them said he knew someone in the local station and would have a word with him, promised that it would all be discreet and that they would send out a policewoman in an unmarked car so the neighborhood wouldn't be involved, and all that. So, reluctantly, I agreed, to my everlasting sorrow.

"That night, about ten P.M., I heard this god-awful noise. An RUC truck, with its two-way radio blaring away, a chained police dog in the back barking madly, and a siren that would burst a water main came roaring into my little, quiet street. I mean, every light on the block went on, every window shade popped up. This monstrosity grinds to a halt in front of my house, and here comes this uniformed dragon lady up my walk. You'd see this apparition and you would lock yourself in Long Kesh and be thankful there were bars between the two of you!

"I go quaking to the door and invite her in.

"'I hear you've been having some trouble with your neighbors,' she says, looking at me as if she has just nabbed the Brighton Bomber in person.

"'Well, yes. Sort of.'

"'Tell me about it,' she barks.

"'Well,' I began . . . and I told her all about the way he stares at me, and the laundry on the line, the phone calls.

"She writes it all down in a little book, then she looks at me.

"'How do you know it was semen?'

"'Well, I, er, you know. You can just tell.'

"'Why do you hang your underwear on an outside line?'

"'To dry.'

"'Bit provocative, don't you think?'

"I began to get her point and I also began to get furious.

"'I hang it outside when the sun is shining so it will dry. The same reason anyone hangs any wet laundry out.'

"'Why do you live alone?' was her next question. I thought then that I might slap her face. The only thing that restrained me was her uniform. So I just said: 'I don't have anything else to say. Good night.' I thought that sounded cold, formal, and dismissive."

"'That's it, then?' she asked. 'Don't want to press charges?'

"'No.'

"'Why'd you call us then?'

"'Frankly, I don't know. Good night.'

"She left. God only knows what she put in her report. Probably that I was a mad whore. 'The wee slut brought it all on herself!' It was one of the most humiliating experiences of my life. I suppose that's what women have to face when they go to court on a rape charge. I was far more upset from my encounter with her than I had been with the guy and his nuttiness. I mean, she really made me feel 'dirty.'

"Well, a few days passed, and one evening as I came home from work I saw my next-door neighbor on his stoop. I started to walk over to say hello, and he immediately went inside and closed the door. I didn't think much about it, but the next day another neighbor, a lady at the end of the block, crossed the street when she saw me in front of my house. It was so obvious it was silly. 'What the hell is going on here?' I thought.

"On Saturday the two little boys from down the street were on their bikes. I saw them riding by and went outside to ask them in for a sweet. That had become our Saturday custom. But they both shook their heads when I spoke to them and looked embarrassed.

" 'We can't come in,' they said. 'Our mum says we're not to go inside your house ever again.'

"I just felt my stomach contract and this time I couldn't stop the tears that started up.

"'Why?' I asked.

"'Because,' one said as they got on their bikes to ride away, 'you're a troublemaker.'

"I had my house on the market within a week and sold it at the end of the month. I didn't say good-bye to a soul on the street when I left, nor did any of them come to say good-bye to me. My friend across the street watched the movers all afternoon from his stoop. He never said a word. In fact, we had never exchanged a word the whole time I had lived there."

Tomorrow

. . . For last year's words belong to last year's language
And next year's words await another voice.
— T.S. ELIOT, "Little Giddings"

WHATEVER THE FUTURE has in store for Northern Ireland, it is lying dormant now within its children. What they become so will their country. Ulster women are the stronger, more dominating force in their children's lives. What they become will be affected in large part by what those women tell them and by the example they set.

It is difficult to measure the damage twenty years of violence in Northern Ireland has done to its children. Psychiatrists have made studies; social workers, teachers, and the parents themselves see the emotional and psychological scars. As Morris Fraser points out in his book *Children in Conflict*, some children in Northern Ireland are more at risk emotionally than others, and, in his experience, there are two categories most likely to suffer: a little girl of ten who comes from an area where there has been heavy rioting and who has a family member who has been hurt in some way by the Troubles; or a teenage boy from a paramilitary family, probably one whose father is imprisoned. But many parents whose profiles fit neither of the above categories have also told me of their child's stress symptoms: bed-wetting, stuttering, nightmares, digestive problems, and, more seriously, antisocial behavior.

I have spent several evenings over the past few years at a youth center in the Ardoyne neighborhood of Belfast, a very beleaguered area that is undergoing rehabilitation now. When I first saw it, it was a dangerous maze of tiny, poor, derelict houses, broken streetlamps, littered walks, empty lots, and boarded-up doorways. Stray dogs wandered around listlessly, heads and tails tucked down, symbolic of the area's despair. An old friend of mine, Bridie Maguire, and her husband, had spearheaded a move to get the youth center built there, and it is now an established part of the children's lives. They can play organized sports on a big gymnasium floor or participate in numerous activities upstairs: pool, video games, arts and crafts, Ping-Pong. They mind their manners or they soon come to loggerheads with Bridie, no pushover, and so there are no serious behavior problems. Nevertheless, the pitch of nervous energy in the building is extraordinary. They run, they scream, they yell, they laugh, they push and shove, they play ball, they just *move* in a manic style. Whether that unleashed energy comes from living in houses that are too small for so many people, or whether it is a sign of the excessive emotional and psychic strain they live with, I don't know. But it's obvious that they are burning up enormous amounts of accumulated tension within the walls of the youth center.

Children have a wonderful ability to absorb whatever is going on around them and make it normal. They also have the ability to forget. I was having lunch with a woman in Belfast, and her grown daughter, who now lives in the United States, joined us. The talk was of the difficulty of raising four children alone, as this woman did when she was widowed very young.

"You suffer each worry alone, you have to wonder if you are doing the right things. You wait up alone for them to come in." She turned to her daughter. "Remember the time you were walking home alone from that dance and someone tried to strangle you?"

The young woman looked completely blank and replied, "What are you talking about?"

"When that man jumped out at you from the telephone box, and tried to strangle you . . . and you ran home so upset! I had to comfort you for hours."

"Mother," the girl replied, "I have absolutely no recollection of what you are saying!"

Both mother and daughter became slightly agitated and also embarrassed. The mother was obviously perplexed and worried that her daughter didn't remember the incident.

"You must remember! We were upset for days. We thought it might be one of those Tartan Boys, because of the way he was dressed."

The young woman's eyes widened. The light bulb had gone on.

"Oh, yes," she said, slowly. "Now I am beginning to remember. I was walking home alone in the dark, and he jumped out from behind and grabbed me around the neck and . . . well, I don't remember much more, but you know, I had *totally* forgotten that."

"Maybe I shouldn't have made you remember," the mother said with a smile. "But it never occurred to me that you would have forgotten it. You were so upset at the time."

Social workers talk about the children's addiction to violence. "They see on the street in front of their homes what most children watch every night on television," one of them told me. "Of course, it isn't nearly as bad now as it was in the early nineteen seventies, where there might be rioting of some sort each night. And it's confined to certain neighborhoods. Many children are growing up in Northern Ireland who have never seen a street confrontation in their lives. I think that is what is hard for people outside the country to understand. They think we are *all* under siege all the time!"

Statistics seem to show that most of the children who grew up in the worst times, in the worst areas, have come to terms with the stress in their lives and have learned in one way or another to deal with it effectively. Valium addiction is endemic, and drinking is heavy (as it is in the Republic; perhaps it is an Irish rather than a "Troubles" problem). But there is no serious drug problem, juvenile delinquency rates are low, and the incidence of serious mental illness is no higher in the North than it was twenty years ago. So the final judgment of the effects of the past two decades on the children will have to be made in some future time.

The current hopes of most parents in the North are that (1) their children not get involved with paramilitary activities and (2) they do well in school, and, once out, find good jobs.

To see how well they are being prepared for this precarious future, I visited St. Louisa's Comprehensive School on the Falls Road during a visit I made to Belfast in January 1987. It has a reputation in Belfast of being one of the best girls' schools in the country.

A guard stopped my car at the gate of the school and wanted to know my business. No chance of a stray troublemaker wandering in.

I told him I was there to see Sister Genevieve, the headmistress. The gate swung open, and I was pointed in the direction of the large parking lot. It's a big school: 2,800 girls, the largest girls' comprehensive in the British Isles. The grounds are swept clean. There is none of the rubble and litter one sees along the Falls on the grounds of St. Louisa's. Inside, the school is spotless: windows gleam, floors shine. The smell of wax and soap bring back more memories, this time of my own Catholic school days, when dropping a chewing-gum wrapper on our own waxed hallway was just short of a mortal sin.

I waited for a few minutes in a little foyer outside of Sister Genevieve's office until she came bustling in, small and slim, intense, friendly, and ageless in the way that nuns are. She is a Sister of Charity of St. Vincent de Paul; her "habit" is a blue wraparound jumper, worn over a white turtleneck cotton jersey. She has a small blue veil that partially covers her hair, and she wears sunglasses. As soon as she began to speak, I thought I recognized a Dublin accent, and she confirmed it.

"What makes St. Louisa's so special?" I asked as we sat down in her comfortable office. "People tell me that everyone in this area wants their daughter to go to St. Louisa's."

Sister Genevieve laughed. "We have very independent girls here; they have to be more independent than other girls their age. That's their history. They haven't always had it easy here, and they know if they want to get anywhere they will have to stand up and be counted. St. Louisa's is their first-choice school. They have to put it down as their first choice. They wouldn't get in here if they put it down as a second choice. They come here at eleven and leave at eighteen. Three-quarters of the girls in the upper sixth [the honors course of twelfth grade] go on to higher education. If they don't get a place somewhere the first time round, they repeat and usually get it the second time. Then they get good jobs. Someone told me the other day not to say 'jobs.' Say 'career openings'! Whatever you call it, they will go into jobs where they will be promoted and can make a career. We don't look for ordinary jobs for them."

"Is it harder to place the girls in career jobs than boys?" I asked.

"No, it's just the opposite here. First of all, our girls have an advantage because they come from St. Louisa's. It has a good name. Some of the boys from this troubled area have a hard time finding jobs; they get so demoralized just walking around with nothing to do that they finally end up taking any kind of a job, even if it isn't going to lead to anything. So we encourage them to come here and take courses with the girls, maybe physics, for instance."

"Why isn't there a St. Louisa's for boys?"

She laughed. "Everyone asks me that. Well, you see, this is a troubled area, but we are kind of isolated right here. And then there is an advantage in having someone like me run a school. I can be independent because I'm a nun. I'm not sure I would say some of the things I say if I had a car or a home and a family that I was afraid would be attacked. I remember asking one of the fathers here once, 'Why do you allow these people to take your cars and so on?' And he said: 'I have only one house and one family. I can't afford to run the risk.'

"Another great advantage of St. Louisa's is the great interest the parents here take in their children's education. Parents here are very ambitious for their children, but Belfast people get a terrible picture painted of themselves. Visitors come here and they say: 'Where's the war? We want to see the war!' Well, most of the people here are working very hard to raise their families and see them do well. Just like people everywhere. There's no bigotry in this school, either. We have English people on our staff . . . we have Protestants. Some of the parents have aspirations to be nationalists, but it's a mixed crowd and that's a healthy thing here in the Falls."

Just at that moment there was a light knock on the door, and six or seven girls came in, identical in their brown gabardine skirts and vests and white cotton blouses. They were attractive and sweet-mannered, reserved but not shy. They had a certain self-confidence that gave them a quiet dignity. When they spoke, it was with a seriousness and intensity that is unusual in a girl of sixteen or seventeen. Their success at school has already given them a sense of command.

"This is the cream of the crop," Sister Genevieve said, smiling, obviously very proud of this group of sixth-form girls. "You can talk to them and get a good idea of what goes on in the school. But they aren't representative! All of these girls will be going on to university next year. They are all senior prefects. They are the school leaders."

The girls brought in tea and cookies, and we sat down in the small office. They were quiet at first, but their answers became more animated as we made small talk and joked. I asked them if they were feminists; they looked at each other and laughed, then turned serious.

"Yes," one answered. "I am. I think we all are. We want a fair deal.

We want to have the same opportunities that men have. Does that make us feminists?"

"You're on the right road," I told them.

"Sister Genevieve is interested in making sure that we get an equal chance as women," another one said. "She pushes us to do our best, to compete with the boys from boys' schools, and that gives us confidence."

"Yes, she expects a lot from us, and we try to live up to her expectations," added another.

We talked about the school curriculum. It was very much like an academic high school in the United States. "What about studying the Irish language?" I asked.

"It's optional. You can choose it as you would another foreign language. It's difficult, and we want to get as many O levels as we can, so that keeps a lot of girls from studying Irish."

"What about social problems in school?" I asked. "Drinking. Drugs."

Sister Genevieve answered that. "There is no drinking or drugs at school, of course. I personally think the girls should be trained for social drinking when they are teenagers. A lot of our problems with drinking here in Ireland is that they don't know how to drink: how much they can drink, the importance of eating with drinking, and that sort of thing. We don't have any drugs here. We can't have dances at night in the school, though, because some of the boys who would come would cause trouble. There is a lot of vandalism in the area. We do have concerts, plays, parent meetings, and night classes, but we just can't have dances. The school is open every night for classes; the people in this neighborhood are so interested in furthering their education. They come in to take all sorts of things: vocational subjects, art, history, poetry. When we achieve peace in this country there is going to be a tremendous new age!"

I asked the girls to tell me about their politics, and Sister Genevieve stood up and smiled. "I don't discuss politics in the school," she explained, "so I don't want to be in on this conversation. But you go right ahead." She turned to the girls. "You can speak freely," she advised, "but wait 'til I get out of the room!"

The girls sat expectantly, waiting for my questions.

"Do you talk politics at home?" I asked.

"Oh, yes." Their agreement was unanimous. "We do. We don't always agree, but we talk. If you discuss politics, you understand what you think. But we can't discuss it at school. That's a very strict rule here."

One pretty, round-faced girl spoke up. "I come from a republican family," she said. "My father is in prison. I think my political views are strongly formed by that. My views would probably be different from some of the views of the other girls here."

Two of the other girls said they had no strong republican attitudes, and they condemned the actions of the IRA vehemently. With tears in her voice, one spoke very emotionally. "We had a bomb planted in our yard once, because we live on the corner and British soldiers pass by. If it had gone off and killed someone in my family, I would never have forgiven them. It does no good to say, as they do, 'Oh, we're sorry that someone innocent got killed.' The truth is, they kill innocent people all the time!"

"What do you think you can do to break down sectarian feelings?" I asked. They looked at each other before one spoke up. "Sometimes we do things with Orangefield [a Protestant girls' school], but I wish we did a lot more. They are very nice girls. We can sit and talk. When you get to know them, they are really nice. Sometimes you hear people around here say, 'Oh, I hate Protestants,' and then you find out that they never met one. They are just brought up that way and they hear that at home. But that would only be an extreme nationalist who would say that.

"The extreme loyalists are the same. We were walking home after a party on New Year's Eve and we had to go through a Protestant neighborhood. A bunch of boys came out and shouted at us: 'We hate you! Why do you come here?' They didn't hit us, but they chased the boys we were with. You'd wonder why fellows the same age as us would hate us, wouldn't you?"

I asked them if they would ever consider the idea of going as an exchange student to a Protestant school, maybe for a month or for a term. They were very excited about the idea, and although they had never thought about it, they believed it would work. But, they cautioned, it would be dangerous going through Protestant neighborhoods on their way to the school. "We could get attacked on the bus getting to the school," they said.

"How would they know who you are?" I asked.

They all smiled. "They would know. Because of our uniforms, for one thing."

Another girl chimed in. "I go to a music school in the center of town. I go there straight from school and people make remarks to me on the way because of my school uniform."

"What if an American girl came to live in Belfast for a term," I suggested. "Say she was Catholic, but she was sent to a Protestant school because it was nearer her home. Would anyone make a fuss?"

They all agreed that no one would care.

"How about other ways of breaking down the myths that grow out of not knowing each other? What else could you do besides school exchanges?"

They looked at one another, but no one could come up with another idea.

"If you met a Protestant boy and liked him, would you go out with him?" I asked.

That made them all smile, but then they all said they would. "But," one added, "I could only marry him if he promised to bring up the children Catholic. They have to make that promise if you marry them."

I pointed out that that was no longer true, that the engaged couple simply arrive at a mutual decision on the children's religious upbringing. They were astounded to hear that.

Sister Genevieve returned at that point, and she suggested that the girls take me on a tour of the building. We made the rounds: classrooms, laboratories, the library, the sixth-form recreation room, the chapel. Everything was well-ordered, quiet.

I complimented Sister Genevieve on the girls as I was leaving.

"They are strong girls," she agreed. "They're articulate, and they know their rights. I say to them all the time, 'Go out and form a new Ireland!' and that's what they are doing. There will be a network of St. Louisa's girls and they will help each other. That's the way men have always done it. That's the way we'll do it."

I was talking to a friend that evening about my visit to St. Louisa's, and telling her how impressed I was with the school and the girls I met there.

"She's a tyrant, that Sister Genevieve!" my friend said. "She's also a shrewd politician. She knows what she wants for the school and she knows how to get it. But she loves those smart girls; she doesn't have any time for the ordinary ones."

I don't know what she does with ordinary girls, but I know that the training and formation of an elite group of young Catholic women in Northern Ireland is one of the most positive and important steps that the nationalist community can take. The best way to slough off feelings of inferiority is to be superior. St. Louisa's is striving for superiority.

The "brain drain" of well-educated young people in Northern Ireland is one of the most serious long-term effects the Troubles have had on the country. Unskilled youngsters either "hang around," living on the dole, or immigrate to England and the United States to look for work.

But now, because of the severe economic depression and the lack of immediate future prospects, the young, educated generation of the North is leaving by the hundreds. Without exception, all middle-class families in the North whom I met have one or more of their university-educated children living abroad. If that pattern isn't broken soon, and if opportunities aren't created to entice the "best and brightest" to remain, Northern Ireland will not only diminish its population, it will lose its chance to play a meaningful role as one of the small, vital countries of Europe.

Not only must jobs be created, but employment must be meted out in a fair and nondiscriminatory fashion. Two organizations in Northern Ireland try to maintain fair employment practices, one between men and women, and the other between Catholics and Protestants. The former is called the Equal Opportunities Commission (EOC), and the latter the Fair Employment Agency. Mary Glass is the Welsh-born director of the Equal Opportunities Commission. She is brisk, fast-talking, and smart, and her lively green eyes sparkle with animation. She is typical of the younger, well-educated, emancipated women of Northern Ireland.

"We aren't really dissimilar here from most other European countries; the length of education has a substantial impact on individual opinion, but men are still less prepared to accept that women have as much to offer industry as men. And there are very few women at the top in Northern Ireland. Allied Irish Bank, for instance, has just appointed its second female bank manager. We have no women judges and only one full-time woman magistrate. Very few women are college principals, and only fourteen percent on our public boards. In many places, professionals are more liberal than other groups, but in Northern Ireland that isn't true. You don't have political and social change filtering down through the middle classes here, so you have to depend on agencies like this one to enforce change. Nevertheless, we are making progress.

"I think that younger women may feel more positive about their role in the work force, but semi-skilled women are still very frustrated. In an opinion poll we took, over half of them said they would stop work if their husbands wanted them to.

"There was dreadful mistreatment of the Catholic population here. When we have Fair Employment Agency meetings [which handle religious-discrimination complaints in the job market], emotions run very high, much higher than in sex-discrimination cases. I would be the first one to say that the discrimination here against Catholics was deep, pervasive, and destructive. But things are better in that area now, as well. The Provos might say, 'Too little, too late,' but I can see substantive change.

"However, the most disadvantaged group in Northern Ireland, according to an EOC Report, are working-class Catholic girls. They don't take physics, computer science, or higher math classes; there is still a colonial attitude here. But the girls themselves are often a disappointment. You try to talk to them and all they are interested in are their boyfriends and a few television programs.

"Contraception is freely available here, but women bear children much longer than women do in the rest of Europe, consequently we have a very high rate of spina bifida and mongoloidism. Most middle-class Catholic women here use contraception of some sort, but many working-class Catholics don't."

I asked Mary about women in politics, my usual question. "Well, the secretary-general of the Alliance Party is a woman, but you're right, we don't have many women involved in politics here. It's not that different in England, you know, although there are more women getting involved in the Republic of Ireland. And women are put off the trade-union movement, I think. Their meetings are like a foreign language to most women! 'Brother' this and 'Brother' that. They quote endlessly from rule books and the meetings go on for hours, and then they haven't moved an inch. That's not a woman's natural style. Most women like action, not talk. But the failure of the women's peace movement taught us that peace has to come through a political process. A lot of women here were very disillusioned about that movement. They not only didn't have the support of the political parties, they had to fight against them.

"Nowadays, the closest thing to the peace movement is the Women's Information Group. They are nonsectarian and they are a support group for each other. They know, for instance, if their boys are in trouble and the IRA are after them, kneecapping them, and they don't go to the police because it's not in their tradition. Where do they go? They get strength from themselves. You see, what most women want is to pay their mortgage, see their children safely raised, put food on the table."

"Would women be afraid to turn to something like the Women's Information Group?" I asked.

"Some of them might be, but one of their women, Joyce McCarten, just walked in their office one day and said to a Provie group, 'Get out!' She's a formidable lady! Now there is someone you should talk to. Generally, though, women aren't a target of the IRA. They are either Mary Magdalene or Virgin Mary figures. That keeps them safe!"

As I left, Mary walked with me to the elevator, and as we stood waiting for it to come, I asked her if she thought peace would bring prosperity to Northern Ireland.

"I think prosperity would bring peace," she replied. "That's what we need here more than anything else: jobs for everyone who can work."

In Love and Anger

MY INITIAL REACTION TO Northern Ireland was confusion and puzzlement. Who are these men who hold their country ransom for a dream? What do they want? Why can't they settle their problems peacefully? What are they fighting about? Why do they hate each other?

My puzzlement turned to irritation as some of these questions were clarified. The problems in the North really aren't that big. There is no Third World misery in Northern Ireland. Their parochial plight shrinks compared to troubles in Ethiopia, Bolivia, Pakistan, Afghanistan. No one is starving in Northern Ireland. There is very little nonpolitical crime. There is no serious drug problem. AIDS has scarcely touched the country. There are no droughts, pestilence, disease. The land is beautiful and fertile. The climate is moderate. There is an excellent public education system and free medical care. There is concern and support for the arts. The population is skilled, literate, charming, and witty. There is no more generous people in the world: the Irish give more to charity, per capita, than any other country in Europe. Their family ties are strong, supportive, and enduring. It would seem that a minimum of good sense, charity on both sides, and a deflated sense of the importance of their quarrel would solve their problems.

The women of Northern Ireland are admirable and likable. When you hear what is inside their minds, their own anger and anguish become real. But despite affection and admiration for their wit, their tenacity, their black humor in the face of adversity, you come back to frustration that deepens into anger. You want to ask: "Why do you let a few men sanctify war? Why hold them up as heroes to your children who need other dreams, other heroes to form their identity? It distorts the imagination of children to have only warriors and martyrs as heroes. Why sing the songs and tell the stories that keep the legends alive?"

Northern Irish don't have a franchise on history, but they make themselves prisoners of their past, like the Greeks and Turks. Every country has its scorched and painful eras; a test of greatness is whether a country can transcend its history and reach out to its future. It must teach its children to widen their concerns, to make themselves part of the struggle for a better world, not just a better Northern Ireland. Over and over again, I heard people in the North say that women were the dominant force in shaping their children's life. If this is true, then the women have even more responsibility to bring up their children with an eagerness to achieve their ambitions and with past hurts buried.

Northern Unionists once dominated their society politically, economically, and socially. The monopoly of Unionist power has been destroyed, and the Unionist establishment has not been able to face up to this. They have to learn a new way of looking at themselves, at life, at their place in the country. They have to learn that they must live side by side, in equality, with the Catholic population. But so far, it has been impossible to coax Protestants into this role. Their tradition is against them. The leadership that would have brought its people toward a fair settlement of their grievances has been denied generations of Ulstermen and -women.

Now members of the IRA want the same kind of mastery that the Unionists once had, and what they can't achieve politically, they try to achieve militarily. Today they are an experienced, committed, skilled terrorist organization. Only a gradual withdrawal of support for them in the nationalist population will diminish their image and lessen their impact. Their chips should be called in. If they truly want to work toward a goal of a united, socialist Ireland, they have a political party and they can work constitutionally toward that goal. It was, after all, the peaceful civil rights demonstrations of 1969 that put the first crack in Unionist discrimination, not IRA violence. If the majority of the population supports them, they will eventually achieve their goal. (However, since less than 50 percent of the Catholic population favor unification, that goal seems very elusive.)

Republicans in Northern Ireland who still feel that violence and military force are the only means that are effective in coercing change in their country often point to the American Revolutionary War. "Look," they say. "You got your freedom from Britain because you waged a war yourselves. Then you come over here and tell us not to do the same thing!" But negotiation and political compromise are more sophisticated tools in the 1980s. Communication is easy and fast. Both sides can know what the other is thinking immediately. Politicians may not be better educated or skilled in their craft, but negotiating techniques are more advanced, and the mutual economies of all the countries involved are more closely intertwined. There is more international pressure on countries to settle their differences.

Their propaganda symbols seem pathetically trivial — flags and emblems, symbols that seem archaic in a modern world — and yet they cling to them for dear life.

In any nationalist movement, the use of or the banning of language becomes a potent propaganda device. The republican devotion to the Irish language contrasts poignantly with the indifference and impatience of schoolchildren in the Republic of Ireland. There, the children are required to study Irish at school five days a week for twelve years. Except for those children whose parents are interested in the language and speak it themselves, or send their children to spend summers with Irish-speaking families (like the Gillespies in Bunbeg), very few of the children I ever knew in Ireland spoke Irish with any fluency. They felt their time would be much better spent mastering French, German, or Spanish, not to mention Chinese or Japanese.

The saddest thing I heard in my travels around the North was women saying, "Oh, we've played a big part in these Troubles." Then you find that their "big role" was banging garbage lids to signal the arrival of British troops, or making sandwiches and tea for the lads.

"Oh, we've really changed and grown because of the Troubles," they say, and then admit that their "growth" is the discovery that they can run their households and raise their children by themselves if their men are dead or in prison, and many times they discovered that they like it better that way. Their "freedom" is an erosion of the cultural and religious traditions that make Northern Ireland unique.

Many women in Northern Ireland think the "national problem" far outweighs the women's issue. But because of the national problem, women are being forced to take on a huge burden, which leaves very little time or space for themselves. The ultimate feminist goal in Northern Ireland should be to create unity among the women there and a common voice that refutes terrorism as a way of life. Until that voice is heard, men will recite those ancient wounds with monotonous regularity to a world grown tired of listening. Their history has given them an addiction to revenge, an addiction as insidious as alcohol or drugs. If they conquer that addiction, they will start achieving their potential, which is great. "Northern Ireland" could become synonymous with cultural and intellectual contributions to the civilized world far out of proportion to its size and population.

Most wounds heal with time. Time is running out for Northern Ireland.

Epilogue [1989]

So many people in Belfast had told me that I should meet Joyce McCarten; hers was a name that came up over and over again when we talked about activist women, women who were in the front line, trying to achieve reconciliation and a viable community life. A Catholic woman married to a Protestant, she has been a leader in the Women's Information Group, an organization of women across sectarian lines who bring one another practical and moral comfort. We spoke on the telephone and agreed then that we would meet when I returned to Belfast the following May.

One evening in May, when I was back in Belfast, I sat talking with my Charabanc friends in their back yard and then later in their kitchen, having a stimulating and, as the evening progressed, hilarious time. That very night, as we sat and laughed and drank white wine, a car with loyalist terrorists drew up in front of the McCarten house, only seventeen blocks from where we sat around the kitchen table. One man apparently sat in the car, ready to drive away. Others burst into the tiny front vestibule of the small row house, guns drawn. Gary McCarten, Joyce's seventeen-year-old son, her "baby," was in the front sitting room. As he appeared in the hall to see what all the commotion was, the gunmen opened fire. He staggered back into the kitchen, which is in the back of the house, and fell into his father's arms. He died almost instantly.

Gary was not involved with any paramilitary or political organization. His murder was apparently a "simple" sectarian murder. He was shot by Protestants because he was a Catholic. Gary was not the first in his family to lose his life because of sectarian violence in the North. In 1972, his cousin died after being dragged out of a wedding reception and stabbed 200 times. His uncle and brother-in-law were both shot dead in the same week of March 1974. His granny, Alice, died soon thereafter of a broken heart.

So I did finally get to meet Joyce McCarten, at the wake of her son. Their small house was filled with people when I arrived, both Catholic and Protestant friends and neighbors. Mary Glass, the woman who had first told me about Joyce, was just leaving. Bishop Cathal Daly had come that afternoon to pay his respects. Joyce was in the kitchen when I arrived and received me with the warm charm that she exudes to all who come across her path. Her face was crumpled and pale, her once-red hair faded, but she smiled as she hugged me, welcomed me, and took my hand in hers as if I were an old friend.

"Come," she said. "Come into the sitting room and see my baby." We walked through the crowd of men sitting silently in the back room, through the little hallway, also thronged with visitors, and into the front room, where the women mourners sat together. Gary was laid out by the front bay window. Sympathy cards filled his casket. He had been due to be married in a few weeks, and he was in his dark wedding suit, with a white shirt and red tie. His wispy, seventeen-year-old's mustache and heavy, dark eyebrows contrasted with the death pallor of his face. Joyce reached out and put her worn hand on his cold forehead. "Here's my boy," she said, and all the sadness of Northern Ireland was in her voice.

Reaching Common Ground [1996]

WHEN I TRAVELED around Northern Ireland in the mid-1980s, talking to women from all "persuasions," I was struck by the factthat so few of them knew their counterparts on "the other side." Northern Ireland is, after all, a small country. If it weren't for the Troubles, women in leadership roles in each community would have the opportunity to meet, talk, and exchange ideas and experience. Instead, most of the women I met who were Catholic nationalists would not have met and talked with their counterparts in the Protestant community. But they knew about one another. They were eager to know if I had met so and so, and what was she like, and what did she say.

They seemed alike to me, in their shared desire for peace and prosperity for their country and for their children's welfare. But during those years of the mid-1980s, a face-to-face meeting would have been considered provocative and could have been dangerous. So I became an informal conduit, passing on interesting bits of information from one group to another.

When I returned home from my two- or three-week research trips in the North and transcribed the dozens of tapes I brought with me from my interviews, I was both surprised and fascinated by the similar points of view many of these women espoused. Here were plain-talking women, full of common sense and fed up with the political leadership that had gotten their country nowhere. Each disdained the posturing of demagogues, who purported to be "leaders" of their community. Many were wary of the influence of the churches and churchmen, both Catholic and Protestant, and almost all were impatient with the relationship between themselves and their churches. They were sick of living in a world filled with violence, mayhem, anger, fear, and death.

Only a very few on the fringes of terrorists organizations were still able or willing, after fifteen years of violence, to cling to their belief in the efficacy of the gun over the constitutional process.

As I sat in my office back home after these trips, listening to the women's words coming through the earphones of my tape recorder, their Northern Irish accents familiar to me by now, I was filled with a growing conviction that here was a passionate force, an energy fed by frustration and fueled by fear, that was waiting to be unleashed. There was a realism, a stark and sometimes brutal truth in their response to the world that had been created around them, a world locked into place by grim history. And they saw the lack of their presence on the political stage.

I felt that if these women of the North could come together on neutral ground, meet each other and their counterparts among the women of the Republic of Ireland and the United States and give voice to their aspirations and fears, they would create a united platform upon which to work for peace, and that in their unity they would be strong.

Years passed while this dream of mine lay untended in back files of my desk, taken out from time to time, more wistfully than with purpose. In the meantime, it was becoming easier in Northern Ireland for women from all sides to gather, to hold meetings, and to begin to build the trust among themselves that they would need to work in unity. Then one day in 1992, I was asked by the British Consul General in Boston, John Owen, to be host at a luncheon party for Lady Mayhew, wife of the newly posted Secretary of State for Northern Ireland, Sir Patrick Mayhew. I was told that she had a far-reaching interest in Northern Ireland and was trying to meet and reach out to all communities there.

It was a small lunch, only six women, including Catherine Shannon of Westfield College and Margaret MacCurtain of University College Dublin, who was in Boston doing a year's fellowship at Boston College. I launched my idea of bringing a group of women from Northern Ireland to Boston, and all the women, including Jean Mayhew, responded with enthusiasm. In fact, by the time we had finished eating, it was as if it had become a "done thing." All we had left to do was trivial: raise the money, get the location, persuade the women to come, find hosts to house them while they were here, organize a Boston group, and map out an agenda!

Time passed and the conference began to take shape. Trips were made to and from Northern Ireland. Meetings were held in Boston, at Hillsborough House in Belfast, and at other sites. Women were brought together who were doing vital work in their communities over the past twenty years—work that, if left undone would have meant the end of a viable life in Northern Ireland.

It was interesting and revelatory for me to see how the women's relationship had changed in the past ten years since I had started research on the book. Many more women of disparate backgrounds were coming together to meet and talk; even more surprising was the fact that many of them—Catholic, nationalist women—would come to Hillsborough House, the home in Northern Ireland of the British Secretary of State for Northern Ireland and a symbol of British power there for centuries. This happy development had come about because of the efforts of Jean Mayhew to reach out to all communities and to try to listen and support the goals and aspiration of them all. She had won the respect and trust of all these women, no small feat in Northern Ireland for anyone!

Women came and sat at the table and talked about the advantage of coming together outside of Northern Ireland. These were, in many cases, women whose personal lives had been shattered by the inhumanity and brutality of life in Northern Ireland; whose husbands, sons, and loved ones had been killed, whose quality of life was very poor, whose educational opportunities, careers, and normal life activities had been stunted by bloody mindlessness of governments and politicians. They were willing to try a new tack, to meet with their fellow countrywomen, to talk in structured workshops and informal social settings.

I have always been interested in politics and puzzled by the lack of formal political participation among the women of the North. All the ones I knew seemed like natural politicians, ready and eager to give of their time to create a better social and economic world. But they were recalcitrant about joining a political party. As Eileen Evason, a professor of political science at the University of Ulster, had asked incredulously many years earlier: "Join the Unionists? Join the SDLP?" The absurdity of this option always brought down the house in a discussion of women in politics.

It was clear that the political options currently open in Northern Ireland were not going to attract women, even the greatest activists among them. Besides, as they patiently explained to this outsider, the onus of being a member of a particular political party in Northern Ireland was to identify one with a religious and political attitude. This identification would damage one's ability to gain trust inside a community.

Back in the United States, our ever-growing group of Irish American women was responding enthusiastically and generously to the plans. President Jon Westling of Boston University was a crucial supporter who offered the use of university facilities, as well as a generous budget to start our fund-raising.

The support and enthusiasm of John and Carol Owen, the British Consul General and his wife, were crucial in each step along the way. With the help of all the women in the conference and the people they reached out to, plus the funds raised from an auction of Irish art, books, and objects, all generously donated by Irish patrons of the conference, we were finally able to raise funds so that we could finance the trip to America of all the Irish women. We did not want any woman to be left behind because she lacked funding.

No one dreamed during the early planning stages of this conference that by the time we would convene in Boston in an unseasonably warm week of November 1994, that the cease-fire would have been announced in Northern Ireland and the country would be, for the first time in over two decades, experiencing the peace and quiet of a country without armed warfare. Borders and barriers were opened; the police walked the streets in ordinary uniforms. The vehicles of warfare, tanks and armored cars, disappeared from the streets. Roadblocks were nonexistent. It was a heady, cheerful, and optimistic time for Northern Ireland. It was with this atmosphere at home that the women convened in Boston.

For three days we met morning, noon, and night at Boston University. We had formal speeches at open sessions, and at closed workshops we discussed mutual concerns. In the evenings we ate, drank, talked, sang, and enjoyed the hospitality of the very generous Boston families who were hosts to the Irish women. We broke stereotypes, we got mad, we became perplexed on occasion, we overcame a few prejudices we had held for years, and we learned a lot about each other. We also tried to nominate one of our women to be the first lay cardinal in history!

We urged the women of Northern Ireland to participate in politics: Shirley Williams, in her very eloquent opening-day speech, set the tone for this: "Please, may I beg you, take the opportunity that will be offered you to put forward your views, your proposals, and your constructive suggestions because this is a crucial opportunity.

"A week ago in the Kennedy School Forum at Harvard, I heard a group of former Loyalist terrorists speak movingly about their desire to make a new start. It reminded me of former South African terrorists both white and black saying the same thing only a few months ago. . . . I conclude by saying that it won't be easy . . . there is much pain, much agony, and much division that we have to put behind us. We all know that we cannot build a world for our children to live in on the foundation of violence. There has to be a better way. And I believe that women are a large part of that better way."

There were moments of high drama and heart-breaking sadness, such as that which we experienced during the speech that the Irish journalist Mary Holland gave at one of the public sessions:

"When I look back over twenty-five years of reporting from the North, it isn't the great historic events which get into the history books that I remember, such as when the cease-fire was called, or the Anglo-Irish Agreement, or the Atkins Talks or the Power Talks. . . .

"What I remember are people . . . and their stories. I remember Michael Kelly's mother telling me how she told her son to wear clean underwear when he went out to march on Bloody Sunday, because if anyone picked him up and he was arrested they would know that somebody cared about him. And then when she heard that he was shot, she remembered nothing for three years. Members of her family told me that she was often found on his grave, scrabbling at the earth, in the dark of the night.

"I remember Annie Harkness telling me of her son, who had come back from the safety of Australia because he was worried about his mother after she had an operation, and how he was blown to bits at Teebane.

"I remember Charlie Butler in the Shankill Road, telling how he dug up three members of his own family and never recognized them out of the rubble of the Shankill bomb.

"And I remember the widows walking behind the coffins with the television cameras, and the children by their sides, bewildered, not knowing what was going on.

"And I remember Mairead Farrell's funeral, and her parents' flowers on her grave. I remember kneeling over the body of one of the soldiers—the naked body of one of the two soldiers who was lynched two or three days after that funeral while Father Reed tried to give him the kiss of life.

"And I know that we have to find a better way of making sure that doesn't happen again."

I had never been in a public forum and seen two hundred women quietly weeping at the end of a speech. For those women in the audience who had suffered personal losses, it was even more poignant, more nearly unbearable.

On the last day of the conference, we met at Wellesley College and at the final wrap-up, one of the women from Belfast stood up, took the microphone, and said: "I am going home a changed person." Her eloquent, simple sentence spoke for all of us.

Rabbi Julia Neuberger, the handsome, dynamic Chancellor of the University of Ulster, gave the opening speech at Wellesley, and with eerie prescience asked the rhetorical question:

"Suppose we could have a women's coalition in Northern Ireland? Suppose the women could change part of the political agenda, suppose they were actually able to insist that they were consulted in all the negotiations, in all the framework agreements?"

I don't think any of us dreamed at that moment that the formation of the Northern Ireland Women's Coalition would be only two years away.

One of the difficulties we had to overcome during the conference had as much to do with the composition of the different groups in terms of class and professional background as it did with religion or politics. Many of the women in the Northern delegation were people from the community level and working-class communities. They are more political because they are living and operating in situations where one must be "political" to survive. It seemed to me that the women from the North admired the women from the Republic for their professional achievements, but felt that they were not as attuned to the problems facing working-class women as they themselves were, having spent, as they have, years in ground-level community work.

There were many strands of relationships we explored during the conference. Not only was it a unique opportunity for Irish American women to glean understanding and insights into the social patterns, political history, and contemporary life of women of Northern Ireland, it was also an opportunity for interaction between women of the North and South of Ireland. Being an American (with no conscious Irish American background until I married), and having lived in the South of Ireland for four years, I have been intrigued and not a little puzzled by the attitudes that Southern and Northern women hold about each other. Aside from obvious family ties or close personal friendships, they approach each other with tense wariness.

In the summer of 1996, I was visiting the novelist and playwright Jennifer Johnston and her husband, David Gilliland, in their home in Derry. I had heard Jennifer participate in a panel in Cork a few weeks earlier, sponsored by "Exiles" Theatre Company, on the subject of "The Artist as Exile," and given her experiences as a Dubliner living in Northern Ireland, I was eager to hear of her views on the way in which women from the North and South view each other.

"I started writing when I moved to London," she began. "It all started by my discovering that I was Irish. It has never occurred to me before that I was anything in particular; I was born and brought up in Ireland, I married an Irishman, so that was the normality of one's life.

"We had a very good life in London and an enormous number of friends, but after I'd been there about eight or nine years, I suddenly woke up one day and said: 'Well, I know what I'm not. I'm not English, and I want to discover what it is in myself that makes me different, because basically it's not education and it's not the language that I speak, so what is it?'

"I think it was shortly after that that I started to try to write, and part of my agenda was to discover why, what was Irish in me, what made me different from the people I was around. That was really my artist in exile bit. Then I came back here [to Derry]. I suppose, because I don't live in Dublin, that perhaps I'm still an exile.

"In the South [of Ireland], we are all 'kings' sons.' What I mean is, there is a feeling that people in the South have a value of some sort, an importance, and this gives them a courage to behave in what one might term (and I'm talking in intellectual terms) an aristocratic way. People who have the courage to behave in that way are much more interesting people. The people here don't have that feeling. They are buttoned up, and their aspirations are to become middle class. The attitude of middle-class people and people of an aristocratic nature are utterly different. So many people here are trapped by their own lack of courage, lack of excitement. This has nothing to do with what's been going on. My God, there has been enough excitement! But it's just that the perceptions of themselves are to become middle-class people. Everybody here wants to be middle class! This is a huge generalization because of course there is a large middle class in the South of Ireland—but basically the people in the South have a totally different, more confident attitude about themselves. This means that they are more interesting, more exciting, more daring people.

"This is one of the things I find makes a difference between women here and women in the South. And I'm speaking of women of all classes, class really doesn't come into this. This perception that they have of themselves here is just totally different and it deforms them. I think you'd find it even if you had a whole bundle of working-class people in the South, they would still have this ease, ease with themselves and ease with the rest of the world. It gives them courage.

"There's something terribly sad about it because we're all Irish people. We all spring from the same roots; by and large after all these hundreds of years we are all coming out of the same melting pot, and yet there is this strange thing. It has nothing to do with whether you are Catholic or Protestant; they all have this same inhibition. It has nothing to do with Presbyterianism. It may be something to do with their inability to recognize what Presbyterianism is all about in the first place, which was all about freedom, and some of them have forgotten that. They have a different perception of what freedom is now. I don't know; I can't ever work out why different nations have apparently different values. It's just easy to stereotype because some of these things are sticking out and hitting you in the face!

"Striving to be middle class, and much more the sense of the importance of consumerism in the North—not that there aren't materialistic people in the South and everywhere in the world, of course—but I do have that sense that in the South there is respect for the cultural achievement, respect for the artistic achievement."

I asked Jennifer if she would prefer to live in Dublin if she could.

"Well, in Dublin I've got pals, I've got cousins, lots of family. Of course, it's not far away by American standards, but it's not just down the road, either. I don't feel an exile here, but I do feel alone. I think it would be the same thing if I lived in County Mayo or County Cork or wherever. I think I would feel the same way. I'm lonely for Dublin.

"There are so many bits of Dublin . . . every time I turn a corner, I think: 'This is part of me,' and I don't have that feeling here.

"But in the end, I live in a country inside my own head, and the things that I suddenly think I want to write about are all to do with the way I see life going on around me. I don't think it matters where I live to do that. The only book I know I wouldn't have written, had I lived in Dublin, was *Shadows On My Skin*."

Where They Are Going [1996]

THE NORTHERN IRELAND WOMEN'S COALITION

IN SOME OF THE LAST few sentences I wrote for this book in 1987, I said: "The ultimate feminist goal in Northern Ireland should be to create unity among the women there and a common voice that refutes terrorism as a way of life. Until that voice is heard, men will recite those ancient wounds with monotonous regularity to a world grown tired of listening."

That goal has now been reached and that common voice is beginning to be heard with the creation of a new political party in Northern Ireland, the Women's Coalition, and the subsequent election of two women, Monica McWilliams and Pearl Sagar, to the all-party talks. The voices of women are now being heard on center stage instead of as muted prompts to the failed actors who pose as politicians in Northern Ireland. One can hope that these and other new fresh voices will replace the old and worn-out voices of the past and bring new life and energy into the political process of Northern Ireland.

One only needs to have followed the chronology of the events of the past twenty-five years in Northern Ireland and to know the names of the players to realize that women have not been a part of this process. There have been good men there doing an unbelievably difficult job of trying to maintain normalcy and achieve peace in Northern Ireland during this time. There have been villains and heroes, demagogues and rabble rousers. There have been "men of the cloth" of all religions. And there has been a statesman or two. But the voice of a woman has not been heard on the broader political stage. Northern Ireland has seventeen members of Parliament and three members of the European Parliament, and they are all male.

Equality for women is coming slowly to Northern Ireland, but what is important is that it is coming. There are changes. There is a female Secretary of State for the Economy, Agriculture and Women's Affairs, Baroness Jean Denton. Rabbi Julia Neuberger is the newly appointed Chancellor of the University of Ulster. Marjorie Mowlam, MP, is the Shadow Northern Ireland Secretary and will be the first female Secretary of State for Northern Ireland should Labour win the next British election. Jean Mayhew, the wife of Sir Patrick Mayhew, the present Secretary of State, has taken her role of "spouse" and turned it into a force for encouraging women throughout Northern Ireland. To be in such a sensitive position as she is and to have won the trust and respect of women from all sides of the religious and political divide are remarkable achievements, coming from a remarkable woman.

Everyone who knows anything about Northern Ireland knows that the women there have been a formidable coalition already. Quietly, without pretense or posture, they have patrolled their streets and neighborhoods, urban and rural, their youth centers and church organizations, and sometimes even their own families, keeping the peace. They have healed pain—mental, physical, emotional, and spiritual. They have put together organizations of reconciliation. They have brought laughter, wit, and common sense into appallingly gloomy situations. They have seen the glimmering light at the end of their grievous tunnel, and they have marched toward it with a steadfastness and purity of purpose. They have been the silent soldiers of peace.

But the times, they are a changin', and these remarkable women have decided that their time has come. As May Blood, a highly respected community worker in the Shankill, put it: "Voters have been taken for granted for years. Many of my supposed leaders never once asked my opinion when they walked up the steps to Stormont to talk about my future. Nobody ever told me what went on at those talks."

When I was in Belfast in the summer of 1995, I had a talk with Marie Abbott, one of the members of the Boston Conference, and we spoke about the encouragement the women from Northern Ireland had received for getting involved in the political process.

"You know, it was interesting after we were in Boston. There was a refocus, an idea of a forum being set up and women wanting to engage with that, or women disagreeing with what was set forth in the proposals by the British government and people getting energized round the idea of politics in the sense of political structures and of parties.

"A lot of women here are political, in that they are engaged with activities and organizations, but they are not engaged in a formal political way. A lot of the debate in Boston was about making that move if people thought they really wanted to, and if they felt they could give allegiance to the structures. I think what a lot of people overlook is that many people here, not just women, but people from the middle classes and professions, don't engage at all with party politics."

It had been impossible, over these past years, for women to be seen belonging to one political party or another, Northern Ireland politics being what they are. They would have damaged their reputations as neutral participants in community life if they had done so. But with an election being held for the first time in over two dozen years, the establishment of the Northern Ireland Forum, and the chance to participate in the all-party negotiations, women deemed it was time to move.

Rather than join one or another of the mainstream political parties, dominated as they are by their male members, they chose to form a new party, open to women of all political and religious persuasions. They reached this decision after having written to all existing political parties in Northern Ireland to ask if they planned to run women candidates. Only Sinn Fein and the small, fringe parties such as the Democratic Left, the Communist Party of Ireland, and the Green Party replied. (Sinn Fein prides itself for including women in its leadership roster, but, at least one never hears a Sinn Fein woman explaining party policy to the public or the press.)

Bronagh Hinds is the Chair of the Northern Ireland Women's European Platform, the group that brought the Women's Coalition together. A number of women's organizations joined in the planning stages from the beginning, including the Centre for Research on Women, the Derry Women's Centre, Democratic Dialogue, the Shankill Women's Forum, the Women's Information Group, and the Northern Ireland Women's Rights Movement. Hinds said: "We heard about parity of esteem as it applies to unionists and nationalists. We want to know what they were going to do about parity of esteem for women in their own parties."

The women had only seven weeks to organize, publish policy papers, raise money, print literature, and campaign. In the end, sixty-eight women ran. They worked together because that is what they have done over the past two decades. They chose to be drawn together by common aspirations rather than pulled apart by anger and distrust. Their commonly held pragmatism leaves little time for recondite constitutional debate.

They realize that many members of the coalition will have split loyalties on mainstream issues, and they do not feel that they should avoid addressing the political and sectarian conflict.

"Politicians have never agreed, so why should we?" Bronagh Hinds questions. "We just know that women have been absent for twenty-five years and that now they can have an impact."

Mary Holland said, in writing about the coalition in the *Irish Times*: "These women are not dewy-eyed idealists who believe that lasting peace can be achieved by the wearing of white ribbons." They are trade unionists, academics, executives in public service, and community activists.

The election was held on May 30. It was an extremely complicated process. The result was that the Women's Coalition was able to get two women elected. During the campaign, one woman involved in the coalition said wistfully: "A dream ticket would be Bernadette McAliskey, a republican socialist from Tyrone, and May Blood, a trade unionist from the heart of the Shankill. What a message that would send to the politicians!"

In the end, those two women did not stand. The coalition polled 7,731 votes, and Monica McWilliams, a Catholic educator, and Pearl Sagar, a Protestant community activist, won two seats.

The two women, and a backup group of policy makers from the coalition, joined the other delegates at Stormont Castle, where the talks take place daily from 10 A.M. to 7 P.M. They are frustrated at the posturing and whinging of some of the other delegates and frustrated at the time spent on trivia: "Where do I sit?" does not loom large on the agenda of these women who have waited decades to be part of the national dialogue. They have found unlikely but helpful and supportive colleagues among the delegates from the Progressive Unionist Party (PUP) and the Ulster Democratic Party (UDP), two small parties whose members, like them, are new to the political process.

"Senator Mitchell is a great addition to the talks," Monica McWilliams told me in Belfast. He and his two colleagues, General de

Chastelain and Harri Holkeri, are well respected by all but the Unionist members of the talks, and Mitchell's negotiating ability and cool, affable style are sorely needed as the assembly moves toward the substantial portion of its work.

The women who created the coalition have not decided where its future lies. I talked about this one day in mid-1996 in Belfast with May Blood, in her bright, cheerful office on the Shankill Road.

"I don't know what we'll do now," she said. "We had great support from many men, and probably would have had more if they had realized that we were going to succeed. We might drop the 'Women' from the coalition and become all inclusive. We have to think about what our best route is."

In the meantime, "The ultimate feminist goal in Northern Ireland" has been met and there is now a common voice that refutes terrorism as a way of life. The Women of the North have spoken out, been elected, and had their positions validated.

The Northern Irish members of "Reaching Common Ground" were hosts to a return conference for the American and Southern Irish women in Coleraine, Derry, and Belfast in June 1996.

This time it was our turn to pack our bags and board the Aer Lingus flight to Belfast. It was a sentimental reunion seeing all our old friends from the Boston Conference and meeting new delegates who had joined the conference in the interim. We took up just where we had left off, and addressed many of the same issues, expanding our American understanding of the political situation in Northern Ireland. Although there was not the euphoria brought about by the cease-fire that had been there during the Boston Conference, there was a new buzz in the air, the creation and success of the Women's Coalition. That was something that had been so eagerly encouraged in Boston that the reality of it created a deep satisfaction among all the delegates, both Irish and American.

Peace has not yet come to Northern Ireland, but the tantalizing prelude to it was there during the cease-fire. I believe it is within grasp, but not until there is new leadership across the land, across those borders of religion and politics and history. The good men must be, after twenty years, worn out. The others, those men who have made the Troubles in Northern Ireland the platform for their own hatred, who have fired the flames of hatred and distrust, should be replaced by decent men and women with common sense and common goals: peace and prosperity for themselves and their children. When and if that happens, I believe peace will come to Northern Ireland.

My hope is that the men and women there will feel free and safe enough to treat each other with the same warmth, kindness, and generosity that they have always shown to me and other strangers.

Glossary

AIA Anglo-Irish Agreement.

Adams, Gerry Leader of Sinn Fein.

Alliance Party Non-sectarian political party, made up of Protestant and Catholic members. Small in number. Founded in 1970.

Andersonstown Large Catholic housing development on the fringe of West Belfast.

Anglo-Irish Agreement (AIA) (Sometimes referred to as the Hillsborough Agreement.) Signed in November 1985 by the British and Irish (Dublin) governments to give the Republic of Ireland a voice in the affairs of Northern Ireland. Strongly condemned by Unionists in the North and by the IRA. Strong support in N.I. from the moderate nationalists and a few liberal Unionists. Official Unionist and Democratic Unionist MPs resigned their seats in Parliament in protest (and ran for re-election). Unionist and DUP members of local councils in N.I. boycotted council meetings. A "joint secretariat" of officials from the British and Irish governments meets in Belfast on a regular basis.

Apprentice Boys An organization of Protestant men in Derry who gather on August 12 to march in celebration of the occasion of the defense of the city in the siege of 1689, when thirteen apprentice boys closed the gates of the city to the army of Catholic King James II.

Armagh Prison The jail in Armagh where most of the women political prisoners were incarcerated.

B-Specials Police reserve force, made up almost entirely of Protestants; disbanded in 1971.

Battle of the Bogside Riots that erupted in the Bogside of Derry in August 1969 after the Apprentice Boys Parade through the city. As a result of the rioting, British troops were called in to Northern Ireland.

Bloody Sunday January 30, 1972, the day thirteen people were shot and killed in Derry by British soldiers as they marched unarmed in a civil rights demonstration.

Bogside Catholic, nationalist neighborhood of Derry.

Campaign for Social Justice An organization founded in 1964 in Dungannon, Co. Tyrone, to collect information about discrimination against Catholics in Northern Ireland.

Corrigan, Mairead One of the three founders of the Peace People in Northern Ireland, for which she shared a Nobel Peace Prize with Betty Williams.

Craig, William Controversial Unionist politician who served as MP for East Belfast and in several ministries in the Northern Ireland government. He lost his Westminster seat to the DUP in 1979.

Cumann na mBan The women's section of the IRA.

Currie, Austin One of the founders of the SDLP, member of the Power-Sharing Executive of 1974. Helped organize the first civil rights march in Dungannon in 1968. Defied a party decision not to contest the Westminster election in Fermanagh and S. Tyrone and ran as an independent SDLP candidate but lost to Frank Maguire.

DUP Democratic Unionist Party.

Daíl The Parliament for the Republic of Ireland (pronounced "doil").

Democratic Unionist Party (DUP) Founded in 1971 by Ian Paisley and Desmond Boal, a Belfast barrister, as a hard-line alternative to the Official Unionist Party. According to Mr. Boal, the party would be "right wing . . . on the Constitution, but to the left on social policies." Mr. Paisley is still the head of the party. The party attracts hard-line loyalist members from both the working class and the middle class.

Derry The alternative name of Londonderry, preferred by its nationalist population.

Diplock Courts Non-jury courts for paramilitary trials, named after Lord Diplock, who recommended them in 1972.

Direct Rule The governing of N.I. from London by the British Parliament.

Divis Flats A high-rise apartment complex in the Lower Falls of West Belfast that has come to symbolize many of the sociological and economic problems of the poor Catholic population of Belfast. Scheduled for demolition.

East Belfast The Protestant side of the city.

Eire The Irish for "Ireland" (pronounced "aira").

Equal Opportunities Commission (EOC) A government body set up to work toward the elimination of sex discrimination and to promote equality of opportunity for men and women in Northern Ireland.

Ewart-Biggs, Christopher British Ambassador to Dublin, assassinated in 1976, two weeks after he took up his post.

Fair Employment Agency A government agency set up in 1976 to promote equality of opportunity for people of different religious beliefs and to work for the elimination of political and religious discrimination.

Falls Road The main thoroughfare of Catholic West Belfast, running from the city center to Andersonstown.

Faulkner, Brian Prime Minister of Northern Ireland, 1971–72 (Unionist Party); Chief Executive in the Power-Sharing Executive, 1974. Minister for Home Affairs, 1959; Minister of Commerce, 1963; Minister of Development, 1969. Retired from political life in 1976, became a Life Peer in 1977. Killed in a riding accident in Co. Down in March 1977.

Free Presbyterian The church founded by Ian Paisley in 1951.

H-blocks Prison blocks in the Maze Prison (Long Kesh), shaped like the letter *H*.

Haughey, Charles Taoiseach (Prime Minister) of the Republic of Ireland.

Home Rule A political movement that sought the governing of Northern Ireland by an Irish Parliament rather than by Britain in the 1870s and 1880s.

Hume, John Member of Parliament for Foyle, also member of the European Parliament. Founding member and leader of the SDLP. Head of the Commerce Department in the Power-Sharing Executive of 1974. Influential in the United States for explaining the role of Irish nationalist politics to Americans.

INLA Irish National Liberation Army, the armed wing of the IRSP. Illegal and ruthless, it has been responsible for many acts of violence in Northern Ireland, Britain, and the Republic.

IRA The Irish Republican Army, known since its break with the Official IRA in 1970 as the Provisional IRA, the Provos, the Provies, or simply as the IRA.

IRSP The Irish Republican Socialist Party. It split from the Official Sinn Fein in 1974 and is known locally as the Irps. Its founder, Seamus Costello, was shot dead in Dublin in 1977.

July 12 Annual Protestant celebration commemorating the defense of Londonderry against the siege of Catholic King James II in 1689.

Lifted Arrested.

Loyalist Staunch Protestants who want to see Northern Ireland remain loyal to the British crown; it is a general description, not a political party.

McKeown, Ciaran One of the three founders of the Peace People in Northern Ireland. Currently a freelance journalist in Belfast.

Mallon, Seamus Deputy leader of the SDLP. Member of Parliament for Newry-Armagh.

Molyneaux, James Leader of the Official Unionist Party, Member of Parliament for the Lagan Valley.

NICRA Northern Ireland Civil Rights Association.

Nationalist One in Northern Ireland who desires unity with the Republic of Ireland.

Noraid Irish Northern Aid, a fund-raising group in the United States that raises money for the IRA.

Northern Ireland Civil Rights Association (NICRA) Established in January 1968 to spearhead a campaign for civil rights for the Catholic population of Northern Ireland.

OUP Official Unionist Party.

Official IRA The remnant of the original Irish Republican Army, which split in 1970 when the Provisional IRA (the Provos) broke away. It is known locally as the "Stickies," and most oldtime Official IRA members are now members of the Workers' Party.

Official Unionist Party (OUP) The largest political party in N.I., established in 1921, which provided the government of N.I. until the dissolution of its Parliament in 1972. It is the party that represents the majority of N.I. Protestants, and almost all of the business and social Protestant "establishment."

Orange Order The largest Protestant organization in Northern Ireland, founded in 1795. Its announced objectives are to defend the Protestant succession to the British throne, and to preserve the civil and religious liberty of the Protestants.

Paisley, Ian Co-founder and leader of the DUP, Member of Parliament for North Antrim, founder of the Free Presbyterian Church. Controversial and charismatic Protestant leader in Northern Ireland for four decades. Rabidly anti-Catholic.

Peace People Established in Belfast in August 1976 by Mairead Corrigan (Maguire), Betty Williams, and Ciaran McKeown after the tragic deaths of the three Maguire children by a getaway gunman's car. Inspired thousands of men and women, Protestant and Catholic, on both sides of the border, to demonstrate and march on behalf of a peaceful settlement of the N.I. Troubles.

Power-Sharing Executive The "cabinet" for the short-lived N.I. government set up in 1974, in which representatives from the Alliance Party, the SDLP, and the Unionist Party all had a role.

Prod Derogatory term for Protestant.

Provo Commonly used name for members of the Provisional IRA.

RUC Royal Ulster Constabulary.

Republican Catholic nationalist whose aims are a united Ireland and the end of British rule and occupation in Northern Ireland.

Robinson, Peter Member of Parliament for East Belfast, deputy head of the DUP. Prominent Protestant politician, typifying the "new breed" of Ulster hard-liners.

Royal Ulster Constabulary (RUC) The police force of Northern Ireland.

SDLP Social Democratic and Labour Party.

Sands, Bobby The first IRA prisoner to die in the 1981 hunger strikes. From April to May 1981, he served from prison as a Member of Parliament (Westminster) from Fermanagh and S. Tyrone.

Saracen Six-wheeled armored vehicle.

Screw Slang for prison guard.

Shankill Road The main thoroughfare of the Protestant section of West Belfast.

Sinn Fein "Ourselves Alone," the political wing of the IRA.

Social Democratic and Labour Party (SDLP) The party of the majority of Catholics of Northern Ireland, founded in 1970. John Hume is head of the SDLP, Seamus Mallon is deputy leader.

Stormont The seat of government in Northern Ireland, five miles outside of Belfast, a palace that is a heavily guarded complex of office buildings and official apartments.

Sunningdale The conference between the British and Northern Irish governments held at the Sunningdale Civil Service College in England, December 1973. Resulted in an agreement to set up a power-sharing government in N.I., with an "Executive" (cabinet) that included Unionists, SDLP, and Alliance members. Brian Faulkner was Chief Executive. The Executive collapsed in the face of a country-wide loyalist strike in May 1974.

Supergrass An informer who, in return for information given to the security forces about former colleagues, is given immunity, a much-reduced sentence, or financial assistance to leave the country.

T.D. Member of the Republic of Ireland Parliament.

Taig Derogatory slang term for Catholic; derived from the Irish form of "Timothy" (pronounced "Tige," as in tiger).

Taoiseach Prime Minister of the Republic of Ireland (pronounced "tee-shock").

Tricolor The Republic of Ireland flag of green, orange, and white; the white was meant to signify the peace between the Catholics (green) and the Protestants (orange).

Turf Lodge Catholic housing development in West Belfast.

Twinbrook Catholic housing development in West Belfast.

UDA Ulster Defense Association.

UDR Ulster Defense Regiment.

UVF Ulster Volunteer Force.

Ulster The name commonly applied to Northern Ireland, but strictly the designation of the historic nine-county province of Ireland that includes not only the six in Northern Ireland but also three counties in the Republic as well: Monaghan, Cavan, and Donegal.

Ulster Defense Association (UDA) A legal Protestant paramilitary group, founded in 1971 as an umbrella association for various loyalist vigilante organizations.

Ulster Defense Regiment (UDR) A part-time defense force, overwhelmingly Protestant, under the command of the British Army and used to supplement the local security forces.

Ulster Volunteer Force (UVF) An illegal Protestant volunteer paramilitary force, responsible for many acts of violence against the Catholic population.

Unionist Party Official Unionist Party.

Waterside The Protestant side of the River Foyle in Derry.

Wee Almost anything small in Northern Ireland.

Westminster The seat of the British Parliament.

Williams, Betty One of the three founders of the Peace People in Northern Ireland, for which she shared a Nobel Peace Prize with Mairead Corrigan.

Women Together A peace movement founded in 1970 to bring together Protestant and Catholic women working for peace.

Workers' Party A republican party with a strong socialist platform. It differs from Sinn Fein in that it disapproves of violence. It became the political party of the Official IRA after that group and the Provisionals split.

Chronology of Recent Events in Northern Ireland

1921 Ireland partitioned into Northern Ireland and the Irish Free State.

1951 Reverend Ian Paisley founds Free Presbyterian Church in Belfast.

1968 Northern Ireland Civil Rights Association (NICRA) is born, begins agitation for political and economic equality for Catholics.

January 4, 1969 People's Democracy March from Belfast to Derry attacked by B-Specials and supporters of Ian Paisley.

April 1969 Terence O'Neill resigns as N.I. Prime Minister April 28 under attack from right-wing Unionists. Succeeded by his cousin, James Chichester-Clarke. Bernadette Devlin elected Westminster MP from N.I.

August 1969 "Battle of the Bogside" in Derry. In subsequent weeks Protestants in Belfast and elsewhere attack Catholic ghettos. British government (under Harold Wilson) sends in British army to restore order. Catholics in neighborhoods form Central Citizens Defense Committee, which soon becomes the nucleus of a revived IRA.

December 1969 IRA splits into Provisionals (under Sean MacStiofain) and Officials (under Cathal Goulding) over posture toward British army and the Provisionals' continued use of violence.

Early 1970 Relations between British army and Catholics deteriorate. Provisionals begin war against British occupation. Moderate Catholics form Social Democratic and Labour Party (SDLP).

March 1971 James Chichester-Clarke resigns as Northern Irish Prime Minister. Succeeded by Brian Faulkner.

August 1971 Faulkner, with British backing, implements internment without trial under Special Powers Act. Four hundred and fifty Catholics arrested, interrogated, and tortured by RUC and Army Intelligence. Catholic support for IRA escalates.

1971 Ian Paisley founds Democratic Unionist Party (DUP).

1971 UDA, UVF, and other Protestant paramilitary organizations begin "Protestant backlash," a campaign of indiscriminate, sectarian assassinations that peaked in 1973–1976 but continue today.

January 30, 1972 "Bloody Sunday." British paratroopers fire on NICRA march in Derry, kill thirteen unarmed demonstrators. IRA popularity soars.

March 1972 British Prime Minister Edward Heath forces Brian Faulkner to resign as Prime Minister of N.I., suspends local government in Northern Ireland, and begins direct rule of N.I. from London.

May 1972 Derry Women's Peace Initiative, demanding the IRA get out of the Bogside and Creggan, two Catholic Derry neighborhoods.

August 1973 British government attempts to restructure Northern Irish government, including provisions for "power sharing." New local elections produce a coalition government consisting of moderate Unionists (under Faulkner), the SDLP, and the small, nonsectarian Alliance Party.

December 1973 "Sunningdale Agreement." Made by the new Northern Irish Executive (the above coalition), the British government, and the Irish (Dublin) government. Right-wing Unionists, Paisley's DUP, and the Protestant paramilitary groups vow to destroy the Sunningdale Agreement. The IRA continues its own campaign.

May 1974 Ulster Workers Council, led by the UDA, organizes a general strike to bring down the power-sharing executive. British government (now led by Harold Wilson) fails to use army to break the strike. Faulkner resigns. The power-sharing executive collapses. Direct rule reimposed.

1974 Irish National Liberation Army (INLA), and its political wing, the Irish Republican Socialist Party (IRSP), breaks away from the Official IRA and begins its own violent campaign.

1975 British government phases out internment. IRA in disarray, bloody warfare among Provos, Officials, and INLA.

August 1976 Peace movement begins in Belfast under Mairead Corrigan, Betty Williams, and Ciaran McKeown.

November 1977 Corrigan and Williams win the Nobel Peace Prize.

1976–1977 Under a de facto truce arranged between IRA and Protestant paramilitaries, violence begins to decline. The number killed drops from 297 in 1976 to 112 in 1977. Sectarian, tit-for-tat murders are abandoned by both sides. Killings of British army, army reserve (Ulster Defense Regiment) police, and prison guards continue.

1976 British government announces that IRA and INLA prisoners as well as convicted Protestant paramilitaries will no longer be given "special status" in prison.

1977–1981 IRA and INLA prisoners are "on the blanket" to protest "criminalization" and the withdrawal of Special Category status.

1981 Bobby Sands and nine other hunger strikers die in prison to protest withdrawal of Special Category status.

1984 Mrs. Thatcher narrowly escapes death in an IRA bombing in Brighton, England.

November 1985 The Anglo-Irish Agreement (the Hillsborough Agreement) is signed.

November 1987 Eleven civilians killed in an IRA bomb blast in Enniskillen on Remembrance Sunday.

Bibliography

Beale, Jenny. *Women in Ireland: Voices of Change.* Dublin: Gill and Macmillan, 1986.

Belfrage, Sally. *The Crack: A Belfast Year.* London: Andre Deutsch, 1987.

Bell, J. Bowyer. *The IRA: The Secret Army, 1916–1979.* Cambridge, Mass.: MIT Press, 1970.

Beresford, David. *Ten Dead Men: The Story of the 1981 Irish Hunger Strike.* London: Grafton Books, 1987.

Boyles, Kevin, and Hadden, Tom. *Ireland: A Positive Proposal.* Harmondsworth, Middlesex: Penguin Books, 1985.

Curtis, Liz. *Ireland: The Propaganda War: The British Media and the "Battle for Hearts and Minds."* London: Pluto Press, 1984.

Coles, Robert. *The Political Life of Children.* Boston: Atlantic Monthly Press, 1986.

Darby, John, ed. *Northern Ireland: The Background to the Conflict.* Belfast: Appletree Press, 1983; Syracuse: Syracuse University Press, 1983.

Devlin, Polly. *All of Us There.* London: Weidenfeld and Nicolson, 1983.

Devlin, Bernadette. *The Price of My Soul.* New York: Knopf, 1969.

Easpaig, Aine, and NicGiolla, Eibhlin. *Sisters in Cells.* Westport, County Mayo: Foilseachain Naisiunta Teoranta, 1987.

Evason, Eileen. *Hidden Violence: A Study of Battered Women in Northern Ireland.* Belfast: Farset Co-operative Press, 1982.

Fairweather, Eileen; McDonough, Roisin; McFadyean, Melanie. *Only the Rivers Run Free: Northern Ireland: The Women's War.* London: Pluto Press, 1984.

Faulkner, Brian. *Memoirs of a Statesman.* Edited by John Houston. London: Weidenfeld and Nicolson, 1978.
Fraser, Morris. *Children in Conflict.* Harmondsworth, Middlesex: Penguin Books, 1973.
Hederman, Mark Patrick. *The Crane Bag: The Northern Issue,* Vol. 4, No. 2 (Dublin, 1980).
Holland, Jack. *Too Long a Sacrifice: Life and Death in Northern Ireland Since 1969.* New York: Dodd, Mead, 1981.
Hooley, Ruth, ed. *The Female Line: Northern Irish Women Writers.* Belfast: University Press, 1985.
Kohfeldt, Mary Lou. *Lady Gregory: The Woman Behind the Irish Renaissance.* New York: Atheneum, 1985.
Levenson, Leah, and Natterstad, Jerry H. *Hanna Sheehy-Skeffington: Irish Feminist.* Syracuse: Syracuse University Press, 1986.
Longley, Edna. *Poetry in the Wars.* Newcastle-upon-Tyne: Bloodaxe Books, 1986.
MacBride, Maud Gonne. *A Servant of the Queen: Reminiscences.* Woodbridge, Suffolk: The Boydell Press, 1938.
MacCurtain, Margaret; O'Corrain, Donncha. *Women in Irish Society: The Historical Dimension.* Dublin: Arlen House, The Women's Press, 1978.
MacStiofain, Sean. *Revolutionary in Ireland.* London: 1975.
Marrinan, Patrick. *Paisley, Man of Wrath.* Tralee, Co. Kerry: Anvil Books, 1973.
McCafferty, Nell. *The Armagh Women.* Dublin: Co-op Books, 1981.
McCreary, Alf. *Tried by Fire.* Basingstoke, England: Marshall Pickering, 1981.
McKeown, Ciaran. *The Passion of Peace.* Belfast: The Blackstaff Press, 1984.
Messenger, Betty. *Picking Up the Linen Threads: A Study in Industrial Folklore.* Belfast: The Blackstaff Press, 1975.
Missing Pieces: Women in Irish History: I. Since the Famine. Dublin: Irish Feminist Information Publications, 1983.
Moloney, Ed, and Pollak, Andy. *Paisley.* Dublin: Poolbeg Press, 1986.
Sands, Bobby. *One Day in My Life.* Chicago: The Banner Press, 1983.
Shrivers, Lynne; Bowman, David, S. J., eds. *More Than the Troubles: A Common Sense View of the Northern Ireland Conflict.* Philadelphia: New Society Publishers, 1984.
Theroux, Paul. *The Kingdom by the Sea.* New York: Washington Square Press, 1983.
Ward, Margaret. *Unmanageable Revolutionaries.* London: Pluto Press, 1983.
White, Barry. *John Hume: Statesman of the Troubles.* Belfast: The Blackstaff Press, 1984.

CPSIA information can be obtained
at www.ICGtesting.com
Printed in the USA
FSHW010209010921
84358FS